THE OTHER SIDE OF SILENCE

The Other Side of Silence

A Life of Ethel Wilson

by
Mary McAlpine

HARBOUR PUBLISHING

The Other Side of Silence: A Life of Ethel Wilson
Copyright © 1988 by Mary McAlpine

Harbour Publishing Co. Ltd.
P.O. Box 219
Madeira Park, B.C.
V0N 2H0

Canadian Cataloguing in Publication Data

McAlpine, Mary, 1926-
    The other side of silence : a life of Ethel Wilson

Includes index
ISBN 0-920080-99-5

1. Wilson, Ethel, 1888–1980 — Biography.
2. Novelists, Canadian (English) — 20th century —
Biography.* I. Title.
PS8545.I48Z76 1988   C813'.54   C88-091378-9
PR9199.3.W55Z76 1988

Printed and bound in Canada
Cover art by Gaye Hammond

For Lucinda and Sarah
and to the memory of a friend

If we had a keen vision and feeling of all ordinary human life, it would be like hearing the grass grow and the squirrel's heart beat, and we should die of that roar which lies on the other side of silence.

George Eliot, *Middlemarch*

Table of Contents

Chapter One

A Beginning

A few weeks before Christmas 1962, I received a short story and a letter from Ethel Wilson, who was godmother to my first child, Lucinda, then three years old. In the letter she said she was sending the child a doll, which had been given to her seventy-two years earlier. She said that she had taken Duchess, as the doll was called, to a doll's hospital in Vancouver, to be mended and made fresh for Lucinda, and that she was slightly disappointed in the result. Then her sense of the absurdity in this human relationship began to rise up and show itself.

"[Duchess] always had a simplicity of fringe & long hair, sometimes braided in a pigtail. But I think that in all these decades the moths must have got into her hair, & the doctor for some reason, after demothing her, made it look fussy & rather vulgar, with a phoney coronet. The doctor held her in high esteem & said things like this—'The Duchess is nearly ready. You may call for the Duchess at half past two'—nearly made one scramble to one's feet."

This was something Ethel Wilson could no longer do. She was crippled by arthritis and confined to a wheelchair.

She was born Ethel Bryant, and the story she sent off that November day is one version of her life.

This true story is about an old tailor named Jan Mortimer, a young English preacher named Robert Bryant, his wife Lila, and their child, who lived in Port Elizabeth, then a small town, on the southern-most tip of Africa.

Jan Mortimer lived in two small rooms with the ghost or spirit of his wife Ellen who had just died in the latter part of 1888. Jan Mortimer did very little tailoring now, partly because—although his fingers were still supple—his joints hurt him and he could not easily bend or stretch or lift things without a great deal of pain. Until his wife died he had the only tailoring shop in Port Elizabeth. Then he was left quite alone and appallingly lonely and he began to realize that the presence of his wife Ellen had made life bearable and happy in their small bungalow and in the shop, but now all was changed. His alone-ness there could not be endured. The only times when he felt an easing and comforting of his days and nights were when he was visited for a few minutes by the young preacher Robert Bryant who had buried his wife.

Since tailoring and living were now so difficult for this silent old man, he decided to sell his little business, or close it up if he could not sell it. No one wanted to buy his business because not many men in Port Elizabeth used to order wellmade and expensive clothes then. So he disposed of his bolts of cloth as best he could and closed his shop, and the wooden sign of *Jan Mortimer First Class Tailor* was burned in the landlord's stove. He then sold the bungalow whose small rooms contained his wife's presence. He kept the bed in which they had with passion, love and sweet contentment lain together, and two tables and her chair and his, and Ellen's chest of drawers, also a very good worktable of Ellen's in which she had kept odd pieces of nice cotton and silk and wool which she used for fancy work and for patching. He also kept a beautiful little doll and a brooch. He then burned up all Ellen's few clothes and suffered great pain, Oh Ellen Ellen. He rented two small rooms, placed his furniture in them and tried to feel that Ellen's essence was with him. He did not say it in such words, but her presence in absence was in the air around him and as he turned this way that way it was his own Ellen who just escaped him. Yet she was there. She was present and he could almost touch her but could not. It was worst of all when he looked at their bed, and lay down, and she was not there not there.

They had had no friends because they were sufficient to each other, and now Jan Mortimer found that to be sufficient is not enough. But he could not help repelling the few people who were kind and made advances to him. It was as though he built a brick wall, and soon the people saw the brick, and turned away and he was forgotten, except by the young preacher Robert Bryant.

Robert Bryant was tall and very handsome. He was dark, and had grown a small beard because it seemed suitable in those days for a young minister with a wife and a baby and a small chapel and a great many young people to help and lead into right ways. He was too busy and often tired, but he stopped to see Jan Mortimer on his way home when possible. He did not stay long as he wished to get home to his serious young wife with her widow's peak of brown hair, and to his baby girl who was, surprisingly, golden fair and rambunctious. His wife Lila had a helpless Kaffir girl called Sasawna to help her with the baby. Lila took her duties as the minister's wife and the minister's baby's mother too seriously. Nearly every night when Robert was out at all his meetings, she wrote to her dearly loved Mother in England, and because she was torn between love for Robert and homesickness and inadequacy she often dropped tears as she wrote. (The baby read these letters 70 years later; she too wept as the picture spread before her, and then she burned the letters.) Lila wiped the tears away quickly when she heard her husband's steps, leaping up the outside stairs, and then she rushed to meet him. She was devoted and sweet but had very little sense of humour. Robert had a sense of joy and fun and humour that fed and lightened her, and brightened young and old people. She loved too dearly, but she felt her inadequacy far too much in this strange place.

One night Jan Mortimer said to the young preacher, "How is Mrs. Bryant? I saw her wheeling the baby and I did not think she looked well." Robert's face changed and he said shortly "No, she is not well," and then he said no more, but went on home to his wife who was not well. The baby whom we shall call E. was healthy, and pink and white and golden, and merry, and naughty. She screamed when she wished to and laughed uproariously when she wanted to, and despite the help and inefficiency of the little Kaffir girl, she tired her mother who was in fact very ill, and about to die.

When Lila died, all the good people in the chapel were very sad for the young preacher, but no one felt as sad as Jan Mortimer whose sorrow had been entirely for himself but now extended to include Robert Bryant whose suffering was very great. Kind women from the chapel rallied round, and his bungalow was no place of rest, but a place of bereavement and absence and also people and confusion. The baby E. had a bit of fever and Robert did not know what to do. He had not found the doctor very experienced. His duties had become involved, his house was a centre of busy kindness, the baby was fretful and did not sleep well. Neither did he sleep. He knelt beside the child's bed and prayed desperately that God would help him to bear what had descended upon him in this loss and all this misery. E. was his only happiness and she was his greatest care. Yet she laughed.

Letters from England came in shoals. He had hardly time to read them. They all exhorted him to leave that country and bring the baby home. "I will take her!" "Bring her to me!" implored the kind voices. But Robert doggedly pursued his way. He prepared and preached his sermons, helped his young people to follow in the good way, and cared as well as he could for his child. He did not know how often the silent man Jan came to his bungalow and worked inside and out, bending and stretching his painful joints. The weather became very hot.

E. now was an active baby ot about two, and gay. Her father's work had reached a point where it could be handed over and connected up with a neighbouring parish. He faced the fact that he must for his child's sake leave Lila, leave Africa, and take the baby home to England, which he did, for secretly he knew he was not strong. He was stationed at a chapel in Wales, and there he, and the little daughter and Robert's maiden aunt, and Mary an angel servant from Lila's old home, lived in the small county town of Pembroke and everything was unimaginably happy, to E.

When Jan Mortimer heard that his understanding kind laughing and now saddened friend Robert Bryant was going away and taking his baby girl who would never think of him—Jan—again, he sat and glowered into the evening, evening by evening he sat glowering. Ellen was no longer so near and he could not summon her.

When Robert and his E. left Port Elizabeth, the people waved and waved and many of them cried but Robert had begun to be almost happy, even though his thoughts were with Lila whom he had taken out there to die.

Jan Mortimer went to his rooms, opened a trunk and took out the little doll and the brooch. The doll was very pretty. Her lips were parted in an enchanting smile, showing tiny white teeth. She had long brown hair cut in a fringe on her forehead and although she had no clothes, she had small red ear-rings in her pierced ears. She was quite new although she was really old. When I saw her today she was over seventy, as I am, but perhaps she is over 80 or 90. I do not know.

While Robert and E. were sailing on the ocean on their way to England, the tailor began to dress the doll, whom he called Duchess. He put the brooch away to keep for himself. He went through the scraps of cotton and silk and some wool that had belonged to Ellen. He selected and then he cut out two sets of undergarments, a red velvet dress with a buckle and bow, and a yellow evening dress. The evening dress and evening underclothes are lost. He embroidered some of the underclothes. When he had finished dressing Duchess he could hardly bear to part with her. But Duchess smiled so radiantly and sweetly at him that he made haste to pack her carefully in a box, and he put in a card which said *This is Duchess*, and mailed her away to Pembroke.

When Father helped E. undo the present from Jan Mortimer, everyone was excited — Father, and E. and Aunt Maria *and* Mary, for no one had ever seen such a lovely doll with such beautifully made clothes. E. was not allowed to play with Duchess very often, but she had ordinary dolls which later she wheeled in her pram, or put into a toy cart which was pulled by Nipper the black dog. But how she loved Duchess. Then Father and she and Mary and Aunt Maria and Duchess had to leave Wales and go to London where Father "had a church," and because Father still had a sort of sleeping T.B. and because he had always overworked, and because he went out to preach when he had a cold and there was pouring rain, he took pneumonia, and he too died. And E., who was not quite sure what dreadful thing had happened to her, was collected by Uncle J. and went with Duchess in her little bag (for she did not own much more than Duchess) first to Mrs. Moon and then to Uncle J., and then to Uncle S. and Aunt E., and then to all the other Aunties, and everybody was very kind, and then with Grannie and an Uncle and two Aunties to Vancouver, in Canada.

For the first part of this moving-about time the smashed-up feeling of Father not being there was very bad. E. did not remember her Mother, so she did not miss her. But Father and she had often laughed so much together that E. used to roll on the floor with laughing. She never never laughed so much ever again. Sometimes they walked to a park to see the animals. And sometimes Father had to whip her a little on her hand, for instance if she told a lie and said she had not taken the chocolate from the drawer and eaten the whole thing when she had. But her life was the happiest life that a little girl could ever have, even if she was rich, oh much better than that, with Father and Aunt Maria and the two dogs and Nigger the cat and Mary and Duchess that old Mr. Mortimer had sent her.

When E. became a schoolgirl in Vancouver, Duchess was getting shabby, but her smile was radiant always. She lay in a drawer with her eyes open, because when Duchess was born, before 1888, dolls did not have eyelids as they do now. When E. became no longer interested in Duchess but in games and books and children, somehow Duchess was relegated to an old trunk. Then I was oh so happily married and Duchess was forgotten. I only saw her when I went to the basement to look for something. Her head was in a strange position but her smile shone through the thin green muslin wrapping. I could not bear to throw her away, and left her in the trunk, and there I saw her again last week and thought of something for Duchess.

This morning I took Duchess, all wrapped up, to the Dolls' Hospital and there I had a very great surprise. She was still smiling happily, but her head was off, and long ago — in Pembroke — I must have tried to push some food between her laughing teeth, for they were a little broken. The ear-rings were gone. Even though she is over 70, as I am, she is still young. The doll doctor is Swedish. She undressed Duchess slowly and marvelled at the microscopic perfection of the sewing of her undergarments. She said, "This doll is a museum piece. How old is she?"

So, I thought, Duchess has become in the passage of years "A museum piece"!

"Duchess is over 70," I said, "or 80, as far as I know." Duchess's head lay sweetly smiling.

"What do you intend to do with Duchess?" said the doctor in an inquisitorial way.

"I am going to give her to my godchild Lucinda for Christmas when you have mended her," I said.

"How old is this godchild?" said the doll doctor, sharply.

"She's 3 or 4 years old."

The doll doctor took Duchess up in her hands and, as it were, withheld her from me jealously.

"You must not give Duchess" (the doll had become Duchess to the doll doctor), "to a child. Give her to her when she is *13*, then Duchess will still be good and intact, and still more valuable!"

"*Valuable*?" I said, surprised.

"Yes. You can get anywhere from $50 to $70 for her today, and in ten years she will be still more valuable. You would be crrrazy to give her to any child, and verrrry verrrry wrrrong!"

"But Lucinda may not like a doll, even a museum piece when she is 13, and I shall be dead!" I said.

"Then you must put her in your will."

So here, Mary, mother of Lucinda, is Duchess for *you*. Keep her with care until the right time. She is part of my life.

November 1962

Chapter Two

A Wedding Photograph and the Seas

In 1951, at a party to celebrate a marriage which was to take place shortly and to end shortly, I met Dr. and Mrs. Wallace Wilson. They were in their mid-sixties; I was in my mid-twenties. They were giving a dinner party, with approximately thirty guests, in a private dining room at the Capilano Golf and Country Club, which lies high above Vancouver on the side of a mountain. It was raining hard that night and I remember looking down, while our car waited its turn to enter the portico, onto the lights of the city and of Lions' Gate Bridge and seeing them shimmer through the sheets of rain.

When I walked into the room, I saw her immediately, and what I remember now is meeting those extraordinarily bright and sharp blue eyes which seemed to fasten on me. She was in a wheelchair. Her husband, smiling broadly and easily, stood slightly behind and to the side of her. We all shook hands and then Ethel Wilson asked after her publisher, John Gray, because she knew that I had just come home from Toronto where I had worked for Macmillan's. We talked about publishing and writers for a good time. She asked after my mother, whom she had known since childhood but had not met for many years. At the end of the evening, when I was fortified by whisky, wines, and cognac, I had acquired the necessary nerve to ask if she would read a story I had written. She said that she could never read anything unless it was in print, which was possibly her escape from such requests, but then she asked me to telephone her and perhaps she could try.

A week later I telephoned her and she asked me to bring my story and come to tea. I came, nervously. She took the typed manuscript and she asked me to sit down. I chose a stool across from her and from the books behind me I picked out Proust's *Swann's Way*. It was a blind choice and was in a blue and white cover, and it was the first time I had taken a look into Proust. I couldn't read it. She asked me for a pencil which was across the room on a polished oak side-table. She was in her wheelchair. I met those bright eyes when I was bringing the pencil to her. She liked the story and that was the start of a friendship which lasted nearly thirty years.

Of course nobody can tell the truth about someone else's life any more than about one's own life. But we can catch glimpses from letters and memories, and quiet, or angry, scenes of openness, and from places and photographs, and lack of photographs.

Through her long life she made and kept many photograph albums, although, oddly, there are no photographs of herself between the time when she was a blonde, cherubic, four year old, and when she had become an unusually tall and beautiful girl of perhaps sixteen. There are daguerrotypes of her father and her mother, which she kept near her in the last years of her life.

Her father, Robert William Bryant, was, as she said, a handsome man. The son of a draper, grocer, and Methodist lay minister, he grew up in the Lincolnshire village of Stickney, the second of his father's eleven children. His mother, Mary, died in childbirth with her sixth child in seven years. Robert was five at the time. Soon after her death, his father married again, which was neither unusual for the times nor impractical for the head of a family, and sired another five children.

Robert, although often ill, finished school in Stickney with high enough grades to enter Trinity College in Dublin. He was not there long, less than a year, and it is not known what he studied or why he left. But when he was twenty, he decided on the course his life would take; he would become a Methodist minister and go out to Africa to preach his faith. Although he seems to have had an instinct for adventure, it was not that alone that sent him to Africa. He was in poor health and his doctor thought the dry air and warm climate there would keep him alive longer than the damp and cold of England.

So in October 1876, Robert wrote in his journal (which is the only piece of his writing that has survived his daughter's death[1]), "I set my face toward South Africa & went on board the 'Dunrobin Castle' then lying in the Thames." He was on the high seas for twenty-one days before entering the harbour of Cape Town. From there he sailed east and north in a small coastal ship, the *Florence*, up along the coast of southern Africa and into the Indian Ocean, passing through a terrible storm before coming into the pretty port of Durban. An old friend of his father's, who was now the mayor of Durban, met Robert on the dock and took him in hand.

For six months Robert relaxed on the lush, nearly tropical coast where oranges, bananas, pineapples, sugar, and tea brought the richness and ease of trade to the port. But he did not become well, and was reluctantly reminded that his "immediate object in going to South Africa was health," so he said goodbye to his father's friend and left for the interior.

He took a bus for three hundred miles, then a farmer's cart, and finally a horse, passing through "country over-run by huge herds of game," and among men who lived in caves and hunted with poison arrows. He reached Harrismith, a border town of the Orange Free State, and rested there for a few days. Then, still generally travelling alone, he went on until, on May 8, 1877, he reached his destination. That was the small town of Bethlehem, and it was to be his home for the next two years and eight months. It had one gaol, one hotel, and two hundred Europeans.

Robert's health improved quickly, seemingly miraculously, but Bethlehem's isolation and "the peculiar difficulties of the work," he wrote in his journal, "weighed heavily upon my heart." Drinking and gambling were "the chief hindrance to the work of God" and the young preacher.

In December 1879 he won a transfer to Pietermaritzburg.

"The first time I saw Maritzburg...I confess I somewhat despised it & was disposed to ridicule its claims to be considered a city," he wrote. "It seemed barely on a level with a third or fourth rate country market town in the land I had left behind me...[But after two years in Bethlehem it seemed] to have grown enormously & when I set foot there again I felt that I was in the world once more...I do not believe that anywhere there is a freer, friendlier, more loveable people than the colonists of Natal."

These colonists, unlike the Boers of Bethlehem, were his own English people.

For three years Robert Bryant had been spreading the word of God, but only as a lay minister. Now he took his orders, and on August 31, 1880, eight months after coming to preach in Pietermaritzburg, he was ordained a Wesleyan Methodist minister and presented with a common-looking Bible with a cardboard cover. "Holy Bible" is printed in gold ink, and on the fly-leaf, with pretty flourishes of plain black ink, is written:

Presented
to the
Rev. Robert William Bryant
at his Ordination

John Kilner	General Secretary
	Wesleyan Miss. Society
Frederick Mason	Chairman
Owen Watkins	Secretary
Natal District	
Pietermaritzburg, Aug. 31st, 1880	

This Bible is not nearly as worn as the small, soft, black leather New Testament & Psalms which has simply a neat, small, but strong signature, R.W. Bryant, at the top of the fly-leaf. Several of the pages have come loose from the spine, but they have not been lost or torn.

Robert's daughter was careful of the few possessions her father left her. Throughout her life she would try to find out more and more about him. When she was a woman of fifty, for example, she was in England and she asked her father's half-brother, Herbert Bryant, for facts. She wrote about this meeting in an essay, "Reflections In A Pool."[2]

Was it true that Paul Verlaine, the French poet "of uncertain character," as she put it, taught her father at the village school in Stickney? Yes, her uncle said, he had for a short time.

> So I said, "Oh Uncle Herbert, tell me some of the things that Verlaine said and did!" and Uncle Herbert said, "I'm sorry my dear, but I only remember that he roared at a very snivelling boy 'Sir! Sweep your nose!' and that's all I remember of the words of the poet Verlaine."

Herbert also told her about Robert's romantic brother whose name was Tom. He too went out to Africa, but he went for adventure and not for God. In the same essay Ethel Wilson tells this story of Tom and her father. (It is interesting and odd that she always capitalized the F when she mentioned her father.)

> Uncle Herbert told me a story of a meeting that my Father had in Africa which I have always pictured vividly in my mind. It was in bright-coloured country and there were Zulus there, and some Kaffirs. A very tall Zulu gave my very tall Father a big Stick of good fortune. But it brought no luck to my Father nor—later—to me...
>
> In this bright-coloured part of Africa whose name I do not know, my Father lived in a rough sort of little bungalow. He had a Kaffir boy and he had a little horse. One day he was riding along an interminable dusty road into the hills to another village when he saw plodding towards him, raising a small cloud of dust, a man who—as he approached—appeared to have been white once and was now very dirty and wore shabby and ragged clothes. My Father was thinking of something else, yet, as he passed the plodding man and gave him a cursory glance and the man looked up at him, he saw something familiar in that sombre face. The man did not stop, but my Father stopped. He turned his horse and looked after the plodding man with such strange and conflicting memories—the family at home, the present scene, the gay departure of the adventurous Tom, the excitement of letters, the gradual decline, few letters, fewer, no letters, no word of Tom, and at last the parents' buried sorrow. Was this Tom?
>
> My Father...rode back to the man who now had stopped, turned, and stood heavily without motion. My Father reined in his horse, looked into the man's face, exclaimed "Tom?" and dismounted.

The man said nothing. Robert took the man's arm and they walked together toward Robert's village. When they arrived at his small bungalow, Robert fed him, gave him his other nightshirt and his bed. When Robert woke the next morning, the man was gone.

> I think, vaguely, that my Father found him again some time later, but I do not know the rest of the story except that after my Father had returned to England with me, Uncle Tom wrote letters, sometimes, and then he died, alone, of enteric fever which spread through Africa, and that was the end of the boy who had left home so gay.

This romantic man could only catch her imagination whereas two of her father's half-sisters captured both her imagination and her love. One was Margaret Bryant, a distinguished journalist and lively woman with a social conscience who, according to an editorial (signed by I.J. in *The Observer* in February, 1942) shortly after her death, was "a worker and a fighter, concealing an iron will under a deceptively meek exterior, loving gay company, helping and inspiring all who came into contact with her, never sparing the 'pygmy body' which housed a gallant soul." It also reported that she "wrote little over her own signature. Yet she was a born writer," and that "the *Encyclopaedia Britannica*, the Ministry of Food [in the 1914-1918 war], the League of Nations, and the Royal Institute of International Affairs benefited by her stupendous energy...She was a periodical and always welcome visitor to Geneva where her visits came to be known as heralding an unusual outburst of activity on the part of the league Secretariat." She must have been a rare person, especially good for an imaginative young woman to know.[3]

The other half-sister was Hannah Waller Atkinson, who married a "feckless clever character," to use Ethel Wilson's words. He was a reporter for *The Times* and deserted her and his children for a woman who, Ethel Wilson said with some glee, drank too much. Hannah had studied piano under Clara Schumann and was considered capable of the concert stage before meeting the *Times* man. Nevertheless, she translated Pushkin's *Tale of the Golden Cockerell* and, with her feckless fellow, Spengler's *Decline of the West*. I don't know when she was born or died, but I do know that the Wilsons visited her in London in 1947 and that then she was crippled and impoverished.

Ethel Wilson said that her father's relatives "had swift perceptions and senses of humours that made life amusing whether rural or urban, but not commercially productive."

Robert Bryant came from a family of independent and free-thinking people who took risks and had little money to spend. The woman he chose to marry was quite different.

Robert met Lila Malkin eleven years after he went out to Africa. In 1887 he was given leave and returned to England. It happened that on this holiday he went to preach in the Wesleyan Conference Chapel in Burslem, one of the grim pottery towns of Staffordshire, and this is where and when he fell in love with this tall, serious woman. She was thirty years old, as he was. She was deeply religious and was a Wesleyan Methodist worker among the people of her town. John Wesley who, like Robert, had been a Lincolnshire man, firmly told his people that in order to come into his society, they must have "a desire to flee from the wrath to come," and that, once inside, they must show their desire to be saved "by doing no harm; by doing good of every possible sort; by attending upon all means of grace."

This Wesleyan worker, Miss Eliza Davis Malkin, happened to belong to a wealthy family. Her maternal grandfather, Joseph Edge, owned a tile and pottery works and although his products were not as famous as those of his neighbour, Josiah Wedgewood, whose Etruscan platters still span the world, he prospered and gave employment to hundreds of the town's men and children.

His granddaughter, affectionately known as Lila, was equally well-known among these people. If they strayed, she helped them return to the paths of Godliness. If they simply went on a holiday, she wrote to them. She was pretty and she dutifully "taught lessons of thrift and self-help to those who needed them," according to Burslem's Methodist minister. When she agreed to marry Robert, she gave her townspeople, who loved her, one of the few surprises she was to offer during her lifetime.

The daguerrotype of Robert and Lila's wedding, which Ethel Wilson kept out on a small, highly polished table when she was old, shows twenty-seven sombre people, most men bearded and all women bonneted, standing and sitting before the brick side of a solid, large house. Dimly seen behind three lace-curtained windows are three maids in stiff white caps and a small boy in a lace collar and they, too, look as if they have just witnessed an accident on the street. The bride is sitting with eyes cast down. The groom appears to be concentrating on keeping his eyes down. Old Joseph Edge sits staring grimly into the camera with his top hat between his legs, his morning coat buttoned tight, and his white mutton-chop whiskers turned downward, like his mouth. His son-in-law, the bride's father, James Malkin, is exceptionally handsome and has a gentle, bemused look about him. The bride's mother, who was to mean so much to Ethel, is small and still pretty.

The wedding was performed on Thursday, April 14, 1887, in the Conference Chapel, and was well attended by the prosperous people of Burslem. Outside in Swan Square, a good number of women with children watched the finery pass them by, and no doubt wished the bride well.

Three weeks later, on May 3, Robert and Lila Bryant came aboard a Union Castle Steamship with friends and relatives there to wish them God speed on their way to Africa. Their first child, Ethel, had already been conceived.

For Lila, who had never wandered far from Burslem, this must have been a frightening voyage. She passed through the gray swollen seas of the Atlantic and out two thousand miles from the westernmost bulk of the African continent. Twenty-nine days passed and seven thousand nautical miles cut her, permanently, from her England before she reached Cape Town.

At last the big ship docked, and Lila and Robert watched her tie up. Lila looked down at the people who had come to the wharf, and she was slightly frightened because they were strange. Hottentots, they're called, Robert said easily. They had sharp yellow faces and wore brilliant clothes. They walked softly, their limbs were loose, they laughed easily and often, and she could not understand their talk. It was a mixture, Robert said, of Dutch and Native. Obviously he was delighted to be back among the hubbub and the colour, and she looked at him again, as though he were a stranger to her. He saw her then, and said, Well, Mr. Anthony Trollope was here ten years ago and he didn't like Cape Town. He called it "a poor niggery, yellow-faced, half-bred sort of place with an ugly Dutch flavour about it." But, her smiling husband said, Mr. Trollope liked Port Elizabeth very much, and said that its public buildings were beautiful and fit for a town twice its size.[4] It was very much like home, Robert said, as it had been settled, only sixty years before, by English men and women, three thousand of them, sailing through terrible seas on three-masted ships. That voyage, he said, had taken them up to three months. Lila no doubt thanked her God that she had come so late. They would only be in Cape Town until the day after tomorrow, and then they would sail for Port Elizabeth on a small boat. Lila might be taken ashore on the back of a Kaffir. She had laughed at her funny husband, but it was true, she might.

Two days later, as promised, they sailed out into the gray Atlantic and then into the clear, dancing blue of the Indian Ocean. The boat turned into Algoa Bay, and Lila clapped her hands with pleasure. Here, above miles of white beaches, pretty Port Elizabeth gently stretched itself up a cliff which rose two hundred feet until it reached a green, grassy plain. And now, in the sea around them, were those lovely dolphins which had accompanied them, it seemed to her, on this final voyage. They rose and chirped and smiled and rolled and slid down into the clear, blue depths and rose again. And over there on the rocks were perhaps a hundred sea lions sunning themselves and giving no heed to the ship or the people, just giving way to their great comfortable snoozing. Lila laughed with delight.

They came ashore, not on the backs of natives but in a small boat which had been sent out to meet them. They drove in a smart carriage through the market square, and many people smiled and called out to Robert and took his hand, and her hand too. The town was pretty, the wind blew gently, and the air, as Mr. Trollope had written, was "as sweet I think as any I have ever breathed." Lila thought she might be happy here.

Their house, the parsonage, was a simple stone bungalow which climbed a sharp hill. It was supported by enormous boulders at the base. As the house rose, the size of the boulders diminished. At the top of the hill, the parsonage sat, briefly, on true ground.

Lila had her Kaffir girl, Sasawna, to keep the parsonage clean and to cook for herself and Robert, which left her free to explore. Often she walked down the hill to watch the big ships coming in and going out, and the country carts, piled high with mohair, being driven along the wood and iron jetties to have their loads dropped into the waiting ships. Port Elizabeth was about the same size as her Burslem, only fifteen thousand people, but it was so busy, far busier than it had been even a year ago. That year, 1886, an Australian named George Harrison had found gold in the great reef running across the veld of Witwatersrand. Now men without wives or children were coming off boats, coming from many parts of the world to seek their fortunes in the open lands beyond Port Elizabeth.

Gold was not the town's only call for riches. Into Port Elizabeth came tall, awkward creatures, birds which could not fly, ugly and comical as anything Lila could imagine. Ostriches, which produced two crops of feathers a year to decorate the fashionable and not-so-fashionable ladies of the world, were sold at Port Elizabeth's open-air auctions for thirty pounds sterling, sometimes more, rarely less.

And that year of Lila's arrival was proclaimed a year of merry-making in all corners of the world because Queen Victoria, Queen of the United Kingdom of Great Britain and of Ireland, Empress of India, had ruled over her empire now for half a century. There was drinking and dancing all over the pink-coloured globe. Port Elizabeth was having the liveliest year of its life, and for that Lila was lucky.

Lila and Robert did not walk out at night, as they had in England, into the garden or out along the streets and into the park. Snakes came out in the cool of night — puff adders, yellow cobras, ringhalls, and others. Neither did they drive out together often beyond Port Elizabeth, because the country was just scrub brush and sour grass, too sour even for sheep, so no farms civilized the land.

And Lila now knew that she was, as she had suspected on that long sea journey, pregnant. That was why she was not feeling well, she explained to herself and to her mother in her letters home. In truth, she had tuberculosis.

Lila gave birth to Ethel in the parsonage on a hot summer day, January 20, 1888, and Robert christened her. She was named Ethel after Lila's younger sister, who had died at the age of twelve, and Davis after Lila's maternal grandmother.

Lila did not seem to recover her strength, and then she was again pregnant. Eighteen months after Ethel was born, she had her son, who was quickly christened Robert Norman. Ten days later, on July 28, after a painful struggle, Lila died. Her son died on August 7 and was buried beside her.

A year later, in July 1890, Robert, now thirty-three, and Ethel, who was two, prayed for the last time together over Lila's and Robert Norman's graves and left South Africa. Neither would return.

Robert had a parsonage in Pembroke, Wales. Maria Riggall, who was his great aunt and was kind and lively, had offered to look after his house and child for him, and it was here that the woman Ethel Wilson remembered being "unimaginably happy."

> Life was luminous and merry and beloved, although I was sometimes whipped on my hands with the back of a hairbrush. I always started to bellow while the hairbrush was still in the air and before it touched me — gently. I became difficult when, in my reading lessons, I (aged 5) could not understand the meaning of the word "the." I asked *"What* is a 'the'?" My Father tried to explain but could not tell me. "But what *is* a 'the'? What does it do?" He could not say.
>
> I remember when I was seven years old sitting happily on the floor of my Father's study while he was busy, trying to read *Ivanhoe* of all things, and getting along pretty well although I could not pronounce the names of the characters in the story. That did not matter. I had to know them by the look of the words.
>
> . . . and because Father still had a sort of sleeping T.B. and because he had always overworked, and because he went out to preach when he had a cold and there was pouring rain, he took pneumonia and he too died.

Robert Bryant was forty. He died at Acton, Co. Cheshire, on June 19, 1897. Ethel was nine.

Now, as she said in the story of Duchess, her relatives on her mother's side came forward to claim her. She went first to Mrs. Moon and then to Uncle John and to Uncle Sydney and Aunt Edith. Later she wrote, "With all [Uncle Sydney's] kind hospitality and Aunt Edith's real goodness, his sarcasms frightened me very much and I became painfully shy." Ethel Wilson would also write of "the strong taste of sorrow in her throat, and in her stomach the cold core of lead that only the desolate know." Somewhere, in all her writing, the unfathomable aspects of human events would be crouched, waiting to spring up.[5]

Ethel's maternal grandmother, Annie Malkin, was now living on the far west coast of Canada, in Vancouver, which was the same distance from England and her granddaughter as South Africa had been when she lived in Burslem and the child in Port Elizabeth. She had seen Ethel, of course, when Robert brought her home to England, before they moved on to Wales, and she had loved her as Lila's daughter. Four years later, in 1894, Annie's husband, the handsome James Malkin, died. Annie was not needed in Burslem now, for her children had grown up, but she was needed, two of her sons said, in Vancouver. So at the age of sixty-three, Annie Malkin, who also had not wandered far from Burslem, sailed three thousand nautical miles across the Atlantic and took a train for more than three thousand miles across the uncivilized magnificent country of Canada to make a home for her two sons. She brought with her two maidens, her flighty sister Eliza, then fifty, and her dutiful, good, but plain daughter Belle, thirty-seven. Annie's youngest child Philip, who was sixteen, came too. He had turned down a scholarship to Cambridge University to join the adventure and his brothers. The group left Liverpool on May 9, 1895, and a remarkable eighteen days later, at noon on May 27, arrived at the edge of the Pacific Ocean. Annie's sons were there to meet them at the station. She had not seen "the boys" for eleven years.

The Malkin men — William Harold, who became a rich man and a respected mayor of Vancouver, and Fred, who did very well through his brother's business — had come to Canada when they were twenty-one and twenty, respectively. They had worked on farms and at various jobs for ten years, always working westward until they could go no farther. They arrived in Vancouver only a year before their mother. A year after her arrival, W.H., as he was known about town (and he was something of a man-about-town in his later life), established "W.H. Malkin Co. Wholesale Grocers, Tea Blenders and Coffee Roasters." His company, which went on to make jams and pickles and other helps to busy housewives and Chinese cooks, gave security to his mother, aunt, and sister.

18

It was three years after Annie Malkin started living in Canada that she heard of Robert's death. Quickly she sent off letters to her sons John and Sydney in England and, probably, to Robert's relative Maria Riggall, who was still keeping house for the child when Ethel was not being passed from well-meaning relative to relative on the Malkin side. Annie was determined that Lila's child should come to Canada, and that she and Belle and Eliza and her sons could give the child a secure home in a new and beautiful country. This country, after all, held the promise of youth, and that was why her sons had come. She prayed for guidance and took up her way. Annie Malkin, small, gentle, and vague when she was not determined, decided to go back to England and collect her granddaughter. Eliza, her sister, decided to come too, and so did her daughter Belle. They all left Vancouver at 1:30 p.m. on March 21, 1898, and settled down among hat boxes and other necessities of travel for the journey eastward. The train was luxuriously appointed with plush seats and polished mahogany walls, and its dining car glittered with white linen and sterling silver and cut glass. Annie kept a leather-bound diary as the train ran smoothly eastward.

March 21...It has been a glorious day. We are travelling most comfortably...

March 22. Breakfast at Sycamous good! 6.50 Dinner at Glacier House where a...[gentleman] accosted Belle saying he had heard her in Homer St. choir...

March 24...Noon. A blizzard all morning, very warm and comfortable. Just now we seem to be stuck in a snowdrift...Train 22 hours late, but we enjoy the delay so far.

March 25. Accident to train full of Klondikers...2 or 3 cars turned over, one man killed. Many sent on to Winnipeg bandaged up but looking cheerful.

March 26....Met with lady going to Cape Town, Johannesburg, had an interesting talk.

March 27...Hear that war is declared between Spain and U. States. Hope it is a false rumour. All our traps together for changing at Montreal where we should be in three hours...All night at Windsor Hotel most Luxurious!

March 28. Got off in nice time for 8.15 train. Belle had no trouble with her Bike, though it looked in poor plight as to packing.

The three women did not stay long in England. That summer they were again travelling west, and ten-year-old Ethel was with them.

"Are there any schools in Vancouver?" asked the orphan, removing her gaze from the prairie which flowed past the west-bound train, and looking up at her Grandmother.

"Oh I think so dear," said her Grandmother vaguely, with her finger in her book. "But there is a very nice young girl called Miss Gordon who lives near us and told me before I left that she is going to open a little school for little girls and that will be nice for you," and the Grandmother added, "she is a Girton girl."

"Oh," said the orphan. She did not know what kind of a girl a Girton girl was. (A pile of white buffalo bones flashed past).

"But is she kind?" asked the inexperienced orphan.

"Oh very very kind I should think," said the Grandmother, "she has fair hair."[6]

As the train moved in to the station I saw...the mountains, the sparsely-manned harbour, the sailing ships, some steamers that had, I suppose, lately begun to enter the harbour. We arrived at the station and were greeted warmly by my uncles. [7]

Chapter Three

The Promising Country

Canada, vast and wild, held qualities which Ethel would always fear and love. It had strange depths that would remain untouched and untouchable, and would suddenly issue up the unexpected. She would write about these properties of her new country—from now on Canada, not Africa or Britain, would be her own country—with humour and also with darkness.

She first met the unexpected in an event which pleased her hugely. She woke up that first morning on the big Canadian train listening to the tiddaly-dum, tiddaly-dum, tiddaly-dum of wheels running along their tracks, and then, as she could stay no longer, she wriggled into her clothes in her upper bunk, snapped open the heavy green curtains that had given her unwanted privacy from the corridor, and climbed down the ladder. She looked where she had left her shoes. They were not there. And then she looked across the aisle and there they were, but they had changed miraculously. They were gleaming from the best polishing she had ever seen. When she told her grandmother about this mysterious happening in the night, she learned that the porter, that large black man whom Ethel had immediately liked for his warm smile and deep voice, had polished her shoes and would do so every night. Yes, he would have come from Africa, perhaps South Africa, but Ethel should perhaps not discuss this with him. His parents and his grandparents would have been slaves in the United States, most likely. But now he was a free man and had dignity, said her small grandmother, who was a devout Christian.

The nice porter, when they pulled into the Vancouver station, put his hand under Mrs. Malkin's elbow to assist her down the three steps from the train to the platform, and Annie Malkin thanked him and discreetly passed him what Ethel knew was a tip. Eliza was helped next, then Belle, and then Ethel skipped down before the porter could help her. They both laughed and she thanked him and said goodbye and followed her family into the station's rotunda where her uncles were waiting.

("They were bent on making up for me what I had lost—which was really everything. Never did I hear a sarcastic word from any of them. I was really jolly lucky when I think of some orphans!" she told a cousin years later.[1])

There was a commotion now, questions, baggage checks, did Aunt Eliza have this or that? chatter, and laughter, and then they were out in the fresh sea air. The child in black mourning was suddenly hoisted high in the air and nearly dropped on a seat in the carriage, and then the women got up and in, and Ethel watched her handsome new uncles step lithely up and sit opposite. Now they were driving smartly toward home.[2]

Squeezed between corsetted thighs, Ethel looked carefully at her uncles, and then she looked out at what she was passing and realized that Vancouver was not at all like London or Burslem, or even Pembroke which was also on the sea. The streets were of dirt or mud, I do not know the weather.

But Vancouver was also the same. The women wore big hats and full skirts, and gloves that buttoned on the inside of the wrists, and purses that dangled or swayed from these wrists, and some of the more fascinating ladies wore boas of ostrich feathers. The men of this city looked bigger, at least some did. Some were very big indeed and were dressed roughly, without hats or canes, with thick boots, and one man, she gasped in surprise, spewed out an extraordinarily long stream of black juice from his mouth. Later she learned that he did this because he chewed tobacco. She was entranced and tried it once, but it had a sharp bitter taste which she did not like, and she was glad to know that ladies did not chew.

Her carriage passed wooden houses with wooden porches and picket fences enclosing the gardens, and when it stopped she saw that her house was of wood too, but larger than most of the houses. The family went inside. In the hall was a pot-bellied stove which, in the rainy and dark winter days and nights to come, would turn red with furious comfort. But this stove was the only unfamiliar in the house. White antimacassars stretched across the backs and arms of stuffed chairs. The dining room furniture was dark, polished, solid. A gleaming silver tea service on a silver tray sat on the side-board. Ethel was allowed to explore the house and the garden, and she walked out through the gate and looked up and down the street, but did not venture farther that day. She had high tea with the family, and while the sun was still well up in the sky, she was told to say goodnight. This was the way of adults with children then, and for several generations to come, so that the children had their rest and the adults had their freedom to talk. Belle, who would always be responsible for the child, took her up to her room and listened to her prayers. Then Ethel jumped into bed and Belle tucked the covers around her and said that she hoped—and Ethel knew that she really meant it—that Ethel would love Canada as much as she did. Belle kissed her niece goodnight and closed the door behind her. Ethel lay quite still for a while, listening to the sounds inside and outside her new house, and to the quiet. She slipped down from her bed and tip-toed to the window, and for a long time she watched lights come on in windows and the sun slip down and the forest darken until it was black against a paler sky. She thought she would be safe here.

Usually twice on Sundays, Ethel Bryant, Miss Eliza Edge, Mrs. Annie Malkin, Miss Belle Malkin, and the three Malkin men would walk out to church. Miss Kate McQueen told me, eighty-two years later, that she clearly remembered her first sight of the new child who lived down Broughton Street. Miss McQueen, who was Ethel's age, then about ten years old, was looking out of her bedroom window on this particular Sunday morning. As usual, she said, she was slow in dressing and her father "was calling up to me to hurry up or we would be late, which he always did, and I saw this gentle procession coming along Bute Street. Everything was very quiet. First came old Mrs. Malkin and then Mr. [W.H.] Malkin. Second, Miss Edge and the young Malkin man [Philip]. And third came Miss Malkin [Belle] who was holding the hand of this pretty little English girl who had long fair hair and was unmistakably English." She said that Ethel was unmistakably English because she walked quietly and her black clothes were obviously English.

They were on their way to the Homer Street Methodist church. But Mrs. Malkin was thinking about the new church which she, in her humble way, was helping to raise on the corner of Burrard and Georgia Streets. This church, which would be Ethel's church for a long time, would be formidably solemn, a gray, wooden, barn-like building without so much as a stained glass window to relieve its gloom. Inside its vault-like darkness, the rows of pews would curve in a semi-circle around the pastor's pulpit, and behind him the choir would sing with proper passion.

Truth has, at least with the sifting and reconstruction of retrospect, the bones of fiction as justifiably as fiction picks the bones of truth. As Ethel Wilson wrote vividly about an incident from her childhood in this church, it is reasonable to drop it into her biography. It was first published in the *New Statesman and Nation*, and then incorporated into her most autobiographical novel, *The Innocent Traveller*. (She said that perhaps it would be interesting for her family to read that novel, even if it were not published.)

In this story, Ethel Wilson explains that a new pastor has come to Vancouver and he has a penchant for revival meetings. The character Rose could be interpreted as Ethel. One of Rose's uncles does not want to go to church, but his mother says, " 'if the Lord should speak to us and bless us, we shall be well repaid'," and, looking with "sweet sincerity upon her household," departs with them all for church.

They walked into the pew, pushing a little, but decorously... There was Rose... small, curly-haired, still wearing the good black in which she had been warmly and suitably dressed following her adored Father's death the year before. They all sat down, then they dropped upon their knees. The uncles remained there for a brief and manly instant. The Grandmother became charged with emotion immediately on closing her eyes. The Aunts communed silently and respectfully for a moment, and Rose stayed down as long as they. On rising they settled themselves on the long pew which curved at the side of the church... Rose looked this way and that with youthful interest. She noted the bonneted old ladies as they stole to their pews, their plain and bearded husbands, the pretty Miss Moores, the fathers, the mothers, the families that streamed in. Most of them dropped to their knees. Fleetingly she wondered what they all really did there. But some, oh horrors, sat smack down and looked round frankly and with interest upon their neighbours...

...here was the Rev. Elmer Pratt, full of zeal, swarthy, black-visaged, and violent of feature. Beneath his black hair shone his bright black eyes... Beneath his large nose sprang and flourished his magnificent black moustaches. Beneath his vigorous chin rose up his high and stiff white collar, with a splendid white four-in-hand tie. The face, coarse and vigorous, was perpetually at war with the sanctity of the starched white collar and tie beneath. He used strange words. Rose, accustomed to the suave tones of her native England, was constantly amazed at the flat and grating voice of the Rev. Elmer Pratt. Whereas the ministers of the Gospel to whom she had listened Sunday by Sunday since infancy spoke gently of the love of God, the Rev. Elmer Pratt thundered about brothels. She supposed that brothels were places where broth was made and decided that the broth must be very bad or the Rev. Elmer Pratt would not be so angry...But once his sermons of wrath and denunciation were over, he became a human and kindly being.

...Rose had never before been to a revival service, in fact there had been some discussion at home as to whether she was too young to come. But, the Grandmother having been saved at the age of five, here she was.

...Softened and vibrating with tenderness...[Rev. Pratt] described to them as if he had been there the Kingdom of the Blessed where they fain would be. Did they not, urged the Rev. Elmer Pratt, as a strong inducement, wish to see their Dear Ones who were undoubtedly waiting for them in the Heavenly Home? "Is there no one waiting for you?" thrilled Mr. Pratt. "My brothers, my sisters, have you no one waiting in Heaven for you? Come now," said he encouragingly, "who has a Father in the Promised Land? Who has a dear dear Father waiting in the Promised Land? Come now, stand! Stand up now, any person who has a dear dear Father waiting in the Promised Land; do not be afraid; stand up, ah, bless you, my brother; bless you, my sister!" Thus exhorted people began to stand up, one here, one there, looking downwards. Rose's heart was ready to burst. Her Father, her dear dear Father, whom she loved better than anyone on earth. Father with the dear voice and the kind laughing eyes, was waiting, waiting. She slipped to the floor and stood up. "Bless you, my child," said the Rev. Elmer Pratt kindly.

Rose burst into tears.

"Let us sing," said the Rev. Elmer Pratt, "let us sing together." And he sang in his grating voice:

> I have a Father in the Promised Land,
> I have a Father in the Promised Land,
> My Father calls me, I must go
> To meet him in the Promised Land.

"Come now," said Mr. Pratt, "all those standing, sing—'I have...' " and everybody sang.

Rose sang sobbingly, sniffingly, to the mute distress of Great-Aunt Topaz, Aunt Rachel, Uncle Frank, Uncle Stephen, [and] Uncle Andrew...The Grandmother, touched and pleased, wept gently beside her.

The child rose weeping twice more, because she also had a mother and a brother waiting for her, and then Rose and her family, like Ethel and her family, returned home to the large Sunday dinner which had been prepared during their absence by "the Chinaman." He with his pigtail, strange clipped talk, soft slippers, and sharp eye was another unexpected and unfathomable particle of Canada. It must have seemed the same to him. He was one of thousands of Chinese men who, not that long before Ethel arrived, came from China to lay the tracks for the Canadian Pacific Railway. He and they were promised high wages, but when the time came to pay, the promises were ignored. Some Chinese men went north to pan for gold. Many, finding no or too little gold, found work as houseboys and cooks in Vancouver houses. They had no money to return to China. They were unhappy men, many of them, who happily smoked opium which was their custom in China. Within their white families they were compliant at least about food, and cooked what their mistresses wanted—suet pudding, roast beef, overboiled spinach. Very seldom indeed did they prepare Chinese dishes, although they cooked those for themselves. They were proud men and not really compliant, some of them.

When Ethel had eaten as much as she wanted, she took her hoop and ran it up and down in front of her house. Then she remembered Mrs. Creary who had a new baby and a smart new English pram. Mrs. Creary wanted to push the pram along a sidewalk and so, because Mr. Creary knew a politician, Mrs. Creary had a new plank sidewalk in front of her house. Her house was not far from Ethel's, and the hoop, although it could catch in the splits between the planks and topple over, was smoother, faster, and far more fun on Mrs. Creary's sidewalk.

The chain gang had laid Mrs. Creary's sidewalk. This was a gang of convicts who were chained together and transported to work in wagons. In 1896 they saved Vancouver $2,996, the chairman of the Board of Works reported on January 13, 1897.

The convicts laid sidewalks with long, rough, thick boards which had been sawed in the mill at False Creek. They cut back the forests to lay the land bare for houses and gardens. They were not attached together when they were working, but their feet were shackled and the guards, who cradled guns in their arms, watched them closely, so they could not escape.

"I was always afraid," Ethel Wilson wrote, "and did not turn to look at the chain gang although I wanted to explore their faces, and understand why this had come about."[3]

They were not important, only seen occasionally and then not looked at.

Equally interesting and much safer sights for Ethel came about on Saturday mornings. She would dress in her best black dress and stockings and boots, and Belle would put on a fresh white blouse which buttoned high at the throat and ballooned out at the elbows, a long dark skirt just high enough to miss the ground and, if raised for a puddle, to show an ankle, and a big hat which was firmly secured by a long pin. They would open the garden gate and walk up the street together. Sometimes they caught the street car, but if the day were fine, they would walk into town.

They usually passed Johnston and Kerfoot, Klondike Outfitters, and Ethel listened to the click of their heels and the oncoming thump of the big men's boots along the boardwalk. They often stopped and stroked the soft noses of the mules who were waiting to be loaded with prospectors' provisions. A few of these animals were thin but most were fed well enough, and groomed, because they were important to their owners' welfare. Aunt and niece walked farther and passed "Arcade Cigars: H.E. Padmore Proprietor." Ethel loved the pungent smells coming from this shop (she would always love the smell of a good cigar) and she enjoyed seeing the elegant young men who came out of this shop and smiled at her, or didn't notice her or Aunty Belle at all. Sometimes they picked up a cake from Black's Bakery for tea, and then, if the weather were kind, they walked north to where they could clearly see, without interruption of house or store, the mountains, the sea, and the train tracks which had brought them to this city. They walked east now, the opposite way from home, along Cordova because this was the liveliest street in town. Ethel loved to hear the guns firing and Aunty Belle allowed her to stop and look in, but only for a minute, at the men in the shooting galleries. The hardware stores gave out sharp, mysterious smells and displayed objects that glistened and asked to be touched. In here was a promising new world of harnesses and kettles, linoleum and lawn mowers, sieves, nails, jugs, glittering spoons to fool fishes, hooks, knives, and bullets. Everything along this street, especially this first summer, fascinated the child, and she wrote about it when she was a woman. Rough, unshaven loggers fresh from up north rolled along the street from side to side, some sad, some amazingly cheerful. And there were "glorious ladies dressed in fashionable black, who sauntered, often in pairs...They sauntered lazily with a swaying of opulent hips and bosom, looking softly yet alertly from lustrous eyes set in masks of rose and white. '...*Look* at those pretty ladies, who are they, just look!' " Ethel sometimes whispered. But Aunty Belle did not look. "She behaved as if she were blind and deaf. It appeared that she did not know the pretty ladies at all. The town was small, and...[her aunt] knew everybody, at least by sight, so this struck...[Ethel] as queer."

On most afternoons that summer, Belle took Ethel down to English Bay, only a few blocks from home. Here Ethel learned to be a powerful swimmer. Her teacher, whose name was Joe Fortes, was a big, barrel-chested, black man who gave swimming lessons free of charge to anyone who wanted to learn — child, woman, or even man. He was undoubtedly the most loved and respected man in Vancouver in those innocent days, although of course he did not enter the houses of the people who loved and respected him. When he died, the politicians of Vancouver put up a memorial to him in Stanley Park, which was an appropriate and not unusual way to honour a man of the wrong colour in or out of the British Empire. Ethel Bryant loved him, and feared him too. She said that she was "one of the cowardly ones who shivered on the raft while Joe roared, 'You jump off of that raff this minute, or I'll leave you there all night!' So she jumped because the prospect was so terrible and so real, and how threatening the wet sea by night, and who knows what creatures will come to this dark raft alone. So she jumped."[4] Ethel grew to love the water, and to swim and dive like a seal. She wrote about it often, always with respect, often with fear.

It was different, usually daft, when her Great Aunt Eliza took her down to the beach. Ethel, as usual, would take her stick and hoop and her bathing costume wrapped in a towel; Miss Edge would, as usual, take her bicycle. She pushed it. She never rode it for fear that it would run away and abandon her somewhere. So the two would set off, but Miss Edge, although maidenly, was not modest and she would stop anyone, no matter where they were going, for a chat. So it took a long time for Ethel to reach the beach. When she did, she ran into a bath house to change. She did not like the dank smells within these wooden huts. Then, with her clothes bundled up, she would run to where her great aunt was engaged in conversation, drop her bundle, call goodbye, and run toward the sea. Later, much later than Belle would allow because Belle would have her eyes on the child in the sea, Ethel would stand, blue with cold, before her great aunt until Eliza's conversation came to a natural end. Then child and great aunt would go home the way that they had come, stopping to chat, and then both would rush into the house to tell Mrs. Malkin what they had each encountered. Ethel's grandmother would smile gently and encouragingly at each. Then, on occasion, her face would light up and she would say, "Praise the Lord, I have a call to make." Mrs. Malkin would hurry out of the room, down the hall, and enter a small room with one window which was placed high above a water tank. Some time later there was a loud and angry rush of water, and Mrs. Malkin would reappear and settle back to hear what Joe Fortes had said from the child, and sometimes about Mrs. Rogers (whose husband owned the sugar refinery) from the adult who did not like to put away childish things.

Despite the possible dangers that were natural to the sea, the opium dens in Chinatown, the men who formed chain gangs, and the seafaring visitors from other ports with other laws, Vancouver at the turn of this century, and for another half century to come, was a safe place for respectable citizens. So it was with surprise that Mrs. Malkin encountered real danger one evening when she was walking home from church. She was alone. (Ethel Wilson, always aware of danger, told this story to her much younger friend Audrey Butler, who told it to me.)

It was raining hard and Mrs. Malkin had lowered her umbrella to buffet the rain and the wind when a large, burly man jumped out of a vacant lot and stood before her, blocking her way. He told her to give him her purse. She was absolutely astonished.

"But my good man," she said, "I have no money. Come under the lamp post with me."

Equally astonished, he came with her under the lamp post. Mrs. Malkin now tried to loosen her purse from her wrist so that she could show him that she had only her handkerchief and her housekey, and no money. In her anxiety she dropped her Bible. She stooped down to pick it up, and then noticed that some of the pages were wet and muddy. Cleaning them off with her black glove, she realized that here was something which might help this man. "Lay not upon yourselves treasures upon earth," she read to him in her gentle way, "where moth and rust doth corrupt, and where thieves break through and steal; But lay up for yourselves treasures in heaven."

With that the robber disappeared into the rain and Mrs. Malkin hurried home. She arrived excited. Someone helped her off with her coat, someone else put on the cocoa, and the family gathered around to hear what had happened. Mrs. Malkin told them, ending her story this way:

"And then, with an unrepeatable word, he went off and I hope that the Bible sank in and that he will not do that again to an old lady."

Belle, no doubt, that night took her mother up to her bedroom, and when Mrs. Malkin was in bed and had said, "Tuck me feet up, love," Belle "reached in her capable and accustomed hands under the bed clothes and wrapped a shawl around the Matriarch's tiny feet...[Belle] was the daughter, the maiden. Never having known the lights and music of marriage, never having known the joy and care of being a mother, she was yet the wife and mother of her household. She was to this home as the good bread upon the table," Ethel Wilson wrote in *The Innocent Traveller*.

"Belle was a little dour and perhaps severe looking, but why not?" Ethel's old friend, Alex Wilson, said to me in 1980. "Look at those people of so many generations—Ethel and Granny and Aunt Eliza, who was a flighty old lady. Belle looked after them all. Granny was known as a saint. She was absolutely good, but she did nothing else. She simply sat there in her white cap and was good."

That September, as Granny had promised, Ethel Bryant became a pupil at Miss Gordon the Girton girl's new school.[5] She was one of six pupils in this first year of the school, which is still in operation. Miss Jessie Gordon, headmistress, was small, pretty, and determined. Her sister, Miss Mary Gordon, was tall, spare, and kindly. (Both Miss Gordons were there when I attended the school forty years later.) Miss Mary was in charge of the school's domestic affairs. Only the Girton Gordon taught, but she employed two other teachers for her six students: Monsieur Dougour-Joutty, who taught French, and Miss Marstrand who, with "shining silver knobbly pins in her fine hair," taught drawing "chiefly by means of the sit-beside system." Miss Gordon taught arithmetic and would often ask Ethel, who was a quick student, to help "little Dot" with her sums.[6]

It is unlikely that the ten-year-old orphan and stranger would be naughty, at least in that first year of school, but those children who were naughty suffered the same punishment I did for the seven years I attended under Miss Gordon's rule. Outside her office door was a wooden box covered in chintz which displayed (faded, in my day) large pink roses. The box was extremely hard, but you did not dare squirm for comfort in case Miss Gordon came out. Oddly enough, for the many many times of sitting there, she never came out, and I was most grateful to God, whose benevolence seemed to have shone upon me so often. I would send up my thanks through the school's daily prayers.

At the end of the day, when the same school bell rang for Ethel and her friends as did for me and mine, Ethel would run out to play Rounders (as we did), or if the rain were pouring down, she would walk and run the ten blocks home. Ethel did her homework first, then sat down to High Tea. She talked and listened to her family and then, so early, Belle would take her up to bed.

Chapter Four

"[Life] . . . is a Difficult Country, and Our Home"

One spring afternoon in 1902, Ethel, who was now fourteen and unusually pretty, came home from school and, as usual, went straight to the parlour and kissed her grandmother and her aunts. She felt a tension in the room, sat down, and asked if there was something wrong.

"No dear, not wrong. In fact, we think that what I am about to tell you will please you."

Her small grandmother, who now took on the appearance of power, told her that the family had talked together and that everyone agreed, although they would greatly miss her, that for her own good she would go to school in England. Miss Gordon's school was good, but Ethel seemed to be an outstanding student and so they thought England was best.

"Where?" the orphan asked, sitting quite still.

"Oh," and now Granny and Belle and Eliza all talked with a rush of relief. Ethel heard that she was to go to Trinity Hall School, which was for the daughters of Wesleyan ministers and consequently inexpensive. It was in Southport, in her father's county of Lincolnshire. It was not far from Burslem in Staffordshire, where Ethel had many kind relatives. Uncle Sydney and Aunt Edith would have her for the holidays, and so would her mother's other relatives, who loved her. (Ethel immediately remembered Sydney's sarcasm and how it had frightened her after her father's death.) The Malkins also understood that her father's half-sisters were now living in London.

That August, Ethel said goodbye to her recently-found family, stepped alone onto the train, alone onto the ship, and sailed for England.

"I spoke last night of pride. Let me recommend it. When circumstances reduce us to being alone and unhappy, pride is a good companion...Pride is cold comfort but good, too," Ethel wrote in her story "The Birds."

> How desperately homesick I was for the first year, but not after that. We worked very hard. We were drilled back to front and back again in the use of the English language. For recreation we panted up and down hockey fields in hateful pursuit of each other's shin-bones;...we whirled about on trapezes; we held debates; we produced plays with ten yards of cheesecloth. Everything else but the human voice, of which we had plenty, was too expensive for us...
>
> ...I can see now the plain devoted face and the thick spectacles of the teacher of Greek history and feel the passion that her dull yet poignant voice and careful falling fateful (about the fall of Athens) *words* raised in us. She had an extraordinary power, that fine plain woman, of using the inevitable *word*. She really cared that Athens fell, and so did we.[1]

Ted Hughes, the English poet, has written about some country which lay not far from Southport.

> The upturned face of this land
> The mad singing in the hills
> The prophetic mouth of the rain
>
> That fell asleep
>
> Under migraine of headscarves and clatter
> Of clog-irons and looms
> And gutter-water and clog-irons
> And clog-irons and biblical texts

Stretches awake, out of Revelations
And returns to itself.

Chapels, chimneys, vanish in the brightening

And the hills walk out on the hills
The rain talks to its gods
The light, opening younger, fresher wings
Holds this land up again like an offering

Heavy with the dream of a people.[2]

Ethel loved the fascinations of light. Later she would write about them often.

Her school, which was celebrating its thirtieth birthday—more in prayers than in frivolity—the year that she arrived, had an imposing appearance of respectability. It was a tall Victorian house of gray stone surrounded by oak, elm, and chestnut trees, and rolled green lawns. A good citizen of Southport had built it in 1872 for his and other children of Methodists for eight thousand pounds. It was slightly eccentric in design, but worthy in its attitude.

Ethel entered the front door for the first time, frightened, early in September 1902. She walked into a panelled hallway and was faced with several doors, all of them probably closed at that moment. One led into the dining room. Another into the drawing room of Miss C.H. Peet, the headmistress. The teachers' morning room was on this ground floor, and so were two gymnasiums and one studio. Below stairs—and she could have heard, then, the cacophony of several pianos producing different pieces of music—were, actually, ten pianos, one classroom, and the science laboratories. The maids did the school laundry there, too.

She was taken upstairs to the room which she would share with either two or four other pupils. If she was worried that she might have a nasty girl in her room, she was comforted by the knowledge that it would not be for long. Every three months everyone changed rooms and/or roommates, which was not so much to share the nasties as it was to prevent (it was not stated but it was known by Miss Peet that these things happened) two girls from knowing each other too well.

Each girl was given her own wardrobe, dresser, and washstand.

Along the corridor were the teachers' bedrooms and also, Ethel was amazed to find, a library which was stocked with more books than she had ever seen in one place. (Vancouver's first public library, built through the funds of the American philanthropist Andrew Carnegie, would open in Vancouver a year after she arrived at Trinity Hall.) On the floor above, the top floor, which had a marvelous view of the sea, lived the prefects and, in separate quarters, the maids.

The desperate homesickness, the frightening loneliness Ethel suffered at first, eased up as she began to notice that there were possibilities for taking liberties here. The rules of respectability and discipline would not wither the spirits of the orphan. She was used to them and that might have given her an edge on how to break them. In fact, because she was not the only one now to be watched, the rules gave her some flights of freedom. She was not always "good."

Below the high land upon which the school sat with dignity, was the gray, usually angry Atlantic Ocean. It could be heard throughout the days and nights, breaking on the stony beach, and the wind came with it and rose up and through the trees surrounding the school. The sea and its wind seemed to beckon to Ethel, and when it appeared that she would not be missed, she slipped away from the grounds of the school and went down to meet the sea. Sometimes she would be accompanied by one or a few other girls, and sometimes she would suddenly strip off her long black stockings, hold them high, and run with them, catching the wind in them, and laughing that high-pitched laugh of hers which made others laugh with, and sometimes at, her. Her friends stood in awe and admiration of her daring-do, for who knew where Miss Peet might be at this moment of revolution?

Miss Peet was not really to be feared. Her strictness was a facade of necessity. When Ethel got to know her, she found a woman who was warm and gentle. And stimulating. Miss Peet loved English literature, and on Sunday afternoons in her drawing room, when the fire had been lit by a white-capped maid, she would gather her girls and read to them from Dickens and Thackery, Jane Austen, Emily and Charlotte Bronte, and other respected writers. She must have stirred Ethel's imaginings and turned her ear toward the beauty and appropriate ugliness (what is more ugly than that word itself?) of the English language. It was now that Ethel started her time as a story-teller. Every day the Trinity girls would be taken on a walk, two by two, in what was known as crocodile style. Then someone would call out, "Ethel, tell us a story," and others would call, "Yes, do," and so Ethel would stir up her imagination and let go of a story.

Miss Peet opened up another door for Ethel. Before she had been appointed headmistress, she had been the school's art teacher. She tried to expose her girls to the pleasures of the visual arts, and succeeded with

Ethel, who would possibly have liked, then, to become an artist. But she could not have been an adventuress in the world of art. "Picasso and his pals," as Ethel branded them in a letter to me many years later, were then causing a stir across the continent of Europe and even in England, but Miss Peet and her company of young Methodists did not notice them.

Ethel Bryant was one of her top students. She took the mathematics prize (*The Imitation of Christ* bound in burgundy leather), the school honours prize (Thackeray's *The History of Henry Esmond, Esq.*, two volumes in soft brown leather), and the music prize (Schubert's works for piano, whose blue leather cover was beautifully tooled in gold). Yet, despite her accomplishments and the fact that she was popular among the students, Ethel Bryant was quite a timid person. According to a school friend Nina Ward (who was interviewed when she was an old woman), Ethel would ask, nearly in a whisper, "Is Irene very nasty to you?" Whoever Irene was, she was a horror to Ethel Bryant.[3]

Ethel did not come home to Canada for four years. Holidays usually were spent with Sydney and Edith Malkin. The girl never did feel easy with them. Perhaps she could not put aside that first connection of their hospitality with her father's death, her sense of abandonment and aloneness, but that was not the only reason for her discomfort. Now a young woman living among many women and girls, she was quick to catch what she called phoniness, and the Malkins' piety seemed false to her.

When she had first come to them as a nine-year-old in grief, she herself had been made most comfortable, with a fire in her room and hot water to wash with. But the child liked the maids of the house, and in the early mornings, when she heard them rising, she would quietly climb the stairs and knock on their door. She was welcomed warmly. She noticed then that their rooms were extremely cold, that they slept in their underclothes for warmth, and that they had no fires.

And now, as a young woman, when she walked along the streets of Burslem, or Southport, or London, she saw people without legs moving on flat, wheeled platforms, begging; and others who were blind and sold pencils or shoe laces; and others who were hideously scarred, or walking about with heavy goiters hanging from their throats. Many of these people would not be deformed if they had the money for doctors, and would not have to beg if they, like her, could be educated. She knew that, and she felt it as a rawness on her own body.

This could have been the start of Ethel Wilson's socialist leanings in theoretical political terms, or social conscience in human terms. In obvious terms, she contradicted herself. She respected to the point of high romanticism the English upper class, particularly the peerage, certainly the royal family. She subscribed to, and had pleasure from, the *Illustrated London News*. (She once showed me a picture of Lady Clementine Churchill, as a bride, clipped from that magazine decades before.) On the other hand, she subscribed to, and loved to talk out, the leftist *New Statesman and Nation*, and not just because her first work was published there. She was far too conscious of herself, or not, for that. These non-aligned periodicals were brought together in her affections by one moral principle which was high in her priorities. People should be kind to each other, and have the same chance to exercise kindness and to live fully. Once she wrote her friend and publisher John Morgan Gray and said that she had been reading Moss Hart's *Act One*, and commented, "[Hart] says so truly 'the rich know the rich and the poor know the poor'—and indeed it has been brought home to me very forcefully that the rich *do* know the rich, and many of them care nothing about the poor."[4]

Her stout Aunt Edith did care, physically, for the poor. When Ethel stayed in her big house, "The Limes," Edith drove out regularly to deliver to the unfortunate of Burslem. Occasionally Ethel drove out with her, surrounded by hampers, in her handsome carriage pulled by a pair of smartly-stepping horses. When Ethel's young Vancouver cousin Philip Malkin visited "The Limes" in the early twenties, Edith drove out in her Armstrong-Sidley with Philip and her hampers. They sat behind a glass partition and she spoke to her chauffeur through a tube. She wore a sprig of white heather, symbol of purity, in her lapel. She was a teetotaler.

"Aunt Edith and Uncle Sydney were hard-working Methodists who made allowances for sinners who had fallen by the way, which included being financially unsuccessful," Philip Malkin told me. This must have been quite difficult for Sydney because he was, in material matters, a very sensible and astute man. When you consider this, you can understand that what once appeared as an aberration in Sydney's behavior was actually in character.

Sydney Malkin had decided to run as the Liberal candidate in his riding and, because of the constant Conservative nature of the electors, there was absolutely no hope of his winning the election. People who knew him were dumbfounded, and those who were fond of him worried about him. But it was really most sensible when you remember that sprig of white heather in his wife's lapel. Sydney could come home from his electioneering smelling strongly of spirits and weaving a little as he walked into the parlour. But he could explain, as he did with gusto, that if a man was to win an election he must go to the places frequented by the voters and that, if sad to say dear Edith, was into the pubs.

As a methodist and a Methodist he was successful. He preached frequently at the church where Ethel's parents were married, and Ethel told Philip that if she could avoid going to the church when Uncle Sydney was preaching, she would do so. But Sydney would make up to Ethel for her loss.

"She told me," Philip said, "that he would return home from giving his sermon and tell her what he had preached. He was not a big man, and he had a ruddy complexion. He would stand before her, feet wide apart, knees bent, clenched fists out front, and say, 'Ethel, I had them weeping. I had them crying. I had them fearing the Lord!' "

If Ethel mentioned that she was planning to visit her father's half-sisters in London, Sydney would say, "So you will be visiting your hoity-toity relations while the rest of us struggle along." As Sydney appeared to be rich, and her Bryant half-aunts not at all rich, the school girl now growing up found that as absurd as it was irritating; but she might have realized that he feared their freedom.

Ethel loved spending time with Margaret Bryant and Hannah Atkinson. They took her to concerts and art galleries, the theatre and restaurants, richness and glamour for the boarding school girl. She loved "Father's two half-sisters...so much, for their unshockability and funniness and cleverness and musicalness...They combined being fastidious with not being susceptible to shock. They wanted me to become an actress. They would help. During my holidays...I was distributed around to both sides of my family. But I saw my intellectual and amusing half-aunts less and less because my maternal Aunt-in-Chief [Belle], in whose kindly care I really was, had a great fear that if I stayed with my emancipated paternal half-aunts I would really go on the stage, and the thought was so terrible. Lost! Forever lost! Years later, when I was a married Canadian, my husband came to know and love my half-aunts as I did; but it was then too late to go on the stage. I had never wanted to, anyway."

Fortunately for Ethel, two Malkins were nearly as unstuffy as the two half-aunts, but not suspected by Belle, of course, because they were Malkins. They were Uncle John and "Aunt John," cousins who had married and at whose house Ethel's parents had become engaged. Aunt John wrote to Belle, saying that they were planning a trip to the Continent and they would very much like to take Ethel with them, if Belle would allow it. Belle did, and Ethel wrote of this remarkable escapade fifty-eight years later in a letter to her friends Alan and Jean Crawley. (Alan Crawley was blind. Despite this disability, and with the

38

help of his wife, he started and edited for many years a small but good
periodical, *Contemporary Verse*. In matters of the mind, he was perhaps
the closest friend Ethel Wilson had in her later years, and she wrote some
of her most open letters to him. This was written in 1962.)

I was taken in an unfinished state at the age of 16. Because none of
the other girls had been to France I did not like to mention this
exploit, or, if I did, it was with the phoney humbleness of James
Gillis the Cape Breton poet who had been twice to Boston but "did
not say it by the way of a boast." When we arrived in Paris we went
to see Mme. Chenier with whom my aunt had been at school.
Mme. Chenier looked at me and said I was pretty but had no chic
and what did my aunt mean by not seeing that I wore corsets. My
aunt looked at me with surprise. It was true. She had four sons but
no daughters, and corsets had not occurred to her—nor to me. I
blushed all the time we were in France because I had no corsets,
especially in the casino at Monte Carlo where I was admitted owing
to my uncle kindly telling a lie and my aunt lending me some
hairpins and a long skirt.

On return [to Burslem] my aunt directed me to go to a shop at
the corner of St. Luke's Square, which is immortal in *The Old Wive's
Tale*, but to be sure not to get anything expensive in the way of
corsets. I blushed (as usual) when I asked for corsets, and again
when the "assistant" said "And what size?" because I had not
thought they came in sizes and did not know. The trying-on was by
guess and by God.

I am glad to have had this slightly historical experience, as few
people today are aware that corsets (alias foundation garments) did
not appear in newspapers and magazines then, and were never seen
by the public except in their effects in the female shape; and that in
very working class areas (such as the Potteries) the lower part of the
corset at that time was not flat, as now, but consisted of a large
curve so that the unbridled stomach could be stuffed into it.
Standing by the counter of that draper's shop at the corner of St.
Luke's Square I was distressed because there did not seem to be
enough of me to fill the curve, and also—owing to the fact that this
was a very grimy manufacturing district—there were no white
corsets (which I had understood to be the only colour), only light
gray, dark gray, scarlet, and black. I longed for the advising
presence of my aunt. Then, suddenly fearful that she might choose
black or scarlet, I chose light gray and walked home with the long

parcel under my arm. On the way home I met Arnold Bennett who was visiting his mother. He was well dressed in urban non-Pottery fashion, you might say well-tailored, for this was his London period. His eyes were dark and grave and if I had been a few years older I would have said [word illegible]. His teeth protruded. I wished to go down on my knees to this great writer but he was thinking of something else and I was still embarrassed by the corsets. My aunt was shocked by the colour of the non-white corsets and I was shocked because I had suddenly become a knight in armour and the armour did not fit. Mme. Chenier would have had hysterics...

During a later visit, when I was twenty-five, my aunt (who like other people in the Potteries did not read Arnold Bennett) kindly took me to have tea with Bennett's sister who lived in a neighbouring small town. She was a delightful woman, a Town Councillor, a Justice of the Peace, emancipated from a certain middle class Five Towns rigidity, and affectionately unimpressed yet proud of her unique Five Towns brother. One thing she told me that I do not forget. In all his long absences in London and Paris, and with all his regulated hours of writing, Bennett never failed to write daily to his mother.

I returned home with my gentle aunt, puzzled. I had never known a mother, but there was something unique and intrinsic—perhaps transforming—in motherness (I thought), for my own memory of old Mrs. Bennett was of a small severe old gray wrinkled woman in a black cape and bonnet walking slowly down the Waterloo Road; yet he loved her deeply. Here was something in human relationships that I did not then understand.

In a P.S. Ethel Wilson, who was then seventy years old, said that she had just re-read "the Bennett bit, and see that in departing from letter writing, a kind of posturing takes place. Interesting."

After four years of forced absence, during which she had been both really and dutifully cheerful, Ethel returned to Canada. She came home to Vancouver in the wild and varied province of British Columbia, which was where she wanted to be, and was able to be, for nearly the rest of her life. Here she was loved, and she loved in return.

Chapter Five

Boredom and Frustration

When Ethel Bryant, eighteen, was sailing home to Canada, Katherine Mansfield, eighteen, was sailing home to New Zealand. Miss Mansfield, who had studied in London while Miss Bryant had studied in Southport, was in a disagreeable mood. She, quite simply, hated to go home and was spiteful when she arrived and until she was free of her family again. Ethel Bryant, on the contrary, was happy and hopeful. She would be again among affectionate relatives. She would, she hoped, meet a young man and marry. And she would again be living in her city. Years later she wrote:

> When the mountains beyond the city are covered with snow to their base, the late afternoon light falling obliquely from the west upon the long slopes discloses new contours. For a few moments of time the austerity vanishes, and the mountains appear innocently folded in furry white. Their daily look has gone. For these few moments the slanting rays curiously discover each separate tree behind each separate tree in the infinite white forests. Then the light fades, and the familiar mountains resume their daily look again. The light has gone, but those who have seen it will remember.[1]

When Katherine Mansfield was nineteen, she published her first story in New Zealand. Ethel Bryant wrote the above in one of her first short stories, to be sent out for publication in England thirty years later, when she was forty-eight.

Katherine Mansfield and Ethel Wilson were returning to their respective British colonies when the world was exploding with ideas and talents. In 1905, the year before they sailed, Albert Einstein had shaken up the scientific world with his Theory of Relativity. He was only nine years older than Katherine and Ethel. The novelist, E.M. Forster, also nine years older, had published his first novel, *Where Angels Fear to Tread*. (Later, Ethel Wilson would admire him as a tightly controlled novelist and Katherine Mansfield would admonish him for not extending himself, risky though that might be.) And that year the wild Welsh painter Augustus John stopped his hell-raising, briefly, to marry his beautiful Ida. In 1906, the year of their return, seventeen-year-old Charlie Chaplin brought down the house at the Folies Bergere in Paris and the composer Claude Debussy went backstage to congratulate him. In 1907, Georges Braque and Pablo Picasso showed a new form of painting, which was named Cubism; pictures on the silent, silver screen were flickering their way across the sight of anyone with a penny or so to spare; dare-devils were soaring to dizzying heights in their flying machines.

Katherine Mansfield wanted to write; Ethel Bryant wanted to paint. But, unlike the rebellious New Zealander, Ethel was an orphan and had to make her own living. Shortly after she arrived home, she took her Certificate of London Matriculation and the official results from the Junior Cambridge Examinations and put them before the admissions officer at Vancouver Normal School. She was admitted to the school and, she would later write, "came under the guidance of the Principal Mr. Burns who was a wit and a very great little man...he taught us all he had time for about life and human relations and language...For the first time I encountered true caustic wit [which later she would cultivate], with surprise and frightened delight."[2] The following year she had her Teacher's Certificate. Naturally, she went directly to the headmistress who had known her as a child, to Miss Gordon the Girton girl. Miss Gordon employed her for less money than Ethel would have earned at a public school. (It could have been for that reason that Ethel only stayed with Miss Gordon for a year.) Still, there was enough money coming in now to do something she dearly wanted to do.

I was determined to continue my lessons in drawing and painting...Having learned that an artist had come to live in an upper room on Granville Street, I went to see her. Since my wages or salary (I like the word "wages") consisted of $47.50 a month at that time...I approached my lessons with diffidence. I had to be very good to justify even this little expense, and I did not think I was very good. The lessons turned out to be uncommonly interesting but consisted not so much of the teaching of painting as of pursuing very agreeable conversation (of which I was very fond but could not at that time afford to pay for). Time would fly by, and we had only talked. I regretfully ceased my lessons — obviously I was not meant to be a painter — and so my teacher, whose name was Miss Emily Carr, lost her least promising pupil.[3]

Probably Miss Carr agreed with her assessment. Doris Shadbolt, who wrote a book on Emily Carr, said that she never came across Ethel's name when she was doing her research. Margaret Andrew, an intelligent friend of Ethel's, said that she believed that Ethel had "no objective feelings about visual art," that her feelings were completely subjective. (Ethel loved the brilliant light of Tinteretto's Venice and the soft beauty of Holbein's wet nurse.) Incidentally, Mrs. Andrew found it interesting that Ethel could not remember really what Miss Carr looked like, although Ethel generally had a keen visual memory for those who interested her.

So she gave up painting and continued to read voraciously. Among her books that are still around from those early times are her father's hand-size, leather-bound volumes of William Shakespeare's plays, several of her father's Bibles, Thackeray's *Book of Snobs*, and Fanny Burney's *Evelina*. And now there was the Carnegie Library which offered up so many worlds of discovery.

Ethel played the piano. She sewed and tatted and went to church, and it was there, at the Homer Street church, that she saw her second famous literary figure, this time the flamboyant Indian "princess" and poet Pauline Johnson. Just as she had been when she met Arnold Bennett, Ethel was overcome. But this time somebody gave her a push and she was "propelled forward to shake hands [with this] buxom, glowing woman with an eagle's feather in her hair."

I heard the words "You may come and see me if you like," kindly spoken.

"Oh thank you," I said in terror, floundering in a turmoil of doorbells, princesses, poets, eagle's feathers, escape and inadequacy (what would we talk about, I feared, already sitting stiffly in a room).

On the way home the sardonic goblin that inhabits and that be-devils and preserves shy people of all ages, laughed derisively. This he did daily, and I did not, could not, ring the princess's doorbell.

Many years later I saw her in a crowded street. She was much much older, yet she had a sad beauty. She was ill, walking very slowly and lost in sombre thought. Memory rushed in and, stricken, I watched her as though I had done it.[4]

Ethel's quickness to watch unusual people and let them affect her was nearly stifled in Vancouver. Her life, really, was confined to her grandmother, aunts, uncles, cousins, a few friends, and the people in her church and school. Here is something which seems to me quite odd. I ask you to leap ahead to a conversation four decades later, but concerning this time in her life.

I had known her for three or four years, and on this day, after work, was at the Wilsons' apartment having tea and drinks (one followed the other quite rapidly). She said something—I can't remember what it was—but it prompted me to ask, surprised, "Did you ever teach school?"

"Yes." That clipped, abrupt Yes was an unmistakable signal that the subject should not be pursued. But I could not leave it because after what seemed, then, to be so many years of talking to her, she had never mentioned it. And now it had just come out by accident.

"Did you like it?" I asked.

"No." She looked at me firmly, and with irritation. The subject fell heavily.

She taught small children for thirteen years, but it seems she didn't make her pupils dislike her, as teachers usually do if they don't enjoy teaching. Unless, of course, those children who were in their seventies when interviewed were seeing her as a celebrity and had forgotten.

Mrs. Gwen Varcoe was in Miss Bryant's 1917 "Baby Class" at Lord Roberts Elementary School. She said that Miss Bryant was "a goddess, tall, blonde, beautiful, like a fairy princess."

Mr. E.R. Austen, who was in the 1916 Baby Class, said, "She was beautiful and gentle. She never disciplined or teased anyone. We all loved her."

Mrs. Jessie de Kou, who was ten years old when she came to Vancouver, frequently went to tea with Ethel at "old Mrs. Malkin's house." "She would tell us stories about Vancouver, especially about Pauline Johnson, to make us feel more at home. She was so kind and nice. She had no reason to be kind to us.

"My mother said, 'Why does that lovely young woman have to teach, and in that awful place,' meaning Lord Roberts," Mrs. de Kou said.

Ethel Bryant had learned self-discipline; to do the best with what you had was a moral rule in her family. When she was hurt, she would raise her face and her eyes would become cold. She was elegant as well as beautiful, as both a young and an old woman. Geoffrey Andrew, who was a good friend of both the Wilsons and was vice-president of the University of B.C., told me that he thought "Ethel hid her loneliness by cultivating her elegance."

Boredom, dislike of her job, and surely the furies which accompany young people in older people's houses, all assaulted her during these times. But she could escape. A small island just a ferry-ride from Vancouver could give her the release that she and her imagination longed for. It was called Bowen Island and was surrounded by opalescent green, sometimes clear blue, waters, depending on the cove, the sea, and the sky, and where she stood, high above or down at the water's edge. Except for a few settlers and the scars of logging (but they were healing quickly in this rainy coastal climate), the island was covered by dark forests where deer, peregrine falcons, ravens, raccoons, rabbits, bears, and other creatures lived. They sometimes showed themselves to her if she were sitting still. Her uncles had bought this property, which led from a small bay up to a broad shelf of land, from a man who had grown hops there. Then, in 1906, they ordered a small, prefabricated house to be towed across Howe Sound, carried in its pieces up the hill, assembled, and nailed into place. Annie Malkin, Belle, Eliza, Philip, Harold, and Ethel (Fred had his own house above another bay) all stayed in this small house. Some slept on the verandah where they could clearly hear the owls and the "innumerable laughter" of the sea, others in tents which would leak. The cove below the house was named Trinity Bay, probably in honour of Ethel's school and, possibly, Annie's faith.

Annie Malkin lost little time in setting up Sunday services in a tent and, no doubt out of respect more than fervour, most neighbours, although many were Anglican, attended. The old Methodist was full of zeal for her Lord. She had been honoured for that. "They" had chosen her to lay the cornerstone for the big Wesleyan Methodist Church on Burrard Street, and they had given her an oak mallet, said to be carved from the tree which sheltered John Wesley when he was giving his final sermon.[5] She herself preached his and His gospel, and told her congregation to pray that "an influence for good may go forth from this church, not only to this city, but to the very ends of the earth." Trinity Bay wasn't that far, but it was on the way.

A steam-propelled ferry, *The Defiance*, usually took Ethel and the family to the island, which is approximately seven miles long and four miles wide. Sometimes, however, Dr. David Wilson would take them in his boat, if there was enough room. Dr. Wilson's daughter, Alex, told me that she clearly remembered her first trip there. She, her two sisters, her father and mother, the Chinese cook, several tents, a cook-stove, the silverware, plates, cups, glasses, beds, coal-oil lanterns, tables, camp-chairs, and a cow were all arranged in an open boat. Her father kicked over the inboard motor, and they started up Howe Sound. The water, she said, was slightly choppy when they set off from Vancouver, but by the time they were in the open water of Howe Sound, it seemed that a hurricane had been unleashed. The small boat plunged and twisted, the cow moaned, the doctor cast about frantic eyes, his wife screamed across the wind for everyone to keep calm, and then, finally, through the white, tossing sea, the Malkins' house was seen briefly on its flat land before the boat plunged again and it was out of sight. Trinity Bay, rather than their own bay, would now be their destination, Dr. Wilson decided.

They came into the small cove and managed to drop anchor. First the cow would have to swim ashore, but the cow, unused to swimming even in quiet places, became alarmed. People were shoving and pushing her into this wild sea. She bellowed. All the people of all ages pushed. All but one. The Chinese cook. He would join her. He could not swim, but anything was better than continued existence with this mad family and so, Alex said, "everyone had to hold on to him for fear of losing him."

So Ethel had the Wilson girls for companions. And then an unusual number of young men started coming to see not just the beautiful Wilson girls, but Ethel as well. They were coming very far out of their way indeed, to call. They sailed into Trinity Bay or boarded *The Defiance*, and then plodded many dusty miles across the island to pay their respects to the blond and beautiful Ethel Bryant. One young man once sent my mother, Helen Law, and her friend, Irene Cowan, into uncontrollable giggles. Both girls were around ten years old and were staying at Cowan's Point (now Point Cowan).

They had been summoned, on that morning, by Irene Cowan's mother, and told to hurry over to the Malkins' house because a Mr. Gomrey, who was, Mrs. Cowan understood, "in the bank," was leaving wih Ethel in a rowboat. The girls were to chaperone them without delay. My mother remembers little more than explosions of giggles while she and Irene sat in the bow and watched Ethel, "looking beautiful," sitting sedately in the stern and Mr. Gomrey rowing with a neck which changed miraculously through ever-deepening reds. My mother said that it was a very short ride. She did not remember seeing Mr. Gomrey again, but neither did she remember seeing John Pethybridge Nicholls at Trinity Bay.

Mr. Nicholls was a small, puckish man, nearly twenty years older than Ethel. He was a great friend of her uncle, Philip Malkin, and had prospered through Vancouver's booming real estate. He, like Philip, was a keen sailor. He also had some sensitivity about books. He gave Ethel's young cousin and his godchild, Ursula Malkin, several books illustrated by Arthur Rackham. (But, of course, Arthur Rackham was already famous and in fashion.)

Mr. Nicholls did not create the fuss that Mr. Gomrey had created. He was a familiar face; he also owned a share of the property the Malkins were sitting on. So Helen Law and Irene Cowan were not called upon, and this might have been how Ethel and J.P. Nicholls became engaged. A fortune teller also helped. Ethel went to see this woman, who was able to see through her dark glass clearly on a Saturday afternoon, and had a cup of tea at the same time because the fortune teller worked in a tea shop. The woman said that Ethel would be engaged in three months. In three months John Pethybridge proposed, and the fortune teller's knowledge was confirmed. Ethel said yes. J.P. Nicholls was delighted. He presented her with a large diamond ring. His friends and her friends and nearly all their relations honoured the young woman and middle-aged man at dinners and cocktail parties, and they entertained, in her honour alone, at teas and luncheons. Invitations went out all over town, and to Burslem and London, and wherever Mr. Nicholls had friends and relatives. The presents—silver, crystal, fine linens—came into the house on Barclay Street, and Ethel, her grandmother, and her aunts opened them with vastly varying joys. Ethel became less and less joyful. She fought with herself, but she honestly did not want to marry this nice, small man. She broke off the engagement, and was deeply ashamed, and desperately sorry for him. And it was shocking to society. But some years later, the shame—and pity—now conquered and forgotten, Ethel attended his wedding and was pleased to see him and his bride looking so happy. She told a young friend about the wedding and said, with those blue eyes flashing wickedly but her mouth in a perfectly straight line, "I was, oh, very embarrassed. I saw my engagement ring on another woman's hand."

Young women of Ethel's age in Vancouver were sometimes sent to Europe to study or simply to travel. The Wilson girls—Kathleen, Alex, and Isabel—were away, and Ethel missed them. Kathleen was studying music in London. Isabel and Alex were doing the Grand Tour of Europe with their parents, Dr. and Mrs. David Wilson, and they had taken with them Amy Wilson of Ottawa, whose father was dead. Amy, who would become important to Ethel, was a soft, sweet girl, quite pretty, who wrote every day to her mother in Ottawa. Her letters reflect not only herself but also attitudes which were common among young women of her class and time. The Grand Tour, by the way, was as common as butter-patties to any family from North America with the correct income and connections, although the latter were not vital. Amy wrote to her mother when they arrived in Liverpool:

When we got into dock Kathleen and Elise Kingman were there to welcome us. They came on board when the gang way was placed. Mother I shall never for-get the meeting. Of course Kathleen was grown up and wore a veil. Her father and mother said they scarcely knew her and auntie said with tears in her eyes "I don't think I shall leave Isabel if she changes so much in two years. Why Kathleen you don't seem like our own daughter at all." It seemed a rather sad meeting to me. She talks at the rate of a mile per minute, and has acquired a sort of English accent, and she has always been undemonstrative. Really she seems like a girl that finds it impossible to show affection in any way, so cold. I have never yet seen her go up to her parents and hug and kiss them voluntarily. Oh darling, I thought of you then, and if I only had you in my arms to hug and kiss, and I prayed I would come back to you in the very same way as I went away, plain Amy without any foreign manner.

That was a small part of Amy's tightly-penned, twenty-four page letter. Nine days later she wrote again, saying, "[I have] become very fond of Kathleen, now that I know her. She is not a girl to be silly over boys whatever — she jokes over them like any other girl, but is not a spec sentimental." Kathleen was a beauty; Amy herself was "a spec" interested in men.

Let me see, was Thursday the last day I wrote you about. Well after I sealed that letter and put it in the mail box on board, we went out on deck and Isabel, the two Heighington girls and Mr. Redpath and myself were all sitting together, when Mr. Rogers, an Englishman came along. By the way I must tell you of Mr. Thomson. I think he was the nicest young man on board; he is about 28, and a lawyer, and is now making his permanent home in Ottawa. He is one of those sensible, plain, true young men. He never told us scarcely anything about himself, but a man told Uncle he, Mr. Thompson [in her excitement she spells his name differently] is a son of Sir John Thomson, once premier of Canada. Sir John met his death by having his hand jammed in the door of a carriage in London while on his way to dine with the Queen, and it turned to blood poisoning and he died in Windsor Castle. Well, this son is so unpretentious. You see. . .[6]

Well, Ethel had been at school in England, and one day, when she had earned her fare, she would go back. But now, now, she was so bored. So why not leave her grandmother and her aunts, and strike out on her own? Why not? She looked into it. There was a demand for teachers up country. She would teach in the Cariboo. She approached her family.

No, said her grandmother, her uncles, and her aunts. Why not? It seemed it was not proper. She returned to her Baby Class, her books, pouring tea for her family and friends and some young men who bored her. She was not happy. She had not been happy since she had broken her engagement to John Pethybridge Nicholls, although she had felt overwhelming relief.

Her much younger cousin Lucille Malkin said, "Ethel used to come to our house and she and I would snuggle up on the sofa — it was velvet with buttons that dug into you — and Ethel would tell me the most beautiful stories. And then the stories stopped. I don't know if I am right, but I associate that with the broken engagement." When Ethel was deeply unhappy, she did not think up stories.

Franz Joseph of Yugoslavia was assassinated in Sarajevo by a Serbian in 1914, and Europe was thrown into World War I. Ninety percent of the young men in British Columbia were British or of British descent. Promptly they went to the recruiting stations. Quickly they were shipped out. Some young women were going overseas. Ethel wanted to go. No, said her grandmother, her uncles, and her aunts. "She saw with envy the young men and a few young women going away to where the war was, and her mind was continually divided," she wrote in *The Innocent Traveller*. She was a dutiful orphan. She stayed and taught the Baby Class. And after school she would walk home, and "as she hurried along the dark wet pavements, life and time continued as usual everywhere under heaven with practiced ease their ceaseless fluid manipulations and arrangements of circumstance and influence and spiked chance and decision among members of the human family. . ."[7]

Chapter Six
An Independent Young Man

W allace Algernon Wilson started his life nine months after Ethel Bryant, on October 10, 1888. His father, who, like her father, was named Robert, was a doctor practicing in Morden, Manitoba, when this first child was born. At first Robert practiced with his brother David in the small prairie town, but a disappointment in politics, and the attraction of a bigger and fast-growing city, and a city by the sea, took David off to Vancouver. When Algie, as the child was affectionately called, was four, his father, mother, and small sister Amy, who was two, moved themselves, their piano, and all their possessions to Vancouver. Dr. Robert Wilson would practice once more with his brother, so he bought a house directly across from David's house, on the corner of Robson and Thurlow Streets. On May 23, four months after he had arrived in Vancouver, Robert Wilson died.

Ethel Bryant was dressed completely in black in Vancouver in the summer of 1898; Algie was dressed in black in Vancouver five years earlier, in the spring of 1893. But Algie felt death differently from Ethel. He did not feel the shock, the outrage, and the unquenchable grief that she felt. She was nine when her father died. He was only four, and his father was a man who was generally too busy to be seen. He was up and out of the house before Algie was awake, and home after his bedtime, as a rule. Algie's mother was far more reliable because she was nearly always visible. But still he suffered from the waves of shock which followed his father's death. The "big people" he loved seemed to draw away from him, particularly his mother, except for erratic, sudden hugs which had no prelude and so were confusing. He wept often from instinct. His mother told him that his father had gone to heaven, and she had told him earlier many times that heaven was a lovely place to be. So, because now she kept crying and behaving so strangely, he thought that she must not have told him the truth. His father did not look that happy either. His Uncle David had lifted Algie up to look down into the coffin, to remember his father, but that man below did not look like his father, he was so white, and his face was set oddly. Algie was glad when he was let down. He ran from the parlour, which was heavy with flowers, and from his father. His father died on Tuesday. On Friday Algie was taken to the Methodist church on Homer Street. He followed his mother into the front pew, which was not where they usually sat, and he tried to tell her, but she didn't hear. His mother was weeping in tight gasps, which frightened him. His uncle, Algie saw with surprise, placed his big hand over his mother's small hands. She was wearing black lace gloves. Her skin was white where the lace opened. Then there was a stillness and the sound of feet in step together, and he turned and saw some men carrying in the coffin which, he knew, held the body of his father. That was where he had last looked at him.

The Reverend Robert Maitland asked everyone in the church to sit down, which they did with a lot of noise. Algie pushed himself back to see if he could reach the back of the pew, and how far beyond the seat his legs stuck out. (It was a matter of how much he had grown since last Sunday.) And then Mr. Maitland took out some sheets of paper and started to read.

> Today with passion-full feelings we assemble to pay tribute to one of God's noblemen and join in sorrowful sympathy with bleeding hearts. What we do is being done at this self-same hour in many a city, town and hamlet, and in many a farm house and many a cottage by the wayside...The grim reaper is no respector of persons. He is not fastidious as to where he thrusts in his sickle. We look out and see old age, trembling upon its staff...[Amy examined her black boots]...We look again and see...the mother crushing to her bosom the blighted flower...[Algie looked at his mother, who was clutching a handkerchief now crushed into a ball]...the beggar leaves his rags, unwept and unmourned; the philanthropist

stricken down while the tears of orphans and widows speak their mute panegyrics...

And so it went, with no beggar in sight and everyone dressed in their best black clothes. Finally, to Algie's immense relief, Uncle David rose to his feet, and so did his mother, and he and Amy were quickly on their feet, and they moved too slowly out of the church and past all those well-dressed people whom he did not know, and, with a surge of gratitude, Algie was out in the spring sunshine.

For many days after, Algie and Amy would watch people come to their house and ring the bell. The maid would open the door to them, but they did not come in; they left black-bordered, small envelopes which were taken upstairs to Mrs. Wilson on a silver tray. The curtains in their mother's room were drawn, even against the sunlight. Then, one afternoon, an extraordinary event occurred. Someone left an envelope and the maid took it upstairs, knocked on Mrs. Wilson's door, and as the door opened, the children heard their mother burst out in rage. They learned, years later, the cause. Their mother had been looking out of her window and had seen that the woman who delivered the note had worn red. "At a time like that!" their mother said, still enraged years later.

Dr. Wilson's widow, Bella, sensibly went home to Ontario.

She settled herself and the children in a house in Ottawa, which was only forty miles from Bell's Corner. Her parents still had a farm near Bell's Corner, where she had been raised. They would not only give her the comfort of being wanted and protected, they could help guide her children into maturity.

Algie, particularly, loved the farm, its freedoms, animals, and its secrets. Mouse-tunnels ran through the hay in the loft, and their makers could be heard scratching across the timbers of the barn. One morning when he had woken, early in December, he saw a red fox running beautifully across the front field, leaving the black imprints of his paws in white snow.

The house had a myriad of pungent smells—apples, freshly baked bread, roasting meat, drying herbs, burning wood, and cold ashes. And it had its own secret. One afternoon he discovered, under a braided rag-rug, a trap door which exposed nearly the entire stone-walled basement if he dropped his head and shoulders down through it. Soon he and Amy were dropping their whole bodies down into the basement, and then climbing back up through the trap door, but always with a sense of danger because, Algie told Amy, they could break their crowns, and both knew trouble was coming if they were caught. Then, when Algie was eight, Bell's Corner, the farm, and trap door no longer existed because both his grandparents died.

Bella was left the money; her brother was left the farm. But her brother did not like that, and so they became enemies, and Bella, Algie, and Amy never returned to Bell's Corner.

Algie was told by his mother, probably when she was weeping, that he was now the man of the house — sons of all sizes were then given that responsibility. But he often forgot. While his mother and Amy had their musical afternoons, singing and playing the piano, even — although Bella was a Methodist — with a Roman Catholic priest, Algie would quietly depart for the Ottawa River. He was forbidden that river. It had been pointed out that it was particularly dangerous if he were alone, when it was absolutely forbidden. After a few hours he would arrive home, late for tea, and make matters worse by frankly telling his mother where he had been, and adding, sometimes, that he had been alone.

His uncle, Dr. David Wilson, sometimes despaired of Algie. There was a time, remembered within his family, when he came from Vancouver to Ottawa with his daughter Alex, to see his brother's widow and children. As there was nobody to meet them at the station, Dr. Wilson hailed a horse-drawn cab, and was clipping sharply through the streets of Ottawa toward Bella's house when suddenly the cab door flew open and, head before feet, Algie catapulted in. He landed sprawling at their feet, looked up with a grin, and bade them welcome to Ottawa. His uncle concluded that Algie was wild and needed a man's hand, but there was nothing to be done about that.

Family lore runs that Algie decided to be a doctor, like his father and uncle, when he was nine or ten. He was walking, it is said, along an Ottawa street one fine spring day, and noticed a brass plate glittering in the sunlight beside the door of a handsome house. He read that this was the surgery of a doctor, went home in time for tea, and announced that he would become a doctor.

In 1909, when he was twenty-one and had his Bachelor of Arts from the University of Toronto, he entered the university's medical school.

"You see how boys change?" his uncle said to Alex in Vancouver.

His uncle was three thousand miles away.

On a winter night, Algie was working late in the laboratory with some friends. He was restless. "Let's," he said, "dress up the skeleton and take him to the pub." They gave the white-boned gentleman a pair of trousers, a shirt and tie, a handsome cloak, scarf, and hat, and, carrying him with his arms across their shoulders as though he were any man's drunk, they walked him out into the street. They hailed a cab, lifted him in, and sat him up, proper and dignified, beside the window. Off they went to their favourite pub. When they arrived, they told the cabbie to wait. They left the skeleton sitting in the cab, partially illuminated by the street light. Occasionally they came out to watch the reaction of people leaving the pub, and when they were happy enough, drove him home and hung him up again.

Dr. David Wilson encouraged Algie to practice in Vancouver. In 1911 he interned at Vancouver General Hospital. He must have met Ethel Bryant, but if so, he didn't pay unusual attention.[1] In 1912 he was restless. There was the world to see, and he wanted his freedom. He would do post-graduate work in England. Bella decided to go over with him, and see him completely settled. On July 12, 1912, Dr. Wallace Algernon Wilson, his mother, Mrs. Robert Wilson, and his sister, Miss Amy Wilson, sailed from Montreal aboard the Royal Mail Steamer *Corsican*. They arrived eight days later in Liverpool, where Amy had docked with her cousins, uncle, and aunt a few years earlier.

The three Wilsons toured France, Italy, and Austria, and on September 16, 1912, saw Sarah Bernhardt at the London Coliseum.[2]

Algie was waiting for a letter which didn't come until late November. And then:

From the Regius Professor of Medicine, Oxford
21st Nov. 1912

Dear Doctor,
    Will you please come to Oxford on Thursday, November 28th on a clinical and academic visit? The programme I suggest is: —

9.50 a.m.	Leave Paddington.
11.30 a.m.	Ward visit at the Radcliffe Infirmary.
1.0 p.m.	Lunch at 13, Norsham Gardens.
2.0 p.m.	Visit the laboratories.
4.30 p.m.	Leave for London.

Sincerely yours,
William Osler
(per secretary)

Whatever that was about — and nobody who I have talked to knows — Algie did not work for, or in any way with, Dr. Osler, although, I believe, he hoped to. Later, as a mature man, he would give the prestigious Osler Lecture. But now he must do what he came for. His mother and sister went back to Canada, and then Dr. Wilson told it this way. (He was so moved and surprised by the occasion of this speech — he was being honoured at a surprise dinner by forty of his colleagues — that he spoke in nearly a staccato.)

I took a course in operative surgery down at Dreadnaught Hospital. Two of us took that course. I remember that it was in the winter and we went down into a room that was stone cold and there was a stiff out on the table. Over on one side was another table on which was *Cunningham's Anatomy* and needles and scalpels and we were to start doing surgery on this stiff. There was a man who was our teacher, or instructor, and he used to appear at intervals out of a warm room. He'd come in and see what we were doing for a few minutes and then he would disappear into the warm room.

After we had tried for a while with stiff, cold hands to do an end-to-end anastomosis on the intestines, I quit. I was only half through the course but I decided that I was not going to be a surgeon. By the process of elimination [he also experimented with obstetrics one debilitatingly hot summer in New York City at the Sloan Maternity Hospital] I became an internist.

Algie went back to the Pacific Coast and put up his brass plate in Vancouver. His practice, perhaps because of his uncle's help, was not slow in starting up. He played golf, he dined out, and he went to the theatre with pretty women, like Ethel Bryant. And then of course came Sarajevo and the Great War.

Algie joined the Royal Canadian Medical Corps on June 16, 1915, when the Fifth Canadian General Hospital, the British Columbia unit, had been formed. He was shipped out to serve in northern Greece. But when the troop-ship put in at Salonika, in November, the weather was too cold to put up camp, and so the unit spent some time, merrily, in the cosmopolitan city of Alexandria, Egypt. Algie's hospital was operating by early December on the plain outside Salonika.[3]

It was quiet then on the front. His patients, generally, were Tommies suffering not so much from bullets and mortar fire as from dysentery, jaundice, rheumatism, malaria, and typhoid. They also were infested with vermin. So, as Dr. J.J. MacKenzie reported in a letter to his wife — he was stationed with the Fourth Canadian Hospital, near Algie's unit — the soldiers "all improve immensely when they get into a clean warm bed and get a good night's sleep."

Algie often walked with his colleagues along the Salika river and up into the hills, where he could see the plain stretching away for miles until it reached the mountains of Bulgaria. In January he enjoyed the sudden blooming of wild crocuses and the great sweep of wild geese returning north to mate in the marshes where they had been born. Algie loved and learned much about wild things. He loved, too, to watch the Vlach shepherds in these hills. They wore cloaks and carried tall crooks; their dogs obeyed their whistles as they drove huge herds of white and black sheep before them.

He slept in a bell-shaped tent with a small coal oil stove to warm him and heat his water. He read George Eliot there, and a small, green-leather edition of Thackeray's *The Newcomes*, which is inscribed with his name and Salonika, 1916. Its spine is tearing and the leather has been softened by much use, but the soft, thin paper is extraordinarily clean. He loved books.

Soon after setting up camp, Algie and some friends went into Salonika. He was walking through the bazaar when he saw something that he thought would please the beautiful but shy, in fact easily frightened, Ethel Bryant. It was a camel bell. He wrapped it carefully and put it in the mail. She kept it near her for the rest of her life.

He fell in love with a nurse when he was overseas, but that is all I know.

Chapter Seven

Squashed Furs and the Furies

Ethel Bryant's diary, if she kept one—and it is probable that she did, if only because it was the fashion—has been lost, or was destroyed when she became known as a writer. But her friend Kathleen (Wilson) Graham, whose Colin was in Salonika with Algie, kept a daily record of the events in her life, and these are worth looking into because Kathleen's, Algie's, Colin's, and Ethel's lives are all intermingled, and because such luxury in boredom is now so strange to all but the richest of us. But it was this way—maids, dinner parties for twenty or fifty, canapés, cocktails with well-selected hundreds, teas, and palaver—until after World War II. Then more women became more educated, occupations more numerous and varied, and the jobs of Nanny and cook general became superfluous. Those who wanted these jobs could demand high pay, which is why only the rich can have and keep their servants.

Here are three days in the 1915 diary of Kathleen Graham:

> October 13—Dull and drizzly. In all morning sewing on a make-over blouse. Afternoon had tea at family's again, and evening visitors. Sang & played a little.
> December 28—Glorious day. Did own work today [most Vancouver maids were given time off on Thursday evenings, when

husband and wife usually went to The Club for dinner, and Sunday afternoons] but dined at Mother's. To town in afternoon & then tea at Ethel Bryant's. Mary & Mother & Mr. Bansk walking home. Miss Gordon [the Girton girl] will see Bal. for a while. Got supper and spent evening at home...

On December 31, 1915, she says that she is too sleepy to "see in the New Year," and that she "finished a book." For some reason she wrote no more in her diary until October 1916. Then she rambled along in an uninteresting fashion until Friday, November 3:

No letter from Colin. Going to give up writing him. Rained hard all day and I never budged outside—except to run out & mail Colin a letter in the evening. Knitted a good part of the day on my sweater. Fussed around the house. Mother [with whom she stayed while Colin was overseas] stayed in bed. Isabel & Reggie [wounded overseas and now home] came for tea. Budgie [her baby] came down to the library. He is at his best up [stairs] in his pen—then he shows off at a fine rate. Spent part of the evening writing Colin & Algie in Salonika & knitted till 10.30—then had a glass of milk & a biscuit & to bed. Very tired. Always feel weary when I have been in all day.

Ten days later she was more cheerful:

Beautiful day. Heavy frost and cold. Letter from Colin at breakfast—was feeling blue about Roumania at the time but says he thinks the war will be over in a year. Had been to a dance, "gay dog." Went into Bawford at eleven. Mrs. Fleck motored me down with Lady Tupper and Ida Cambie. Went to bank. Walked home feeling brisk. Played with Budgie. After lunch had a rest: Mgr. of P.C. Permanent was here to lunch. Called on Mrs. Henman & spent afternoon at Isabel's, who was receiving. She had 19 callers. I poured & was busy. Wrote Colin after supper & knitted.

Wednesday, December 13, she reports:

Dull but not raining. Got two big letters from Colin. Felt happy all day after [Colin] had been to London, saw a questionable play & bought me white fox furs—not black, the dear...

And on Tuesday, December 19, when the day is over, she writes:

Cold. Slept late. Washed & did a lot of things badly needed doing. Then went to a meeting of the D.O.E. [Daughters of the Empire] at the Tuppers to arrange the Party. Found my furs when I arrived home. Disappointed at first—all squashed. Felt like weeping, but on comparing them later with Isabel's found little difference. Poor Colin. Am glad I didn't write him right off the bat. Had a lovely tea & went over to Mabel's after to see furs & then to a boring evening at the Armours. He sat & played solitaire & she talked of everything 5 times over.

This was written by one of the liveliest and prettiest young women in Vancouver. It is not surprising that her friend Ethel Bryant wanted to leave town.

Perhaps because so many British Columbia men were away fighting a war, their women got down to business. In 1914 they raised their voices. The Legislature in Victoria heard them and gave them the vote. Then they turned their attentions to the drunkenness of some of the population, and a law prohibiting the selling and purchasing of alcoholic spirits was passed. Many citizens distilled gin in their bathtubs, occasionally with fatal effects, and bootleggers started up big businesses—offering home deliveries. These changes, naturally, irritated many people, and one who was particularly put-out, simply because he did not like anyone telling him what he could and could not do, was Mr. B.T. Rogers, founder and owner of the B.C. Sugar Refinery.

At the best of times, Mr. Rogers was inclined to release his ill temper into his world, which was duly cowed, and when things really became unbearable he drove down to his 168-foot steam yacht, *Aquilla*, and cruised with a good store of liquor through the often stormy waters of the coast. *Aquilla* was designed to take it. She had passed through worse waters before reaching Mr. Rogers, although she needn't have done this if he could only have waited less than two years for the Panama Canal to be completed. He couldn't wait, however, so she battled her way through the terrible waters of Cape Horn to reach him. She had been well tried.

Sometimes "B.T.," as he was known, took out his wife and his children and his children's friends, depending on his temper. There was one time, in the summer of 1917, when he took his son Blythe and his daughter Elspeth. Elspeth was allowed to take a friend and she chose Helen Law, the girl who got the giggles in Mr. Gomrey's rowboat. The cruise went pleasantly for the girls, who did not see Mr. Rogers too often, until, after a week at sea, they passed through Vancouver's harbour and were coming in to tie up at the B.C. Sugar Refinery's wharf. Now, according to Helen Law who was then about nineteen, they saw lines of "rough looking men" watching *Aquilla*. Elspeth and Helen stood on deck and watched these men until a sailor came up and said that Mr. Rogers wanted them to come to the saloon immediately. They quickly followed the sailor. Mr. Rogers was standing, waiting for them. Those men they had seen, he said, were strikers. Now listen closely. They were to get off the *Aquilla* and, looking straight ahead, mind, they were to walk straight through those men. They were to keep their eyes straight ahead. Not look at the men on any account. They were to catch a street-car home. No, Williams (the chauffeur) would not be coming. They were to do precisely what he had told them to do. Yes, he and Blythe would be coming too, but not until later, not until they were safely on the street-car. She remembered Mr. Rogers taking a small gun and putting it in his pocket.[1]

Helen Law's friend Alex Wilson married Blythe Rogers, and her friend Irene Cowan married Ernest Rogers. That was the way then, as it is now. The socially acceptable married the socially acceptable with few strayings, and it was the same with the socially unacceptable. Ethel Bryant would follow the norm.

She knew the Rogers, of course, and would have known that Blythe had joined up and been sent off, but that he had only reached Ottawa before he was kicked by a horse and sent home on a medical discharge.

Every night now Ethel checked the evening paper for the men she knew, older than Blythe, like Algie Wilson, who were overseas. Every night, lists of those killed in action and those missing in action were published in the newspaper.

In the summer of 1918, and then, even more hopefully, in the autumn, it looked as if the Great War would end. Women set their minds to imagining meetings at the railway station, and debated with themselves about what to have for his homecoming dinner. They looked closely into their mirrors to see if they had changed. They did not think long on that. Armistice was first announced on November 6, 1918. One of Ethel's Baby Class pupils, E.R. Austen, told me about that cruel mistake.

> Three of us, all boys, were in Stanley Park and we heard the boats whistling and people shouting and we asked a man what it was all about and the man said that the war was over. But that was on November the sixth and it was the false Armistice. We came home, to my house, and I said, "I don't feel very well," and one boy said,

"Get away, get away from me," and he ran away. For the next five days I don't remember anything. I woke up at night on November the eleventh. There was blood on my pillow. I had been haemorrhaging from my nose. I heard street-cars clanging and horns honking and people running up and down the street. My father was by my bed. I asked what all that was. He said, "It's the real Armistice."

That nine-year-old boy survived "Spanish Influenza," which crossed Europe and North America killing more than a million people, half a million in the United States alone—more than the Great War killed. It came in three waves to Vancouver. Two of them, in the summer of 1918 and in January 1919, were quite mild. The middle wave struck in October.

From October 18 to November 19, 1918, the Mayor of Vancouver banned public meetings. Passengers on incoming boats and trains were checked and watched carefully. Children were told to stray no further than their gardens. By the end of that November, three thousand cases and three hundred deaths were reported in Vancouver, and by the end of the epidemic there were eight hundred deaths.

King Edward Public School, where Ethel was teaching, closed down to the children and opened up to the sick. Desks were carried out and hospital cots carried in. Doctors and nurses, short of staff because of the war, appealed for help and Ethel Bryant volunteered.

She was given a long white gown, with slits for her eyes, which covered her from her head to her feet. She filled containers with disinfectant and scrubbed the woodwork, beds, and floors. She emptied bed-pans and ran errands, and then Professor Percy Elliott, who was managing the instant hospital, took a look at her and made her his special assistant. Kate McQueen, who ten years before had watched Ethel walking up the street on her way to church, was on the day shift. She said Ethel Bryant, "who did not of course know me but I knew her," was unusually kind. She remembered "Miss Bryant coming into my ward and she said, 'You have the tidiest ward'." Although sixty-two years had passed, Miss McQueen smiled with pleasure when she told me that.

"Miss Bryant had a presence," she said.

Then Miss Bryant caught influenza and was taken to her bed. By the time she was up again, the men were coming home.

One afternoon in 1919, when she was thirty-one, she came into the parlour, told her grandmother she was going out, and stooped to kiss her goodbye.

"Where are you going, dear?" asked her grandmother.

"To the tea dance at the Vancouver Hotel," Ethel said.

"And who is escorting you?"

"Dr. Wilson."

"But how kind of old Dr. Wilson," said her small grandmother, looking very pleased.

"I didn't tell her," Ethel Wilson said to me years later with a laugh of delight, "that it was Wallace and not his uncle, old Dr. Wilson."

Chapter Eight
A Death and Love

Her year of 1919 was filled with life-lasting events. She was to start falling in love, to start writing, and to again feel the agony—but this time it would resolve itself into nearly an ecstasy of freedom—of death.

Her grandmother Annie Malkin, Ethel clearly saw when she was lying in bed recovering from Spanish Influenza, was far more frail, slower to move, possibly even more vague in her strangely serene way. She was now eighty-six, and Ethel realized with sudden sharpness that she loved this small person immensely, and that any happiness and security which she now had was largely owed to her grandmother. She knew that her grandmother would soon be on her way but still, like all people who love, Ethel could not guard herself against the shock of facing death straight on.

Annie Malkin died on March 17, 1919, in her bed with her white cap on, her Bible beside her, and her courage intact. She had nearly unswervingly, she believed, served her God and her family through three generations, and now she perhaps praised her Lord that she could go to His shelter. She was leaving her house in order. Her orphan granddaughter was good and beautiful, her sons prospered, her daughter Belle was good and responsible, and her sister Eliza would go her precarious way quite safely, one could presume, as she had been going that way in safety for the last seventy-four years. So she slipped into "some abyss of memory," but not yet, not yet for Ethel.

Ethel was now thirty-one, sensible, responsible, shy, quick to laugh, quicker than most people to stifle crying. She did something that seems out of character but of course can not be. She said No. No undertaker was to be called in. She knew what to do. She had worked in a hospital and seen people die. She would not have some man who made death his business touch her grandmother. Men who dealt in death must be base, even if they were necessary in a society which hid from death. She had seen death. She would prepare her grandmother, and so she did.

After that and some time of grieving, the shock of death wore nearly away, and Ethel's duties diminished. Her aunts agreed with her that the house was now too large, and they understood, really, that Ethel should perhaps live with others closer to her age and temperament. Belle, still quick and reliable, took her old, but still quick, Aunt Eliza off to live in an apartment, and Ethel Bryant was, at long last, free. There was a vacancy at the Langham Hotel. She took it. It was a residential hotel, respectable and inexpensive, and within easy walking distance of her school.

I don't know who suggested it. Harold could have, or one of his brothers, or Belle, or it could have been Ethel's idea that W.H. Malkin Co., Wholesale Grocers, Tea Blenders and Coffee Roasters, run a serial—stories for children—as a way of advertising. If it were Ethel, Harold Malkin would have asked her to write them, she would have declined in modesty, he would have encouraged her, and, I am sure, paid her. She was, after all, known in the family as a teller of tales and she could, after all, use a little more money. So three times a week the school teacher put aside her pupils' exercise books and settled down to write a new installment of "The Surprising Adventures of Peter by E.D.B."[1]

It was stuff as stirring as the best of boys' and girls' stories in English books of the time, full of pirates, heathen murderers, camels, the high mountains and hot deserts of the Far East, a midnight visitor, bearded and long-since dead, named Sir Richard Fenn, a boy named Peter, and Chum, "his own black dog."

"My wig," said Peter, "there's lots of work here for me." Peter was looking at the driftwood thrown up on his beach by last night's storm. He would collect it for firewood. And that was how he found the jeweled treasure box, and why the late Sir Richard came to his room at midnight, and so the second episode was kicked off and running with the plot.

There is charm, excitement, and humour in these children's stories, and they run innocently along until Peter leaves Tibet and enters China (where he gives victims of the plague "ease and comfort"), and then the plot behind the stories is boldly revealed. Episode 22: "On the Value and Comfort of Tea":

> [The Chinese Prince] said that a man might drink many cups thereof and yet it would not harm him, but that the sole effect, when made with care, was to warm, cheer and comfort the heart and body of man. He told us, too, that it made for great solidity of friendliness between those who partook of it together. Indeed, he said, it is a priceless boon.

So ended Episode 22.

Today, with our attentions so often concentrated on the freedom of the mind, and our sometimes compulsive motions to try our talents, it seems odd that Ethel should stop writing then, and for many years. But it was not strange. The Katherine Mansfields were far stranger in their time. Isak Dinesen, who had much the same Victorian-Edwardian upbringing and was just three years older than Ethel, would not write to be published until she was forty-six. But she, like Ethel, "always" told stories (Isak Dinesen tried hers out on her sister Elle when they were in bed, until Elle "would have to ask her to go to sleep or keep quiet.") Isak Dinesen, like Ethel, took art lessons when she was twenty. And she too did not want the fame of success and never really felt at ease with its flattery.[2]

While they were pretty women and still young, Isak Dinesen and Ethel Bryant were much too engaged with life to think of writing. Dinesen was in Africa, Ethel at the Langham Hotel, which was just as liberating as Africa. One of her pupils, white-haired Mr. Austen, told me that his aunt, Bessie Rowan, also lived at the Langham. She told him that Ethel Bryant was extremely popular, that nearly every night, when everyone had sat down to dinner, the telephone in the hall would ring. The diners would fall silent and watch one of the maids cross the room to answer it. Before she could say "Hello," someone in the dining room would say, "It's for Ethel." That remark would be followed by laughter. But the call nearly always was for Ethel.

Included among these callers, with much interest on Ethel's part, was Dr. Wallace Algernon Wilson. She found him not only a good dancer. He was an interesting man. And very attractive too, she thought. He had a kind and pleasant face.

His cousin, Alex Wilson, noticed this growing interest between the two and observed it closely. She told me that Algie was "clever" about Ethel. "He was very wise. He courted her gently and slowly. He was very careful."

If he were invited to a dinner party he would ask if she would be there, and if that were the case, he would telephone Ethel and ask if he could take her. He also took her to concerts and to plays. They walked in Stanley Park, and on hot weekend afternoons went swimming down at English Bay. Often they just went for a drive, as a rule obeying the fifteen miles-per-hour speed limit in the city, but often ignoring the twenty-five miles-per-hour limit once in open country. Each was delighted with the fact that the other, too, loved the country.

After the war, Vancouver, like so many North American cities, was booming. New buildings were rising, more streets and sidewalks were being paved, and the boards from the old walks were being discarded. There was enough lumber to serve eternity, it seemed then, and cutting down trees put a lot of money in a man's pocket if he worked hard. Driving or walking out together, Algie and Ethel noticed these new arrangements being made to their city, and spoke of them with usually mutual pleasure or displeasure.

On one of these comfortable and yet exciting outings, Ethel noticed a new sign and it puzzled her. She spoke now without much thinking to Algie, and so she turned to him and said, "Look—you see?—it says Public Convenience. I wonder what a Public Convenience is?" And then it struck her like a bolt of lightning, and she blushed fiery red. But Algie, being wise, did not appear to notice the sign, or Ethel's blush, or even hear her words.

She and Algie exchanged books because both were avid readers. Algie introduced her to George Eliot, whose complete works he had bought during the War. Sometimes they read to each other—something short that they thought might please the other—and it is possible that Ethel read him a little of Oscar Wilde:

"...if my name was Algy, couldn't you love me?"
"I might respect you...I might admire your character, but I fear that I should not be able to give you my undivided attention."

From then on, except when they were sharing, or perhaps (as with the "Public Convenience") not sharing, a joke, she would never call him Algie. Just Wallace. And, in moments of affection, "Waas."

Wallace's mother and sister were now living in Vancouver, and Ethel saw them frequently. From her own childhood, Ethel had kept Hilaire

Belloc's *Cautionary Tales*, whose pages, even today, are worn but flat and clean.[3] Surely she must have read this caution to him.

> Young Algernon, the Doctor's Son,
> Was playing with a Loaded Gun.
> He pointed it towards his sister,
> Aimed very carefully, but
> Missed her!
> His Father, who was standing near,
> The Loud Explosion chanced to Hear,
> And reprimanded Algernon
> For playing with a Loaded Gun.

Amy, Wallace's sister, although sweet and lively, could irritate Ethel.

In July 1920, Wallace asked Ethel if she would marry him.

He proposed in a field of lupines, she told a young cousin. He proposed in a garden under a tree, she told me. They are compatible. In a cigar box, which I saw many years later, were dried red carnations and a scrap of paper on which she had recorded, because she might forget the exact words, "I love you and I want you to be my wife."

She sent her letter of resignation to the Vancouver School Board on July 26.

On January 4, 1921, a night of heavy rain, W.H. Malkin stopped his car outside the Langham Hotel, ran into the foyer where his niece was waiting, and escorted her under his black umbrella to the car.

> When I was getting into Uncle Harold's car on this streaming wet wedding night, a handsome young English schoolboy who was staying with him said solemnly, "Miss Bryant, the Nuptial Hour Approaches!" I was shaking with fright, but when on recovering from the wedding I told Wallace, we both thought it was very funny & have so often used it—to catch a plane, a boat a concert, etc.[4]

The Vancouver *Sun* ran this account of their wedding in its social pages.

> The marriage took place at 6:45 p.m. Tuesday at Wesleyan Methodist church of Miss Ethel Davis Bryant and Dr. Wallace Wilson. Miss Bryant, who was given away by her uncle, Mr. W.H. Malkin, made a charming bride. She wore a becoming costume of

navy blue gabardine handsomely trimmed with Russian sable. Her hat was of silver lace with navy ostrich trim and French flowers; and her corsage bouquet was of Ophelia roses. Although the wedding was quiet and the bride and groom unattended, a large number of friends were present at the ceremony which was performed by Rev. R.J. McIntyre. During the signing of the register Mrs. Clelland sang Foster's "Of Love."

Ethel had wanted a quiet wedding, without bridesmaids or a reception, because she hated a big social show, and because she was not particularly strong. The Spanish Influenza had left her permanently vulnerable to anaemia. But most important, this marriage was private to Wallace and herself. (Yet many years later, when I was about to go on a honeymoon, she insisted on sending a letter to her friends Roderick and Anne Haig-Brown, because, she said, she knew that we would like them very much. I mumbled some words of reluctance which made her say, "You may think that you want to be just with your new husband, but that is not enough." Why she did not find it enough, I do not know.)

Twenty-odd years after her wedding she told a friend that she had been "a very nervous bride" and had said to Wallace on their winter wedding night, "Oh darling, thank God you don't wear long underwear," which, like Public Conveniences, must have startled both of them.[5]

They had decided not to go on their honeymoon after the wedding. One reason was that Wallace recently had been appointed Chief of Medicine at Shaughnessy Hospital and he was anxious about leaving his hospital at that time. (She told me that this appointment made it financially possible for them to marry.) Certainly equally important was the fact that in the summer they could go together Up-Country to a sparkling small lake, where Wallace would teach Ethel how to cast a fly for the quick, elusive trout. For many weeks of many years she was to spend times of contentment on this lake. She was to write about it too, calling it Nimpish Lake, Three Loon Lake, Blue Lake, and Lac Le Jeune. It was, when they first went there, called Fish Lake, and is now known as Lac Le Jeune.[6]

So, in the summer of 1921, they packed two split-cane rods and boxes of flies and light gut-leader, and placed them and two suitcases containing books and some rough clothes in Wallace's automobile. Wallace lit a cigar — as he always did before taking a journey made for pleasure — and pushed the button to start the motor. It stopped. He got out, went into the box of tools which was strapped to the running board, found the crank, put it in at the front of the car, and cranked. The engine started, it stopped, he cranked again, and when the car was trembling with eagerness—although letting out the occasional, alarming cough—he jumped in, slammed the door, and he and Ethel headed northeast. Hours later they drove along a precarious, narrow road with hair-pin turns above an angry, swollen Fraser River. And finally, when night was coming down and they were high above the river and had left behind the most dangerous turns in the road, they drove up to Brody House, which sat at the edge of a bank of the Fraser River in the small town of Lytton.

A man came out to the car and took their suitcases and Ethel up to their room while Wallace registered. They still had nearly an hour before they had to be down for dinner, Wallace said when he came into their room. He poured two glasses of rye whisky and water, and together they stood at the window and saw the confluence of two great rivers, and the trellis bridge poised over these opposite and opposing waters.

It is true. Say "Lytton Bridge"—and the sight springs clear to the eyes. There is the convergence of the two river valleys and the two rivers. The strong muddy Fraser winds boiling down from the north. The gay blue-green Thompson River foams and dances in from the east. Below the bridge...the two rivers converge in a strong slanting line of pressure and resistance. But it is no good. The Thompson cannot resist, and the powerful inexorable Fraser swallows up the green and the blue and the white and the amethyst. The Thompson is no more, and the Fraser moves on to the west, swollen, stronger, dangerous, and as sullen as ever.[7]

Early the next morning they had a large breakfast and again drove northeast, and they saw "the wind flowing through the sage" and heard "the occasional wild and lonely cry of the loon clattering through the trees." They drove on through country which was sometimes wooded, sometimes barren, until they were only a few miles from the cowboy town of Kamloops, where the train stopped to take on cattle and bring them down to the slaughterhouse in Vancouver. But they turned sharply to the right about twenty miles outside of Kamloops. Now they drove along a deeply-rutted dirt road which led them high into wooded hills and then, quite suddenly, they saw, below them, Lac Le Jeune.

And when I got there, I tell you my heart rose up the way it does when you see your favourite lake away up in the hills all shining and saying Come on, Come on, and the sky all blue and the reflections of the forest upside down in the water and everything as innocent as a kitten. That lake is nearly forty-five hundred feet up and even in summer after hot days it can be cold and you can have storms like winter but there's a smell of the pines there and especially when the sun's on them and even when the rain's been on them, and all the way up there's the smell of the sage too. And right away when you see the fish jumping and hear the loons crying on the big lake or Little Lac Le Jeune Lake you know — well, it's heart's desire, that's what it is.[8]

Here they were extraordinarily happy.

Isn't it strange. . . nearly all stories have been about love or fighting and all love stories have been about faithless, unhappy, or frustrated love. No one can write about perfect love because it cannot be committed to words even by those who know about it.[9]

Every day in any weather they took out their clinker and they cast their flies among the tule reeds or out in the centre of the lake where the fish were leaping (although sometimes these fish, they knew, were teasing and would not accept their flies) and where the trout swirled the surface of the water.

At night after dinner they sat with the other guests and the owners of the lodge and talked mostly fisherman's talk, and Ethel listened carefully. Then they would say goodnight and go upstairs to their room. Sometimes they read for a while.

One night Ethel left Wallace reading in bed and went to the outhouse which was not far behind the lodge. She felt and saw, dimly, the trail, and then the outhouse appeared. She went in and closed the wooden door. Just as she was sitting down she heard with horror the latch fall on the other side of the door. She pushed the door, she jiggled and kicked it, but it did not budge. She could not call for someone to come because that would be so terribly embarrassing. She refused to panic. She would sit down and wait for Wallace; he would soon miss her, and then he'd worry. And then he'd come running up the path, calling her name. She smiled. He would come soon. She waited for a very long time. The night was cold because even in summer, four thousand feet is too high to hold the heat of the land. Her feet were bare and she wore only her nightgown and summer dressing-gown. She became more and more furious with this nearly brand new husband of hers, whom she had left comfortably, warmly, in bed, reading a good biography or history or whatever it was he was reading. Perhaps he had fallen asleep. Certainly he was not missing her. She heard a man's footsteps, but they were not Wallace's and, oh, horrors, the man tried the door, and then he said, "Is someone in there?" and she had to say she was, and that she was locked in. It was the owner of the lodge and he let her out and apologized for the unreliable lock, and she said no, it was of no importance, no she hadn't been there long, but she was glad he had come along. She thanked him again, and then, her feet stiff with cold, she stumbled along the path and up the steps to the lodge and their room, opened the door, and there was Wallace, still reading. He had not noticed her disappearance, but her reappearance was not ignored.

It is not uncommon for people to hate to come home from holidays; Ethel was certainly reluctant to come home from this one. She was coming home to her mother-in-law. Her sister-in-law Amy had married Ernest Buckerfield and they now lived in a flat. Later the Buckerfields would move into a house in Shaughnessy Heights, but there was no room for Bella there either. So for the next six years, Wallace's mother continued to live with Wallace in the stone-and-timbered bungalow, which was not large and was shared now by his bride.

"At the age of thirty-three," Alex Wilson told me, "and after living with her grandmother and her aunts, she felt, I think, that she had done her duty and now life was to be enjoyed and she should be free to enjoy it. Old Mrs. Wilson was a dour woman without a sense of humour."

Wallace was a busy internist, with a growing practice. Ethel was kept busy, but in a way which "quite terrified" her—" 'teas' they chiefly were, of all abominations—1 a day 2 a day 3 a day & everyone talking more & louder & faster. As a young doctor's wife I did my best," she wrote in a letter to her friends Alan and Jean Crawley.

She read when she was home, and occasionally played the piano. Her mother-in-law frequently played the piano and sang. Her sister-in-law, Amy, also sang when she dropped in for tea.

"The human voice," Ethel said more than once, "is my least favourite instrument."

When Ethel was growing up she was told to keep control of herself. So she did now, a woman in her thirties. She did not rage. She became silent. Her smile became a little stiff, her blue eyes a little more piercing. She took to her bed quite often.

And then Amy and Ernest built a new house on Marine Drive in Vancouver, overlooking the Fraser River. It was a big handsome house with an enormous garden. Bella Wilson paid for the building of her own room, and in 1927 moved in with the Buckerfields.

Ethel seemed to regain her health.

Alex Wilson said that silence of Ethel's and her withdrawal signalled "a little nervous breakdown." She said it recurred in 1929, when the Wilsons were on a trip and there was a plan to visit some people in England, and Ethel did not want to do this.

"It was like a depression. But when the problem was cleared up, and she didn't have to stay with those people in England, the little breakdown disappeared," she said.

Ethel was a smart orphan who had been properly brought up.

Chapter Nine

Visible Worlds

Oh, Bella wasn't all that bad. She disappeared, sometimes for months, making her way about the North American continent, visiting friends and sometimes travelling with them for short distances. So at least occasionally Ethel was free of her mother-in-law's sober goodness. And, of course, the Wallace Wilsons were very pleasant to have around, so two or three evenings a week they played bridge with friends and cousins (" 'Cards' were unknown in [Grandmother's] house...I don't know why 'cards' were taboo but they were"[1]) and on other evenings they would be entertained or entertain at dinner.

On Wallace's days off they went alone together on long walks—not talking hurriedly as they had when he was courting, but now as an easy couple, "sometimes in perfect silence." They walked sometimes in the rain, in their gumboots, along the dykes of the Fraser River, where ducks and gulls and other seabirds came to feed and nest. And they walked, without shoes in the summer, along the long white beaches which surrounded their city, and here she became "aware of the incorporeal presence in air, and light, and dark, and earth, and sea, and sky, and in herself, of something unexpressed and inexpressible that transcends and heightens ordinary life, and is its complement. Without it, life is uninformed."[2]

They went to the theatre whenever they could when Wallace was not on call. In the first nine years of their marriage, Vancouver jumped in population from 124,000 to 242,000, and it had an extraordinary (in quality) number of visiting artists. The Wilsons heard violinist Fritz Kreisler and pianist Paderewski. They were in the audience when Nijinsky danced and when all three Barrymores—John, Ethel, and Lionel—trod the boards of the Vancouver Opera House (plush, pretty, and owned by Canadian Pacific Railway). And John Barrymore came again to play his Hamlet.

> Polite and fashionable Vancouver attended, flattering William Shakespeare by evening dress or at least by a "fascinator" over the head, and even by a sprinkling of tiaras and pearl dog-collars.[3]

Vancouver could attract these artists because it lay conveniently on a natural circuit. Travelling from the east, they would finish in San Francisco and then turn north, without much time or trouble, to play Vancouver before returning east.

The Vancouver Symphony Orchestra, which was started in 1919 through the interest and financial backing of Mrs. Rogers ("B.T." of the Sugar Refinery's wife), with some ill-sounding horns which persisted until after the end of World War II, played the three Bs—Bach, Beethoven, and Brahms—and, rarely but noticeably, a few short, modern pieces. These, to Ethel, were worse than the human voice, and in Wallace's copy of *Tom Jones*, which she was reading in the Twenties, she underlined: "now, on some hollow tree, the owl, shrill chorister of the night, hoots forth notes which might charm the ears of some modern connoisseurs of music."

She was becoming more free, losing more and more of the uncertainties of her childhood and her womanhood. She now smoked openly, and too much. She told stories about her grandmother and her aunts at dinner parties and teas, and friends laughed and said, "Oh Ethel you must write that down," but she was too busy living.

Often the Wilsons were invited to dinner in a handsome house with seventeen rooms and two-and-a-half acres of gardens, which stood among others of its kind behind high hedges along South West Marine Drive. It was built by Alex Wilson and her first husband, Blythe Rogers, and was named Knole, without shame, after the great house and gardens in England.

One night Wallace dropped Ethel off under Knole's Porte-cochère and

74

drove away to park his car. She met him in the hall, and together they went into the drawing room for cocktails. It was a large party, the men in black tie, the women in evening dress, possibly with a sprinkling of tiaras. There was, as usual, much talk ("Her talk, so voluble and kind. It always runs before her mind," said Ethel's Shakespeare), and then the butler announced dinner and people slowly passed into the dining room. This room was resplendent with red carpet and red velour curtains, and a French-polished mahogany table which on this night was set for twenty-two and shining with English cut-glass and heavy silver. Ethel and Wallace were separated, as husbands and wives could talk to each other on most occasions, and Wallace found that he was seated beside a young woman whose name—he quickly glanced at the place-card—was Maidie Daniel. Mrs. Daniel, he learned, used to live in Vancouver, but was now married and living in San Francisco. She had noticed his place-card: Dr. Wallace Wilson.

"Oh," she said, "are you related to Alex who was a Wilson?"

"Yes," Wallace said, "I am her cousin."

"I have not seen him for many years, but I knew an Algernon Wilson who was Alex's cousin. Are you by any chance related to him?"

"Ah Algernon," Wallace said, dropping his eyes mournfully, "Algernon has gone to heaven. But Wallace," he said, suddenly looking at her with bright eyes, "has taken his place."[4]

Through Wallace, Ethel was learning the freedom of fun. "It was not until I was married that I learned it was possible to enjoy life without passing a moral judgement on it," she told a magazine interviewer in 1947.[5]

Still, something was missing. They did not seem able to have children. Many of their friends have told me that they thought that the Wilsons did not want children. I, by the same instinct (both friends and I can only call on instinct), think they did want them. Both Wilsons were extraordinarily attractive to children, and children are extraordinarily quick to sense those who can and cannot be trusted, and who do and do not like to be with them.[6]

In the 1920s Vancouver was small and the social register was smaller. Many people did not mind their own businesses any more than they do now. One day a man whom Wallace had known for some time said to him, "Why haven't you and Ethel any children?" Wallace answered with a good-natured smile in order to confound the man for his impertinence, "Oh, Ethel doesn't want to ruin her figure." The man was left where Wallace wanted him, in speechless wonder. A woman who was extremely fond of Ethel, and whose affection was reciprocated, told me that she asked the same question and that Ethel answered abruptly, "I taught children for thirteen years." Her friend dropped the subject. But Ethel once mentioned their childlessness to a young woman whom she was beginning to love as a daughter. She did not say it outright, but she implied that they were unable to have children.

"I said to Wallace, 'Would you like to adopt a child?' and he said, 'Whatever for?' The subject was never mentioned again," Ethel said.[7]

She had a game which delighted small children. She would touch her elbow and, her mouth closed, emanate a sharp trill, then touch her ear, another trill, her foot, another trill, and then she would have the child touch those parts and let out another trill, and the child would laugh and so would she, and usually they were now firm friends.

"A child is still one with reality. Nothing intervenes. The light that falls on each day is the first light that ever fell. It has not even a name but it is part of the world of his bright senses. Sounds, objects, air are all his own. They are himself, an extension of himself," she wrote.[8]

Wallace's way was different. He was slightly brusque with children, but he was a man they went to easily. When Ethel's godchild, Lucinda, was about four, she disagreed with me about birds regurgitating to feed their young. We were on our way to tea with the Wilsons. She said that we would ask "Dr. Woozy." She did and she was right. Then Wallace fascinated her with true stories about birds for perhaps twenty minutes, while Ethel and I listened. He stopped suddenly, rose and went to a drawer, opened it, took out something unseen, and suddenly presented a chocolate bar to the child. And before we left he dug into his pocket and money passed from the big to the small hand.

In the Twenties, servants and cooks were treated with courtesy—in kindly houses—but kept separate in an unspoken agreement between the master, mistress, and the children. This was the rule in Vancouver as well as in England. It could have been Ethel's memories of the maids at the top of Uncle Sydney and Aunt Edith's house, but it was more likely her and Wallace's natural curiosity and courtesy that made them bring people who worked for them into their lives. In their early years of marriage they had a series of young Japanese houseboys. One who was loved by the Wilsons was Tom Tokunaga. Forty years after he had gone, she wrote about him.

When my husband returned from what is called the First War we soon engaged a handsome Japanese schoolboy of about seventeen named Tom Tokunaga to live in our house and to work for us after school hours. This we did chiefly so that he could answer the telephone if we were both out. When a young doctor is working hard and building up a practice it is a very bad thing if the telephone rings and there is no answer. The doctor is not notified of trouble and patients are — quite rightly — affronted. In those days there were no fancy arrangements whereby a doctor could be reached by telephone when there was no-one at home. So I attended to the telephone during the first part of the day but, when Tom came home from the high school, he did some housework before dinner, which I had got ready, and at night I was free to drive out with my husband on his calls while Tom did his homework and answered the telephone very well indeed. As Tom left school and us for a full-time job, he was succeeded year by year by four other Japanese school friends of his, and so for five years we employed the part-time service and happy company, in turn, of five young men who would be the flower of any nation.

Tom was distinguished in appearance, strong, quick, graceful, with classical features, and he loved the plays of Shakespeare. He became an engineer and returned to his country. After the next war, which is called The Last War, my husband and I feared that Tom had died, as we heard of him no more. He had a remarkably concise way of speaking, and several of Tom's utterances are ours today.

We lived in a small stone house full of fireplaces — perhaps the oldest house in the west end of Vancouver... We had a kitchen stoep, or stoop. We had at first no refrigerator, but on the stoep was a small wooden contraption called the meat safe. The meat safe, standing in the open air, was for the purpose of keeping the meat safe and also a multiplicity of eatable odds and ends. It had three shelves which were always overcrowded and it was surrounded by wire netting. One night at dinner Tom brought us our pudding, but not the custard which I had made that morning. Some of our elders and richers bought cream, but we did not. Creamo had not then been invented and so I made custard, from supposed duty, not from love of custard.

"Oh Tom," I said, "the custard?"

Tom gave his involuntary almost imperceptible bow. "I am sorry," he said, "Meat safe had many contents, and in endeavoring to extract custard, by Series of Combination of Events, it spilled." (One saw at once the tippling impinging dishes and custard flowing, dripping down.) Dear Tom, he could not know how useful his words have been to us during the global and domestic complications and vicissitudes, the unexpected pleasures, and the series of combinations of events over forty years.[9]

Because he, too, loved Shakespeare, Tom read aloud with the Wilsons after dinner. It was the Wilsons' life-long habit to read Shakespeare aloud, another bond between them.

"Shakespeare knows everything," Ethel would say with the emphasis of conviction. She read from her father's hand-sized, leather-bound books, which had been his heritage to her along with a few Bibles and approximately $200.

Wallace had George Eliot, and then there was Trelawney and Flaubert. Somewhere, when she was reading, she came across the phrase, "good is as visible as green." She became excited by that and looked up John Donne and read more, and Donne, with his clear-sighted wisdom, became nearly as important to her as William Shakespeare. Wallace loved history—she started to look more deeply there—and the worlds of nature, which she also loved, so they shared these books. Her curiosity about the English language started in her father's study ("What is a 'the'?") and was encouraged in her grandmother's house ("books were as common as tea cups"). Now she had fallen in love with a man who was leading her into even more worlds of discovery.

When in 1927 Amy and Ernest Buckerfield moved with Bella into the grand new house on Marine Drive, the distance between them and Ethel was too great even for a good healthy walk, so loyalty and affection came more easily. Ethel and Amy started writing letters to each other which, despite the existence of the telephone, was still the civilized manner of communication. Amy was a sentimental person who, throughout her life, kept memorabilia; she kept some of Ethel's letters. Among these were six letters stuffed into a single envelope. In the first, dated Saturday a.m., Ethel says that this is "just another pass-time letter, but I haven't as many interesting things to tell you as you have to tell me." She chatters about Amy's relatives and some mutual friends, and says that she is "so tempted to go out and rake leaves with the gardener, it's a lovely occupation, but will reserve my quota of strength for a possible walk with W. this p.m." And then she says, "Well, I lay down my pen—no I don't—wouldn't it be funny if we lived ninety years ago—*thus*"

Mumba Parva
Dumpshire

3/3/1817

My dear sister-in-law yr. missive recd. by last week's mailcoach wh. alas suffered delay on acct. of the deplorable condition of the roads gives me inexpressible relief & Joy...

This letter, which is signed E.D. Wilson, and the five that follow, open up a world (shared by two sisters-in-law) of friends, domineering but kindly husbands, maids, cooks, and an unwanted relative. They are concerned with the elopement of Sir H. Stukely's daughter, Dora, and Axton, the riding master for E.D. Wilson's seven daughters. Sir H. Stukely suspects a go-between, whom he determines to track down. Here is the sixth and final letter:

My dear Sister-in-Law

O my dear Sister-in-law prepare yr. Self for this Shocking News. The Gilty Person on whom Sir H. Stukely's vengence is set is none other than yr. Willful Niece Camilla. O my dr. S.i.l. could I ever describe to you the Sene in our Hall yesterday when I innacently descending the Stares was confronted by this Angry Man. In vane did my Husbd. explane, & in vane did I protest, but He wd. have None of it & Stroad out Shutting the door with a Slamb & Left us There. Since then I have took to my Bedd & have only now had my first Food a little Beaf Tea. It apprs. that Camilla that Wicked Girl had a great Affection for Dora S. who to Speak the Truth is a very Lovely Young Woman. And when She (Camilla) requested that she might visit Miss S. at the termination of her Riding lessons, under the Gise of speaking french for ½ an hr. with her, Miss D.S. haveing visited the french Capital last Jan. I readily agreed, seeing that Camilla could then canter Home alone, Being but a matter of a few Minute ride. It apprs. that on Severall Occasions Miss S. & young Axton gained a few Minuts together, the Twins being left Loytering in the Drive, & More Over that Camilla was constantly Barer of Letters & Toakens, wh. she did with a very good Will. All this has now come to Light, through a chance Remark of Bell Miss Stukely's maid carried to Mrs. Lambkin the Housekeeper who fourth with Reported it to Sir H. Stukely who There Upon questioned the maid with great Severity. I have not yet seen my Daughter but her Father says Upon his taxing her with this she cryed Bitterly, but said she was Glad she had done it & wd. do the same again. I am astounded by the Coolness of my own Daughter who these Many Days has carried in her Boosum so Serious & Secret a Matter. So far my dr. Wm had delt with her, so great was my Upset, but Now I must Arise. I am not Well & Do not know what to Do.

Beleeve me my own dear Sister in Law
yr. affect. Sister-in-law
Eliza D. Willson

Post Scriptum I am Upp but Distrakted. Camilla rode away on her pony this p.m. & has not Yett returned. Estella Wormley who dropt in for a moment to Commiserate with me says she gest this all along but Dursent Breathe a word.

At the top of the letter which accompanied these six fragments of fiction, Ethel wrote a P.S. to Amy: "I think for pastime & amusement I'll write a series of letters called 'My Dear Sister-in-Law' & send them to a magazine. I'll probably peter out when it comes to doing it." There is nothing to indicate that she did write the series.

Ethel's great-aunt, Miss Eliza Edge, and aunt, Miss Belle Malkin, were about to experience a great event. Miss Edge, in 1923, was seventy-eight. That November, to avoid the Christmas mails, she sent off her annual Christmas card to Queen Mary at Buckingham Palace. She told Her Majesty that she was about to become eighty, which was true enough, and that she was planning to visit England during the coming year. She did not mention that she was going with her niece Belle, probably because Belle was only sixty-five, and in any event, it would not matter to the Queen who she was travelling with, or even probably that she was coming, because she was extremely busy and had a good deal to occupy her mind. But apparently it did matter that Miss Eliza Edge, who had founded the knitting group in Vancouver, Canada, to which Queen Mary had extended her patronage during the Great War, was coming to England. Her Majesty's secretary wrote to Miss Edge and asked her to come to tea, alone, with Her Majesty, specifying the day and the hour. Imagine! Just Miss Edge and Her Majesty.

But by the time Eliza and Belle had stepped off the train in Canada, and off the boat in Southampton, and then off the train in London, imagination became too much. Now Eliza was in the hubbub of London, dizzying to an aged person who had become accustomed to the softness of a city cut off from the world by mountains and sea. The nervous excitement could not be handled. She sent her regrets to Her Majesty, saying that she was not well. Her Majesty, apparently very sorry that the appointment had to be cancelled, asked her secretary to arrange a day and hour when Miss Edge was better. And that's how the innocent traveller went to see the Queen. This event—not omitting the fact that Miss Edge's brother, John, who accompanied his sister to the palace, would have liked to meet the queen but was asked to wait in another room—is told in truth in *The Innocent Traveller*.

Then Eliza, Belle, and John went on to do the Grand Tour of Europe, and in Florence, Eliza bought a copy of John Galsworthy's *The White Monkey*, which had just been published a month before, on November 11, 1924. It was for Ethel, and she would send it on to her in time for her thirty-sixth birthday. But she did not mail it off. It seemed that Belle was not well. They must get Belle home. The doctor said she was very ill indeed. Belle, of course, made the arrangements, and they took the ship back across the Atlantic, then the train across Canada, and by the time they were home, the pain had become severe.

Belle had cancer; a long illness and slow death. She did not die until 1926; it was agonizingly slow. When her death was coming, Ethel was near her, sitting in a chair, watching her and knowing what a good aunt this emaciated person had been. She leaned forward and looked into her aunt's eyes, which were now dull from exhaustion, and said, "Aunty Belle, Aunty Belle"—her aunt looked up—"you do know that you are the best friend I ever had and am ever likely to have." Belle's eyes cleared and she sighed, and "she seemed to be thinking 'My life has been worthwhile after all.' I don't know why or how I said it. It seemed inspired by God," Ethel said.[10]

Chapter Ten
Sub-Visible Worlds

Ethel had become acquainted with the terrors of death, and sometimes she could put them aside. But with living she could not dodge or delay the terrors. These, nearly always new to her, came simply because her husband's importance was growing in the city and, in fact, across the province.

Wallace Wilson has been described by his friends as "a dedicated doctor," "a humanitarian," "an extraordinarily generous and good man with a keen social conscience," and "an excellent administrator." It is not surprising, then, that in 1928 he was invited to become the next president of the British Columbia Medical Association (his uncle, David Wilson, was the first president of the Vancouver Medical Association in 1898), and that he accepted. Ethel was pleased for his sake, because it was an honour, but not for herself. More often than ever now he was late coming home, and "his lateness made the house too quiet."[1] And she found her new existence as a social being a terrible strain.

"I think 'social life'...is a most peculiar erection built of imponderables and invisibles," she wrote.[2]

She now faced two to three hundred people at a time, grinning and screaming at each other at teas and cocktail parties, more complicated canapés, more expensive hats, and more exclusive snobbery. The other ladies in hats and the men in expensive suits did not notice the strain. Her beauty and sometimes most surprising quickness of tongue charmed them (only a few noticed those quick blue eyes and felt uneasy), and they did not suspect her. She had been taught that when you show uneasiness you make the other person uneasy and that is unkind. So when she was nervous, she did not do what she felt like doing. She did the opposite. She gushed. (Some women imitated her gush.) She milled among people whose smiles seemed set in concrete, and her own smile felt as if it would crack into a thousand pieces and clatter to the floor. She chatted and laughed (those who imitated her gush thought her laugh dreadfully shrill) and drank cocktails, but only two, and swallowed small round sandwiches which were formed in wheels (two or three different fillings lay between thin layers of bread, which were wound around each other) and flat, ordinary sandwiches, far more delicious than the wheels, which were paper-thin and filled with simple goodness like cucumber or tomato or egg. She herself made such sandwiches for tea and took them, with her silver tea pot, into the garden, even when she was alone. She liked the things, not the effects.

Nevertheless, she was known as an excellent president's wife. People found Wallace more charming, of course; he was warmer, easier. Perhaps she was just a little cold, a little too sharp, although nobody could remember anything she said that was unkind. (Several people told me that she had a very cutting tongue, and yes, they remembered what she had said, and they repeated it. But it was not malicious, and when they heard themselves repeat it, they realized that. But there was sometimes the way she said something which made you pause.) She hid behind her elegance, as her friend Geoffrey Andrew had said. And behind that facade, the writer, who would emerge in ten years, was watching, listening, storing up.

Quite often Ethel took to her bed during the year of being president's wife, and later too, even when she had no rigorous social duties. It could have been the anaemia. But active, imaginative people sometimes take to their beds in crises, small or large. It gives them time and silence to think.

Then, with such enormous relief, the year was over. Now came the prize. They were to go to Vienna where Wallace would do post-graduate work in internal medicine. Coming with them were Colin and Kathleen Graham. Colin would do graduate work in eyes, ears, nose, and throat. Kathleen and Ethel would be free to wander, go to concerts, visit art galleries, sit in outside cafes, window-shop (little buying for students' wives), and explore. But first, and even more exciting—in fact thrilling—they would all go to the Middle East. They would sail through the Adriatic, the Mediterranean, and Aegean seas, walk in the Holy Land, Egypt, and Greece.

> The isles of Greece, the isles of Greece... Many an evening she saw the Grecian islands melting away, mauve and pink and purple and a dying grey, into the darkening sea. "The wine-dark sea,"... What had she expected to see? Sea the colour of wine? No. At this moment the colours of the Mediterranean slid from steel-blue into sapphire into indigo into purple into bronze, and this, this was the sea which the Hellenes had smitten with their oars and which Odysseus had sailed for adventure and for home... [They sailed] down the Adriatic Sea, past the shores where Nausicaa played and the shipwrecked Odysseus slept, round the tip of the Peloponnese and north to the Piraeus,... [and then they saw] the height of human truth and beauty, the small hill of the Acropolis, in Athens, and upon it the ruined Parthenon.[3]

They climbed the Acropolis with a guide named Socrates and Wallace said to this man, "Are you indeed Socrates?" and the guide said, "I am not Socrates himself, but I am his favourite nephew." She told me that was a true story. She put it into *The Innocent Traveller*.

Now she started to take notes. She did not write a diary, as did her friends. She simply made notes, quick moments of discovery.

> Up the broad steps and up the stony hillside. The five serenely handsome maidens (at the temple of Erechtheum) stand arrested in their ritual dance for twenty-three hundred years. We perishable ones look up at them supporting with modest dignity the southern portico of the small temple. There is a different kind of air and time on this low hill. The wind blows freely through the warmly pale pillars and through the sublime ruins of the greater temple. Pericles walked here and talked here and looked across to Hymettus and to the sea. When the sunset smote Hymettus, Socrates took the hemlock and drank.
>
> Nearly everything that is significant in thought and form, nearly everything that is beautiful in thought and form, nearly everything that is beautiful in principle and in prospect is in the air that blows through the Acropolis.[4]

They took a ship from Piraeus to the Holy Land. Now they would find the places where Jesus had walked. They were outraged by the hawkers who badgered them to buy rosaries and relics. Some pulled at their clothes; Wallace roared at these. Then they visited the Garden of Gethsemene, where Jesus had been taken prisoner, and it looked to Ethel just the way she thought it must have been in Jesus' time. No hawkers. A simple, silent place. She dropped to her knees and kissed the ground. Then she picked a wild flower growing there and put it in her father's Bible. And she snapped two sprigs from an olive tree in the garden and put these in a handsome, inlaid box.

From Palestine they sailed across the Aegean to Egypt and then up the Nile. The river was broad and brilliantly blue, and its banks were lush green with spring. They stopped in Cairo and spent several days there, and then went on to Alexandria where Wallace had played during the war. But this Egypt was wildly disturbing to Ethel, a confusing muddle of romance, ugliness, poverty, history, disease, flies, blindness, withered limbs. They drove out to the Valley of the Kings and stepped down into the darkened tombs, which were airless, quite terrifying to Ethel. But she said nothing and stayed beside her husband. Then they climbed out of those tombs and walked again through free air and saw the sky.

Their driver started back across the desert toward the greenness of the Nile. Then, for no immediately discernible reason, he stopped abruptly in the desert and honked his horn. (This incident must have sat heavily on her mind for many years before she was relieved of it through writing. She called the story, first, "Buy a Little Hand," finally "Haply the Soul of My Grandmother.")

After that sudden stop, "they saw on their right, set back in the dead hills, a row of arches, not a colonnade but a row of similar arches separated laterally a little from each other and leading, evidently, into the hills..." (In this story, Marcus can be seen as Wallace, Mrs. Forrester as Ethel.)

The driver then signified that if they wished they could go up to the tombs within the arches. Without consultation together they all immediately said no. They sat back and waited. Can Marcus be ill? Mrs. Forrester wondered. He is too quiet.

Someone stood at the side of the car, at Mrs. Forrester's elbow. This was an aged bearded man clothed in a long ragged garment and a head-furnishing which was neither skull cap nor tarboosh. His face was mendicant but not crafty. He was too remote in being, Mrs. Forrester thought, but he was too close in space.

"Lady," he said, "I show you something" ("Go away," said Mrs.

Forrester), and he produced a small object from the folds of his garment. He held it up, between finger and thumb, about a foot from Mrs. Forrester's face.

The object...was a small human hand, cut off below the wrist. The little hand was wrapped in grave-clothes, and the small fingers emerged from the wrapping, neat, gray, precise. The fingers were close together, with what appeared to be nails or the places for nails upon them. A tatter of grave-clothes curled and fluttered down from the chopped-off wrist.

"Nice hand. Buy a little hand, lady. Very good very old very cheap. Nice mummy hand."

"Oh g-go away!" cried Mrs. Sampson, and both women averted their faces because they did not like looking at the small mummy's hand.

The aged man gave up, and moving on with the persistence of the East he held the little hand in front of Marcus.

"Buy a mummy hand, gentleman sir. Very old very nice very cheap, sir. Buy a little hand."

Marcus did not even look at him.

"NIMSHI," he roared. Marcus had been in Egypt in the last war.

He roared so loud that the mendicant started back. He rearranged his features into an expression of terror. He shambled clumsily away with a gait which was neither running nor walking, but both. Before him he held in the air the neat little hand, the little raped hand, with the tatter of grave-clothes fluttering behind it. The driver, for whom the incident held no interest, honked his horn, threw his hands about to indicate that he would wait no longer, and then drove on.

She played the dark unknown, the little hand alive with its fluttering grave-clothes, against the brutally brilliant skies of Egypt. She said that she knew nothing of and cared much less for symbolism. She was aware for her art and her life. She had faced the terrors and she knew she could never be really acquainted with them.

Ethel Wilson admired E.M. Forster who, in a talk to the Bloomsbury "Memoir Club" in 1904, said something with which she must have agreed.

The original experience—of the kind called human, but really fatuous and shallow—is of no importance and may take any form. Soon it goes, and the continual births and deaths of such are part of the disillusionment and livingness of this our mortal state. We do constantly invest strangers and strange objects with a glamour they cannot return. But now and then, before the experience dies it turns a key and bequeaths us with something which philosophically may be also a glamour but which actually is tough. From this a book may spring. From the book, with violence and persistency that only art possesses, a stream of emotion may beat back against and into the world.[5]

They left Egypt and went to Vienna with the Grahams, and here, she told me, she spent "a deliciously happy" year. A glimpse of this happiness is caught in her story, "We Have to Sit Opposite." (Again, Mrs. Forrester could be Ethel Wilson and Mrs. Montrose, Kathleen Graham.)

Both Mrs. Montrose and Mrs. Forrester were tall, slight and fair. They were dressed with dark elegance. They knew that their small hats were smart, suitable and becoming, and they rejoiced in the simplicity and distinction of their new costumes. The selection of these and other costumes, and of these and other hats in Vienna had, they regretted, taken from the study of art, music and history a great deal of valuable time. Mrs. Montrose and Mrs. Forrester were sincerely fond of art, music and history and longed almost passionately to spend their days in the Albertina Gallery and the Kunsthistorische Museum. But the modest shops and shop windows of the craftsmen of Vienna had rather diverted the two young women from the study of art and history, and it was easy to lay the blame for this on the museums and art galleries which, in truth, closed their doors at very odd times. After each day's enchanting pursuits and disappointments, Mrs. Montrose and Mrs. Forrester hastened in a fatigued state to the café where they had arranged to meet their husbands who by this time had finished their daily sessions with Dr. Bauer and Dr. Hirsch.

This was perhaps the best part of the day, to sit together happily in the sunshine, toying with the good Viennese coffee or a glass of wine, gazing and being gazed upon, and giving up their senses to the music that flowed under the chestnut trees. . .

No, perhaps the evenings had been the best time when after their frugal pension dinner they hastened out to hear opera or symphony or wild atavistic gypsy music. All was past now. They had been very happy. They were fortunate. Were they too fortunate?

Perhaps.

Chapter Eleven

Power

For more than a year the Wilsons lived in an ancient city and travelled at leisure through the tidy, peopled countrysides of Europe. Now, in 1931, they were on the enormous train crossing wild Canada. "Look. Oh look," one said to the other as their train swayed and curved past miles of empty white beaches which stretched around Lake Superior. If this lake were in Europe, they agreed, it would become the playground for the world's most fashionable people and be ruined. Here it was, empty to the sight, but so alive behind those rocks and trees, and so immense that they could not see the end of it. Then, for two days, they passed through the prairies, whose emptiness was punctuated by a water tower or a grain elevator or a house far off from the train, and they agreed that you could only know this beauty by walking through it because only then could you feel the wind and smell the dryness and observe the small, delicate flowers which were so brilliant. Then they entered the foothills of the Rocky Mountains and saw snow under the sun, lying across jagged peaks, and something physical stirred in her. She had come this way three times before, always full of expectation. She knew they were approaching British Columbia, some pockets of which she and Wallace knew nearly intimately, but even these were beyond intimacy because they were unpredictable. And now they were in British

Columbia and they were passing sage-brush and tumbleweed, jackpines and polepines, roaring rivers and high virgin timbers, and then they were down into the valley of the Fraser River, running through its fertile lands toward the city, their home, the sea, and those mountains which, too, are always topped by snow, and look scrubbed and polished after the rains go their way and the sun falls sharply on them.

They stepped off the train and tipped the pleasant black porter, walked quickly through the passageway and out into the rotunda, and heard their names called. Here were Amy and Ernie Buckerfield, Wallace's mother, many Malkins (a few older but most of them the same), and everyone laughed and hugged each other. They started toward the cars, and as they crossed the marble floor of the vaulted rotunda, they saw the same people they had seen from the train windows. The hobos, poor bums. On the train, flashing past, they had seen those men sitting near the tracks around fires, or asleep, or smoking, or drinking canned heat, which would kill some of them soon. Once, when the train had pulled into a station, they had got off to stretch their legs and watched as a guard's light swept across the roof of a car and settled on the figure of a man who lay still, dead it seemed, for seconds, until the guard yelled at him and he got up and climbed down and was sent, with threats, away from the train and into the darkness.

The Wilsons did not suffer — financially — from the Great Depression. Wallace was one of 106 physicians and 136 surgeons, out of more than a thousand applicants, to be admitted to the Royal College of Physicians and Surgeons in June 1931. He had set up his practice in the tall art-deco Medical-Dental building on fashionable West Georgia Street, and his practice was large enough to enable him to forget to send bills to people who could not afford a doctor. Fifteen percent of Vancouver's 40,000 were "on the dole." Bums coming to the Wilsons' house were fed and given odd jobs if they could be found. In the large handsome house next to the Wilsons lived several children and their parents, who were having a hard time. Several times a week, when they were going out, Ethel asked one of the children if she would be kind enough to sit with the dog for the evening.

Fifty years later I talked to that child, now past middle age and prosperously married, and she was frankly amazed and openly amused to think that she had been asked to baby-sit a dog. She still did not connect this with her family's welfare. She said that she was "handsomely paid" — she thought it was a dollar a night, which was generous (housemaids were paid $10 a month). She said that she would sit with the wire-haired terrier, Rorrie, in the study. Before leaving, Wallace would light a fire for her, and Ethel would bring out cookies, sometimes sandwiches, and a glass of milk, and one of them would point her attention to the oak table where lay recent editions of glossy magazines from England — *The Tatler*, *The Illustrated London News*, *Country Life*. She remembered the house as being "tiny," but it still stands at 1238 Connaught Drive, and it is not small. (I don't know when the Wilsons moved from the stone-and-timber cottage on Beach Avenue to the more fashionable slopes of Shaughnessy Heights, but they were in Shaughnessy after they returned from Vienna.) It is a neat, stucco house with two gables above the front door, and it looks down on an open park with large shade-trees. One is an old California Oak whose branches spread out far from its trunk and whose large green leaves are always moving and have a brilliant fragility. Even now the park is a quiet place and seagulls still come here from the sea. There is a constant breeze here, even on a slow, hot, summer day.

The house's living and dining rooms look over the park and beyond it to the city, and beyond that to the mountains. The kitchen, master bedroom, and study, where the child sat, look onto the garden. From a vacant lot nearby, the Wilsons took twelve dogwoods and planted them in the garden. Eleven flourished, which was a joke because they thought they'd be lucky if two would continue to grow. But they left the eleven because, in the spring, dogwoods give yellow and then white circular flowers, in the summer, delicate dancing greenery, and in the winter, dark twisting branches which appear to be fragile but are not, and are supplicant to the sky.

The Wilsons also flourished. Wallace was soon to be named, he and his colleagues thought, chief of medical staff at Vancouver General Hospital.

"Wallace had an engaging personality and was a delightful speaker," said Dr. Frank Turnbull, a neurologist.

"As a consultant," said Dr. Donald Williams, a skin specialist, "when you see patients you see how their doctors manage them and how they manage a certain situation. Wallace provided his patients with a very high quality of care and he had an exceptionally good way with his patients."

"He was an excellent administrator and certainly an honourable man," said Dr. A. Taylor Henry, a surgeon.[1]

In the 1930s, the medical profession was solid and placid. A doctor's knowledge contained mysteries, and doctors were in no mood to open up the mysteries. "Doctor knows best" was accepted by children and adults. If, by chance, a doctor's ability were doubted, there was little his patient could do. He could seldom bring a lawsuit because doctors stuck even more closely together than they do now; it was awkward to get another opinion because this meant that the patient had to confront his physician with his distrust. All this was bringing about a quiet rebellion among Canadians and their elected representatives, and more and more frequently the latter spoke of medical insurance schemes. Actually in British Columbia, a medical insurance act had been on the statute books for nearly a decade, but it had not been framed. The doctors thought it never would be, certainly not in their lifetimes.

In 1934 the doctors were warned. The Honourable George Weir, then the provincial minister of education, had headed a public health commission in Saskatchewan. Soon he would become B.C.'s minister of health. He told the B.C. Medical Association, which was meeting in Kamloops that year, that he was appalled at the injustices, injustices which the medical profession instigated, among the poor people of British Columbia. Weir told the doctors that their days of "rugged individualism" would soon be over. He said that he intended to see a bill for compulsory medical insurance driven through the legislature.

"He spoke out of the side of his mouth. He was not an appealing speaker," Dr. Turnbull told me. "But he gave us fair warning. After that meeting Wallace and some others got together and decided that the medical profession needed a more effective organization so that it could fight the government if it came up with the wrong scheme."

The next year Wallace read two important papers to the BCMA. One was the prestigious Osler Lecture, which he titled "Concerning Goitre and Its Ancient Background," and which had fun as well as substance. The other was "The Wilson Report."

Isn't it about time that we removed our individualistic heads from the sands of inertia and did a little realistic looking around and a little active educating of the public along the lines of what we believe is right with reference to the coming of socialized medicine?...Democracy pure and undefiled does not yet exist. Ignorance and intolerance are not yet peculiar only to other forms of government and there is such a thing as the autocracy of the majority or what Lord Acton called "the tyranny of numbers" and bureaucracy *can* be a curse to those who live under its shadow...

...No positive health plan will succeed that leaves without its scope the general practitioner and the sooner that fact is accepted by the people, the profession and Public Health authorities the better...

...Do not misjudge. No attempt is being made to argue against pre-payment plans for the provision of medical care but it must be pointed out that such plans in no way guarantee an elevation of the standard of the health of the people...

...Individually and collectively while living up to our standard of ethics we must form a part of organized Medicine...

Medical treatment under insurance was an excellent idea, but only if the scheme included preventative medicine. Public education and more action from the provincial Department of Health were vital to its success. And, Wallace said, only if the BCMA were included as an adviser would it be in a position to support the bill.

Wallace Wilson was ignored. In 1936 a medical insurance plan was introduced in the B.C. Legislature. Quickly Wallace got a copy. And then, Dr. Turnbull said, "Wallace and others on his committee got hold of one of the world's leading economists—I forget his name, he was English—and a couple of other economists. They reported back that the bill was impractical, that the money available would not cover the costs, that the system would break down. Wallace's committee sent these reports to Patullo [B.C.'s premier] but the bill was passed. As soon as this happened a special meeting was called. It was the largest attended meeting of doctors in B.C.'s history (approximately 250 attended; now a big meeting would mean 2000) and it was a packed house. Only two men voted in favour of the bill.

"Wallace Wilson sent a wire to Patullo, who was then in Ottawa, saying that the medical profession refused to work under the Act. Patullo wired Victoria to shelve the bill sine die [from this day on]. The bill was never promulgated.

"Wallace's prestige was now extremely high," Dr. Turnbull said.

Then George Weir became minister of health. Quite naturally he was indisposed to Wallace Wilson. In 1937 the new Chief of Medical Staff for Vancouver General Hospital was to be appointed. Dr. George Lyall Hodgins ("Lyall Hodgins spoke out of the side of his mouth, like George Weir," said Dr. Turnbull) got the job.

Dr. Hodgins had supported Weir and the government. The job was his but, according to Dr. Williams, he was "black-balled" by his colleagues.

Wallace left Vancouver General Hospital, where he had been a senior member of the staff since 1922. He was named Chief of Medicine at Shaughnessy Hospital and became a consultant in internal medicine at St. Paul's, the second largest city hospital.

"But his profile was low for the next few years," Dr. Turnbull said.

In the distance of time it doesn't seem too low. Wallace was invited to speak to the Board of Trade that February, and in April he and his committee were honoured at a dinner held by the College of Physicians and Surgeons. Lyall Hodgins did not attend. In November he received the Prince of Good Fellows Award from the Vancouver Medical Association, and he was chosen to be the Canadian delegate to the Royal Medical Association's meeting in Plymouth in 1938.

Wallace went about his rounds now as he always had, and sometimes Ethel went with him if he were called out at night. They drove into the parts of town where prostitutes and bootleggers conducted business, and into Chinatown where opium dens were illegal but open because of police corruption. They also drove into the world of large gardens and broad boulevards.

Peggy MacIntosh, whose husband MacGregor had been seriously wounded in the Great War, said she had to call Wallace in the middle of the night quite often. She watched for him to drive up, and then watched as he took out his bag and came up the path. Sometimes, she said, Ethel was sitting in the front seat. She asked me if Ethel had ever had "a nervous breakdown." I said I didn't know, but why did she ask? Well, she explained, when she saw her, Ethel nearly always had her head slumped down. And when she asked Wallace if Ethel would like to come in, he said No, politely but firmly, that she was happy in the car.

Ethel was taking notes while she waited for her husband. It was her secret. She was starting to write. She had, she said, "a compulsion to write," and she could not explain how it came about. It came with worry or loneliness, but it also came during happiness. It was simply a compulsion which probably had been formed by reading, and came from frustration and pleasure and anger and happiness.

In that year, 1936, Ethel showed three stories to Reggie Tupper, who, she told me, was the best-read man she knew. (He was a prominent lawyer, and married to the former Isabel Wilson, Wallace's cousin.)

"He liked them and he said, 'Send them to the best. Send them to *The New Statesman and Nation*,' and I did."

All three were accepted. The first, "I Just Love Dogs," came out in 1937; the others, "Hurry, Hurry" and "I Have A Father In the Promised Land," in 1939.

"Uncle Phil dear," she said to Philip Malkin in Vancouver, "I have something to tell you. It makes me feel very good. I can hardly believe it. The other day I sent three little sketches to *The New Statesman* and they've accepted them all."

Her uncle said, "Well. This is delightful. You're a writer. Fine, just fine."

A few months later, Philip Malkin went to London on business. As he was stepping out of his hotel, the Savoy, a double-decker bus was coming toward him. In the front of the bus was a banner, "Read Ethel Wilson in The New Statesman and Nation."

"Well, I nearly fainted, right on the sidewalk," he told his family.[2]

Chapter Twelve

Only Them as Could Afford It

In 1938, before she packed for Europe to accompany Wallace (who was to attend the Royal Medical Association meetings), Ethel went downtown and bought, among other things, a blue leather book whose pages were lined and edged with gold. It was handsome, not fancy, and it would be useful for jotting down observations and ideas. Writers kept journals, which was very sensible of them, and she was now, at least temporarily, acknowledged as a writer.

It is a curious book, most of it still empty. In the front she has written "June, 1938." Many pages follow, completely blank, and then, "Boston. June 24. Saturday." She writes that she and Wallace have arrived in Boston and that she journeyed out to Cambridge alone to see the famous glass flowers at Harvard. "Incredible." She came back to the hotel, slept, then "out in heat and taxid to the ship. Very contented & happy. Such a good night. Oh my dear Wallace."

Two days later, aboard the *Scythia*:

> Fog. Lots of. Both completely happy. Large plain cabin. Every comfort. Divine service, so heartfelt. Ten times around the deck. Met Dorothy (Pound) Plaunt. Sherry. Lunch. Boohoo goes the foghorn. Algie and I rest so comfy.

She had not been to England for twenty-five years. Then she was alone.[1]

On July 5 they arrived in England and were met at the dock by Margaret Nowell, "such a brick to get up so early, waving red hanky—sat with Margaret in train, same nice crisp lovely Margaret, same champion skier—the one that had T.B." From the train they took a taxi to 22 Ryder Street, where they had rented rooms for the London visit, unpacked, took a walk, and bought tickets to that evening's performance of a play starring Alfred Lunt and Lyn Fontaine. She writes that there were several letters waiting, one from her old Vancouver friend, the beautiful Marion Ward, another from Sylvia Lynd who was, herself, a writer, and was married to Robert Lynd, who was literary editor of the London *News Chronicle*, and was a staff editorial writer for *The New Statesman and Nation*. (Robert Lynd wrote under the initials "Y.Y." for seven Guineas a week, which was then decent pay. But for many previous years, he and other contributors received pittance. The editor, Kingsley Martin, had assumed that all his writers had private incomes.) The Lynds had invited Ethel and Wallace to "din & garden party." There was a letter from her father's half-sister Hannah Atkinson, and then Ethel wrote:

> Oh, I never said, I talked to Margaret [Bryant, the journalist], very quietly thrilling to me. Then a word with Hannah this morning. Her gentle voice quite recognizable after all these years.
> So many chimney pots! Toits de Londres! Run burglars run & climb & escape."

She had seldom been so happy.
She and Wallace went to the House of Commons on July 7.

> Sir Stafford Cripps & the Labour members fought every inch of the way—it seemed to us they had every right on their side—but were deafeated at division...Sir S. Cripps I fell for entirely.

She says that she has telephoned Sylvia Lynd. "Din 8 on Thursday—gave me instructions, & said that Jack (!) Priestley & Rose Macaulay would be at din & perhaps some others. Very exciting & most sweet of her."

The next day started pleasantly, but before lunch was over she had what the Irish call "a turn."

Sir Arthur Newsholme came to lunch. The merriest most genial healthy agreeable man of 81. Told me some interesting history re my Father & a possible stepmother for me. Thank God Lady Newsholme advised Father as she did, or I'd have had a stepmother, a wild stepbrother, no Wallace, and I wouldn't be where I am now having the best time in the world.

After Sir Arthur departed, she took Wallace to look at a suit she had seen that morning, and wrote, "I can hardly write for blushing that I ordered two suits (one is my Xmas & birthday present from W.) a loud purple etc. check cardigan, & an olive green tailored. Then home to rest & plan our itinerary."

The next evening, after a day at Lords, they visited her father's half-sister Margaret. Ethel wrote in her journal:

Yesterday we were in Fairyland & in Grimland. Fairyland was the Eton & Harrow match at Lords. Grimland was my little Aunt Margaret's flat in a colossal & dark & ancient pile in St. Pancreas. Her little party with its assembly of hard-working little people who had always run about & worked among piles of dark flats all their lives, & always would, saddened me, especially in comparison to the waistcoats at Lords...

The flat, spare, small, immaculate, severe, in good taste, few objects but nice, but cold, restrained, & grim. Margaret gave us coffee & the other aunts arrived & my cousin Tony who, poor boy, appears to be a half-wit, tho he can't be as he has his BSc... There was the hospitality of sherry, & refreshments & I knew how much this little party meant to the tired, busy little Margaret in her straitened circumstances. Ella's [Ella Fell from Vancouver] lovely lunch in the Guards Tent was nothing compared to these little sandwiches & lemonades, & I got very depressed as I thought how much more of London lives at the St. Pancreas level. Hundreds live at the Lords level, thousands, perhaps, & thousands or millions below that level.

Well, nobody's happy all the time, & nobody's unhappy all the time, & that's what it amounts to.

The following Thursday evening gave a very different scene.

Friday July 15. The most delightful evening in the world at the Lynds. I was only sorry that Rose Macaulay was not there after all, for after the first shyness of meeting her, I was looking forward to it. It was the most kind and hospitable din. party, beautifully done, just as though we were friends of theirs, not strangers being introduced to someone.

Taxi'd to Keats Grove. *Charming* little street *off* Hampstead, small delicious houses. Door opened by sweet elderly woman, housekeeper probably, & shown into beautiful little room with windows at both ends, soft beigy green misty warm colours, wide boarded floors with deep warm brown polish. Mrs. Lynd came in looking simply *lovely*, a black taffeta dress with knife edged pleating, nearly high to the neck with colossal sleeves, & tremendous skirt, beautiful lines, & little slippers made of little black straps. She looked so fragile, but has tremendous vitality & charm. Then came Y.Y. polite & inaudible. Late in the evening he warmed up for a good garrulous evening, but then we felt we should go. Then the Priestleys. She very pretty, smart young mother of 6, learning Russian, & I should think, her husband's encourager & critic, a very clever serene young woman. We liked Priestley very much, despite rumours to the contrary. Knows what he thinks, & says so, like a Yorkshireman, is amusing, & has a very sweet funny little smile. Of course he was among friends & he & Mrs. Lynd play & laugh & talk together.

(About twenty years later she told a CBC radio audience that she was afraid of Priestley, and in 1965 she wrote to Margaret Laurence about the evening and said that "Priestley held the talk all through dinner.")

Then Mr. & Mrs. Joyce Cary from Oxford. He writes, good novels about Nigeria Mrs. L. [Lynd] says (I think she must be very kind to young writers). Mrs. C [Cary] is very pretty & serious & domestic, have 4 big sons. Sherry. Dinner in tiny dining room with fireplace over which were plaster (Camberi?) — cool — pale. Candles. Long narrow table with low dish of pink roses in centre, pale blue tablecloth & glasses — pale green glasses on cream shelves — books everywhere. The housekeeper & a butler waited. Marvelous din. Lobster claws with mayonaise — cream mushroom soup — roast duckling — the best ice cream I've ever tasted with something queer on it — mushroom savoury — strawberries & cream — hock — brandy. Rapid talking from Mr. Cary, laughing from Sylvia Lynd, pleasant rumbling from Priestley, Mrs. P. completely natural & charming.

Left the men. Soon they came. P [Priestley] talked to me a little severely about repertory theatre in Canada, & creating our own letters, reviews & theatre etc, not deriving from anyone else, not being self conscious about ourselves, but going ahead. I told him we were still adolescent, but though we haven't achieved anything indiginous yet except in painting I thought it would come & is coming. It came down to this partly—I want you to see *my* plays in Canada—you should support Repertory.

Then came a hugely tall young man called Campbell [probably Patrick Campbell, the writer and columnist]. Stammered but didn't mind. *Very* nice. Some peer's son I gathered, as Mrs. L scolded his father for not doing more in the Lords. Then came a *very* fashionable & smart young woman, very soignee, the right curves, the right skin, the right jewels, & a supreme right violet chiffon dress. She was Lady Rooke (*I* say) & Lady Butler (W. says). Evidently writes, speaks in public, but very snappy & witty & a Great friend of S.L. Never a book was mentioned, & only when we were without the men *The Situation* [Hitler and Germany] & then very seriously. The Priestleys left, & the Carys for their train, & suddenly it was after 12, & the evening began. I felt a little freer & not so silent when the great P had gone. W. and I had our little whiskies, & Y.Y. got funny & Irish, & the young man seemed to think it was foolish to think of going as he often stays into the night—however I felt it was an imposition—the Lynds walked us down the dark lane to Keats' house—the Lynds' house had been in Mrs. L.'s family for generations—we all piled into Lady Rooke's car, & she drove us wittily into town whence we taxid home.

I found three supremely satisfactory hats awaiting us from Miss Fry. So *wasn't* it a good day?

Now Wallace went off to Plymouth on his CMA business, and Ethel went to Burslem to stay with her Aunt Edith. Her Uncle Sydney was now dead. In her journal Ethel wrote, "[Edith] seems to me to be on the brink of something, very dazed & forgetful, but won't consider staying in bed. I do hope nothing happens." She also hoped nothing would disturb her happiness.

She went to Alford to visit her father's grave and simply wrote, "All very good."

Margaret Bryant went with her to see Nott's Castle where there was "an ancient inn (1189); scalloped out of rock on wh. castle stands [is written] 'The Trip to Jerusalem'." Their guide, whose name was Minnie

Wilcomb, told Ethel and Margaret that Charlie Peace, the murderer, used to hide out in that inn—"Of course ee didn't murder *pore* people, only them as could afford it, rich people & the like." Years later Ethel mentioned this incident in a letter and added, "I had never thought of the rich in that light, had you?"

Wallace's job took them to Scandinavia. She found it extremely expensive, which is about all she said about that.

Back in London, on Tuesday, August 16, she wrote, "The German manoevres began yesterday & one million men are under arms today. Everyone is saying that everyone is torn. Those in the know—but what is 'The Know.' A good lunch..." She would not be disturbed.

The next day:

> Sustained by the gently obdurate W, I determined to beard the N. Statesman in 10 Gt. Turnstile. I was terrified & felt a perfect fool, & I was quite sure I'd not know how to begin & they'd say, "Oh yes, really?" For stimulus I wore my new green Finnegan suit & hat, & for placebo I took a grain of phenobarbinol. We took a taxi...

For four-and-a-half pages she rambles on excitedly about the taxi driver being unable to find 10 Great Turnstile, and then:

> Well, I palpitated into the N.S. Office & was going [to accept the fact that] the Lit. Ed. was too busy for words. But he saw me, and it was Raymond Mortimer, & he was one of the nicest people I've ever met. I tried not to overstay, but some others came in, & R.M. asked such heaps of questions, & I do hope I wasn't too frivolous & I told them about the phenobarb & they laughed a lot. Well I had a grand time—Kingsley Martin [the editor] wasn't back from Ireland—but I didn't mind *that*.
>
> Then I met W. outside Lincoln's Inn, just outside, & we went to two old silver shops off the Strand to look for a tea pot, & then to lunch in Likes in Maiden Lane. So nice, so posh, so dear, so full of old prints, so 1793.
>
> ...bought my tea pot in Holmes, Bond St. of all places. A pet.
>
> What fun. In one day such a funny incident [lost in the taxi], the nice encounter at the N.S., & a little silver tea pot.

On September 8, the next and last entry, they are on the train and have stopped at Sicamous, B.C.

Trip over...W. & I glad to be home—such a happy time—lovely voyage—

Hitler had marched into Austria that spring. He was making increasingly threatening gestures, but Ethel, although aware, preferred not to notice. She was conspiring with her discoveries and her happiness, and she was exercising what Stendhal said was "the great art of being happy, which is here practiced with this added charm, that the good people do not know that it is an art, the most difficult of all."

Chapter Thirteen

Before the Storm

"Is Mrs. Wilson in?"

"Hopsum you holum lie."

"I beg your pardon?"

With enough fury to force the telephone far from the bewildered one's ear, Chow Lung, the Wilsons' cook, bellowed "HOPSUM YOU HOLUM LIE!" and with his rage reaching down to his small, slippered feet, he stomped into the study or living room or bedroom or dining room or out to the garden, and bellowed, "Missy Wilson!"

She rushed, for fear of further irritation, to the telephone and explained, in hushed voice, that "Hopsum you holum lie" means, in polite terms, "Perhaps, hold the line."

Chow Lung, who wore a pigtail and posed with lit cigarette and an authoritative yet graceful stance when Wallace snapped his picture, was an ill-tempered servant. Like other Chinese men in Vancouver, he spent his loneliness by passing evenings and free afternoons gambling and smoking opium in Chinatown. As both preoccupations increased, so did his ill-temper.

Chow Lung's regimen over his small household gave Wallace and Ethel laughter as well as sharp irritation, and provided Ethel with incidentals for the outside world. She told of how she liked spitting on her iron to test its heat, a practice which Chow Lung despised. In some extraordinary way, even if he was out of sight of the pantry (she checked before she started to iron), he would know that she was doing it again. He would come storming into the pantry, his face furious, and bellow, "No spitty iron!" She demurely dropped her eyes in obeisance. She tried it again, on other days, but unless he was in Chinatown he would reappear with the suddenness and terror of a genie.

There was the day when Chow Lung came to her when she was reading in the study. She did not hear him come in, and was startled to find him standing over her with the telephone book raised high in his hands. He looked as if he was threatening her, and he was.

"That man in kitchen," yes, she had heard high-pitched, angry Chinese words coming from the kitchen, "he go now. He my cousin two thousand years ago." He shoved the telephone book nearly into her stomach and waved it up and down. "I see many Wilsons here. How come you not invite them here?" She saw hundreds of Wilsons arriving in confusion, and Chow Lung looking proud and immensely satisfied that he had made her do her duty. But she didn't; both their dreams died.

Chow Lung had been hired after Ethel ran a newspaper advertisement for a cook general. This was in the Dirty Thirties, and around a hundred white women and Oriental men answered the ad. Before Chow Lung appeared for his interview, Ethel was sitting with a large woman who had presented her with some excellent references. Ethel really found pleasure in looking at good-looking (spiritually and physically) people and, although she knew this might, or might not, be unfair, she was bothered by those who weren't. This woman, extraordinarily large in size and with a grating way of speaking, "would not suit," Ethel knew, but she could not think of how to tell her this with kindness. Suddenly she was inspired. The woman noticed the change in her expression and stopped talking.

"My husband," Ethel said, "is terribly fussy about his meals. I am afraid that I can only hire a Cordon Bleu cook." Those who could afford cooks in this far western corner of the Empire flourished on roast beef and suet puddings, so this woman, Ethel was confident, could not say that she "was acquainted," as she might have, with the Cordon Blue school of cookery. But Ethel was too confident. The woman smiled broadly, happily, in shared understanding.

"I sure agree with him, Madam," she said. "Poor cooking sure puts my stomach right on the bum." That became one of the Wilsons' private phrases. Chow Lung followed and was quickly hired.[1]

It was all so leisurely and pleasant for Ethel. Her mornings started with breakfast in bed while Wallace ate his in the dining room. Then when Wallace left, around eight, Ethel pulled out her letter-sized pad of paper, sharpened her pencil, and started to write. She would stop around noon, before lunch. She sent off another story to *The New Statesman*, and it was rejected.

"They did not like it and I don't blame them," she told me. She destroyed it as she did nearly all her rejected work, and all that she herself found inadequate.

"I was aware," she told a CBC audience later, "that if I had a talent (and I was not at all convinced of it), it could be measured with a teaspoon, not even a liqueur glass—that would be too heady—whereas I knew other talents that flowed with the power of a river."

Her literary loves were deep, and they were frivolous too. Hilaire Belloc she adored for his wisdom out of whimsy and absurdity, and so did she love Daisy Ashford of *The Young Visitors*. For courage, a quality she greatly admired, and fine writing, she turned to Mary Kingsley, the proper Victorian who travelled without proper trepidation through West Africa, then The White Man's Grave, to collect fetishes and fishes. Joyce Cary, the gentle humanist she had met but not yet read at the Lynds, was high on the list, and so was "that wonderful terrific old I. Compton Burnett," whose icy fingers probe and prick family relationships. Ethel Wilson had been a grateful orphan, but she had not been blinded by gratitude. And then there was the master of innuendo, Henry James, the giant Proust—although she became uneasy, possibly impatient, with his homosexuality. She allowed me to borrow her volumes of *Remembrance of Things Past*, but suggested that I skim over the areas where his homosexuality takes over, not because these were shocking, simply because they were not as clearly brilliant, as objective, and so were diminishing of Proust.

Ethel Wilson was an Edwardian who lived out her childhood and youth among strict Victorians. She would write of sexual desire and fulfillment, but not of sexual love with explicitness; not because of prudence or prudery, but because it was difficult and possibly unnecessary.

"I have just been reading Gogol's *Dead Souls*," she wrote me in 1956. "Gogol can write that long & famous & *real* book without one sexual episode, and so can a lot of other people & yet, I do really think, it's a fashion or obsession to haul it in now—& sometimes I think it's because a writer finds not much else to write about. I think Gogol could have hauled it in too & Chekov probably—but there's such an awful lot besides."

When Nabokov's *Lolita* was the cause of battles among literary critics, libertarians, and prudes in the late 1950s, Ethel mentioned in a letter to George Woodcock that she had not read the novel because, she said, "I dislike the subject however sweetly it is discoursed upon—the sweeter the worser." It seems that what mattered was the worser, because she could praise the handling of sexuality in other writers. In Helsinki, during that summer of 1938, she had picked up D.H. Lawrence's *Lady Chatterly's Lover* ("Lady Loverly's Chatter—I think it sounds comical"), which was then banned in its unexpurgated edition in England and America, and would be for another decade.

"How well he wrote some parts," she commented to her friend Alan Crawley, "particularly the orgasmatical, & how dreadfully banal other parts...I really do wish that D.H.L. had been able to profit financially" (as Nabokov was profiting then).

James Joyce's *Ulysses*, with all its frank imagery, gave her no discomfort. There was so much more.

"Joyce could not have done what he did with language if he had not already been an easy master of the use of the sentence; from there Joyce sought and made his way into countries of deep dreams from which no syntax had yet been reported," she said in 1958 to the Vancouver Institute.[2] Here was sensuousness but not pornography, a great experiment without self-consciousness. Ethel abhorred self-consciousness in writers.

She distinctly disliked Ernest Hemingway. His style to her was obviously self-conscious and embedded in affectation. She could not trust it. She mentioned this in a letter in 1962 to the then-young writer Margaret Laurence, whom she encouraged because her work had "warmth and colour," and because she used "words which are the fruit of a natural gift." Hemingway's style, she said, "has been the model for innumerable young writers—and their undoing I think..."

> Did I ever tell you of a page of Hemingway that went something like this:
>
> > 'Gimme a drink.'
> > 'He wants a drink.'
> > 'He's drunk.'
> > 'I said gimme a drink.'
> > 'Who says he's drunk?'
> > 'Aw say, cut it out.'
> > 'Hell, gimme a drink.'
>
> and on and on.

Although she pooh-poohed PhDs on occasion, she did regret not going to university. But the woman who had been taught to make the best of everything found some good in what was missing, too.

> The individual who is self-educated (that is, educated without the authority of—for example—a university) is fallible in opinion and prone to diffidence; but there is a strange secret earned authority resident in that individual which is in the nature of a perception, and will not be denied. There are peculiar pleasures in being self-educated which, in lieu of the less peculiar pleasures of being educated, are extraordinarily fresh and rewarding. (Of course one goes without one's cloak—I mean the authority of learning—and so one is vulnerable.) After living for a while one meets *Hamlet*; and each reading of *Hamlet* sends new freshets of light and darkness through the mind; and with the twentieth reading, the fiftieth—still new freshets flow. One does not stumble; one is led into the depth of the living by the hand of the word.

"Are you writing?" she asked me. I now had a husband and four children.

"No."

"Too busy living," she said.

She, unlike Edith Wharton, did not find social life suffocating. She, like Wharton, wrote about it with sharpness, but she truly enjoyed it, even when she didn't enjoy it.

Nan Cheney and her husband, Hill, arrived in Vancouver from eastern Canada in the autumn of 1937. She was a medical illustrator, Canada's first, and he a radiologist, one of Canada's first. They took a house on Connaught Drive, three doors down from the Wilsons. They met the Wilsons naturally, as medical people.

Before World War II, Vancouver was isolated from the rest of the populated world by the sea, which stretched to the Orient, and by the Rocky Mountains, which barred natural exchange with the eastern part of the continent. People who did different things, and thought differently, came to Vancouver in transit and usually disappeared without notice. People like the Wilsons, who read avidly and had some ideas, were rarely come across in Vancouver, and so when Nan Cheney mentioned to Ethel that she knew Marius Barbeau, the distinguished but not, in the west, famous ethnologist, Ethel paid attention. Nan said that he was coming west in the summer of 1939 and would stay with the

Cheneys, and Ethel said that she would be so happy if she could meet him. So in the summer of 1939, Ethel was invited to tea with Marius Barbeau.

"Ethel," Nan Cheney said, "was very good-looking, very tall. She arrived looking as if she had just stepped out of a dress shop—a lovely hat, white gloves—very smart. Marius Barbeau was startled when he saw her, and she him.

"He was a funny looking little man. He had on a French Canadian suit you know? of beige and pink stripes. It looked as if he had slept in it across Canada. And he had an electric blue tie. His hair was long, for those times—quite long, and it was turning white. It curled below his collar.

"I can see Ethel now, looking down on this apparition. That probably set him off. That day he was so funny. But she didn't find him funny. She wanted to have a serious talk with him. She left the house feeling very flat."

Yes, Nan Cheney said, she liked Wallace better than she liked Ethel. "Oh everyone was crazy about Wallace. He was a wonderful man. I think a lot of women were in love with Wallace. Ethel was, oh, a little cold." Nan Cheney was even then, in her eighties, a beautiful woman. We talked of other things and then came back to the subject. She hesitated, and then said, "I'm sure there was nobody else in his life but Ethel. He seemed absolutely devoted to her."

Ethel knew they liked him better. She hid behind her elegance and knew that he liked her best. In an article which the poet Dorothy Livesay wrote about her and sent to her before mailing it off to the publisher, Ethel changed a word, "assurance," which was used to describe the result of her upbringing in her grandmother's house, to "a sense of proportion." She was keen to the mistake, and she understood it.

Mrs. Wallace Wilson appeared to be assured at parties, where she was known to gush. This made it possible to hide her shyness and to stop other people from feeling uneasy. She was aware of other people's feelings and their motives, even if their society was different from hers. One of her favourite writers, George Eliot, said, "If we had a keen vision and feeling of all ordinary human life, it would be like hearing the grass grow and the squirrel's heart beat, and we should die of that roar which lies on the other side of silence." Ethel Wilson had a keen vision. She was able to realize what was important, not just to her own life, but to other people's lives. Although she lived within the rules of her peculiar society, she refused to be snagged by its pretence. It was not possible for her to embrace that pretence—her friends might have felt much easier if she had done that—because, although she was probably not thoroughly conscious of this, then she would lose her freedom and her ability to see clearly.

Often she went alone—this was unseemly for someone in her society, because it would appear that she had no friends—to the movies in the afternoon. She particularly liked the vulgarian and comedian George Formby, and her sharp, trilling laughter would be heard all over the theatre. Ethel could take and offer delight in the eccentricities of the human body. Many women she knew found the body as vulgar as they found George Formby. ("I once shared a compartment on a train from Montreal with a lady who said, 'Pardon me but I suffer from flatulence' and proceeded to rip off a blast. . .")

When she learned that I was pregnant, again, she surprised me by writing that she knew of a woman who tried many contraceptives but they seemed to have no effect. After delivering her fifth child, this woman waited for her doctor to appear at her hospital bed. When he came, she told him that he really must find something, somebody *must* have discovered something more reliable. To her surprise, his face broke out in a smile of delight and confidence.

"I have found something for you," he said warmly.

"Oh you darling," she said, nearly overwhelmed by hope. "What is it?"

"Very simple. You simply take a glass of water."

Her face fell in disbelief. But then she thought about it and remembered that he had no sense of humour.

"Before or after?"

"Instead."

Until that story came through the mail, I had thought Ethel Wilson was strictly correct.

In September 1938, Britain's Prime Minister Neville Chamberlain proclaimed "peace in our time" to a world which was relieved. Six months later, Czechoslovakia fell without a struggle to Hitler's demands. On April 8, 1939, Mussolini marched into Albania. On May 9, Hitler and Mussolini signed a pact. On September 1, 1939, Hitler invaded Poland. On September 3, Great Britain and France declared war on Germany. Seven days later Canada declared war, and again in Ethel's lifetime, young men and women hurried to recruiting offices and were shipped off quickly to England.

In the summer of 1940 Adolf Hitler sent three thousand aeroplanes to fly over the sensitive areas of England and, if necessary, fight off England's eight hundred planes. The Germans came at night and dropped many of their bombs on the industrial Midlands. The Wilsons immediately sent off letters to Burslem, asking that two small cousins be sent to them to stay for the duration of the war. They waited, but the boys did not come. Their parents decided that the risks of being torpedoed on the Atlantic were too great.

That winter Ethel ran into an old friend, Dorothy Lamb, and mentioned to her that her young cousins were not coming. Dorothy said that two of her relatives and their Nanny had just arrived, and they had with them a sixteen-year-old English girl whose name was Audrey Butler. She said that she was a little concerned about this girl, although she was living with a wonderful family, was perfectly safe, etcetera, but if she and Wallace perhaps...

Ethel went home and talked to Wallace. Wallace's sister, Amy, knew the Thomsons, who had taken in Audrey. The Buckerfields invited Audrey Butler and Graham Thomson, who was then known as Patty and was Audrey's age, to Christmas dinner. They came, and so did Wallace and Ethel. During the evening, Patty lost her handkerchief and mentioned this to Audrey. It would have been ill-mannered, the girls knew, to disturb the "grown-ups," and so they discreetly looked around for the handkerchief. Then Audrey noticed that she was being watched by a pair of sharp eyes. She flushed and said to Patty, "I'm sure this person," she blushed more deeply because she couldn't remember her name, "umm, she will see that you get it back."

Ethel Wilson replied, "This person, umm, is Mrs. Wilson."

Audrey thought she was stuffy.

Chapter Fourteen

A Possible Child

However Ethel felt once about having children, she embraced the change now. Audrey Butler arrived to live with the Wilsons late on a Saturday afternoon a few weeks after Christmas, in 1941. She came straight from a tea dance.

Wallace took a look at her and said that she had the measles. It was not a bad case—he comforted her with his sympathetic smile—she would be fit in a few days. But now he suggested that she go straight up to bed. Ethel took her upstairs and showed her that this top floor was entirely hers. Here was her own bathroom. This room, on the south side of the house, was her study. It would at least catch all the light that a winter day offered on this Pacific coast. And across the hall was her bedroom, with twin beds in case she wanted a friend to stay the night. It had three windows looking across the small park that was usually deserted except for the occasional neighbourhood dog and seagulls who, still, strangely favour this park for walking and resting. Through darkening trees, Audrey could see the outline of the mountains and, below them, the city centre, where lights were now shifting and sparkling. Audrey thought that this woman, whom she had suspected of being stuffy, was really very kind. She fell into a warm sleep easily and quickly.

The next morning she woke up to Ethel pulling the curtains. She had brought up a breakfast tray. Ethel sat down beside the bed, and she and Audrey started to know a little of the other. Ethel said that when those measles disappeared, perhaps they should go shopping.

"At sixteen I was enchanted by the thought of new clothes," Audrey Butler told me. (When I spoke to her, she was in Alberta briefly on business for her Roman Catholic society, and was a woman in her mid-fifties.) "I had gained weight since coming to Canada, and this was a very good opening gambit for Aunty Ethel to make. Clothes were fun. Not delving into a person's personality etcetera. Both Aunty Ethel and Uncle Wallace accepted me as I was and never tried to change me."

Before a week had passed, Audrey went downtown with Ethel and came home with new clothes. That weekend she drove out with Ethel and Wallace for one of their favourite walks, along the Fraser River dykes, with the two wire-haired terriers, Johnny and Tuppence. The dykes had been the setting for "Hurry, Hurry," the ominous story published in *The New Statesman and Nation*.

[In] the stubble fields behind the high dyke, and in the salt marshes seawards from the dyke, and on the shallow sea, and over the sea there were thousands of other birds. No people anywhere. Just birds. The salt wind blew softly from the sea, and the two terrier dogs ran this way and that, with and against the wind. A multitude of little sandpipers ran along the wet sand as if they were on wheels. They whispered and whimpered together as they ran, stabbing with their long bills into the wet sands and running on. There was a continuous small noise of birds in the air. The terriers bore down upon the little sandpipers. The terriers ran clumsily, sinking in the marshy blackish sand, encumbered as they ran and the little sandpipers rose and flew low together to a safer sandbank. They whispered and wept together as they fled in a cloud, animated by one enfolding spirit of motion. They settled on their safe sandbank, running and jabbing the wet sand with their bills. The terriers like little earnest monsters bore down upon them again in futile chase, and again the whispering cloud of birds arose.

The dogs and the woman, who narrates the story, find a wounded hawk, whose eyes are fixed on the woman and are "bright with comprehension," and a man who is running in panic from the woman he has just murdered.

"I remember Uncle Wallace striding ahead," Audrey continued, "and Aunty Ethel and I talking. She said there was absolutely nothing that I could tell her because she knew life was absolutely impossible before the age of thirty."

Audrey laughed. "And then with supreme tact on her part we talked about my spotty face—no, it was not measles, it was acne—and my lanky hair. She said she had a wonderful hairdresser who could do wonders for spots through electric treatments, and could cut hair beautifully, and so I went to her. This hairdresser adored Aunty Ethel. She told me that when she was married, Aunty Ethel arranged for flowers to be put in their bedroom." (People on small incomes could not afford the high cost of hot-house flowers, and people in Ethel's social class seldom thought of servants and working girls once they were out of sight.)

Audrey told me about a mysterious woman whom Ethel used to meet regularly for lunch. She did not know her name, how old she was, where she came from, or what she did outside of having lunch with Ethel every Thursday in the dining room of a downtown department store. Ethel called her Miss Cosychat. This was her name, Ethel said, because when they were about to part and were shaking hands, she always said, "Goodbye Mrs. Wilson. I'm so looking forward to our next cosy chat."

Probably Wallace also knew very little about Miss Cosychat. Ethel loved the game of secrecy if her imaginative world was active. She might have had literary plans for Miss Cosychat, perhaps she even used her somewhere. She always kept her writing life secret. Once she mentioned to her publisher, John Gray, that she excluded her husband from this private occupation, but added, "Of course if I were in a real spot of 'literary' indecision, W. could help me, he would. As things are, he doesn't mind that I play my cards close, which I prefer."

"She had among other qualities one which was really unusual," Audrey Butler continued. "You knew that she would never lie to you. She might swing away from a subject, but she would not lie."

She sometimes did, though, as Audrey remembered. One morning Ethel was in bed, watching Wallace tie his bow tie. She stretched and said, "Wallace darling, did Chow Lung tell you that they took away the front steps last night and now there is nothing there at all?"

Wallace dropped his hands, turned, his face became dark.

"Have they indeed!"

He marched out of the bedroom, down the hall, opened the front door, paused, and yelled back, "You're crazy!" It was April Fool's Day.

On that day of another year, she sent her husband rushing to the window of the Hotel Boccalioni to see the lions below, walking in the streets of Rome. Her half-aunts would have been pleased that their faith in her talents as an actress had been confirmed.

It was a delight to Ethel that her love of play-acting was shared by this developing woman/still child Audrey Butler. It may have seemed nearly an omen, certainly extraordinary luck, that this young woman seemed to have a true affection for the works of William Shakespeare. The bond between them, in Ethel's mind, tightened.

Now, on easy evenings, Ethel would bring out one of her father's red leather volumes, Wallace one of his blue leather books, and Audrey would read aloud with them. They went, as far as Audrey could remember, through each of Shakespeare's plays during the time she lived with them.

Something else about Audrey must have pleased Ethel, who many years before had won the music prize at school in England. Audrey mentioned that she and her father used to sing and play the piano together. Ethel, she said, then "made it a practice" to sit down at the piano to "play and trill" while Audrey "boomed."

Audrey said that the Wilsons were extraordinarily generous with their affections. And with their money. After she finished high school, they sent her to the University of British Columbia, and "made it easy for me to accept by explaining their financial position," she said.

Her friends came to the Wilsons' house, sometimes staying the night, sometimes just for dinner. Audrey would warn them about Wallace. She said he had this habit. It would have been alright if her guest had been a boy, but her guests never were. He would carve the roast with the skill of a medical man, and when the guest's plate had been passed to her, he would say "with abruptness, a touch of shyness—'That'll put hair on your chest'." She and her friend consequently blushed. Wallace, who was a sensitive man, must have found fun in this because he continued to do it.

Audrey stayed with the Wilsons until 1943, when she joined the Canadian WRCNs. She was sent to eastern Canada, and then overseas. She did not return to Vancouver for four years.

At first Ethel welcomed her back with great warmth. But, Audrey said, the atmosphere quite quickly began to change.

Audrey felt that Ethel wanted her full attention and loyalty and, to Audrey, that signalled choosing between her parents and the Wilsons. She said that she chose her parents, naturally. Audrey said that she did not know Ethel's interpretation of the discord. Ethel still became silent when she was distressed, as she had when she was young. Now, Audrey said, small things happened; it seemed that Ethel resented Audrey's presence. Audrey felt, for example, that Ethel resented having to serve fish on Fridays. She said, "[Ethel had] a lack of interest in me and my future."

And then Ethel "put" Audrey in a boarding house with the magnificent name of "Queen Mary's Coronation Hostel for Gentlewomen Born in the United Kingdom and Seeking Employment in British Columbia." She stayed for a year, often visiting the Wilsons, and then returned home to England.

When I was living in London in 1956, Ethel wrote and asked me to look up Audrey Butler, whose life, she said, "was certainly torn up by the roots when she was shoo'd off to Canada. However, God was good to us both, and we loved her and she loved us, and we still all do, and our lives were mutually enriched thereby."

Robert William Bryant

Eliza Davis Malkin

The marriage of Robert William Bryant and Eliza Davis Malkin in Burslem, April 14, 1887

Behind Lila Malkin is Eliza Edge

Front Row: Philip Malkin, Annie Malkin, James Malkin, Robert Bryant, Lila Malkin, Edna Edoe, Joseph Edoe, Mrs. Joseph Edoe

Ethel Bryant with her mother

Ethel Bryant and her father

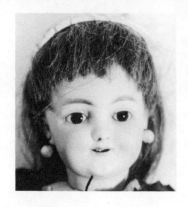

Duchess

Ethel Bryant as a child in England

Wallace Wilson and his sister, A

Ethel Bryant as a young woman

Ethel Wilson, Audrey Butler, and Johnny, outside the house at Connaught Drive, summer 1941

Wallace Wilson

Chow Lung at Bowen Island

Little Rock, Bowen Island

Ethel Wilson's publisher, John Morgan Gray, and his family

Ethel and Wallace

Chapter Fifteen

Literary and Other Eggs

Worlds War II never showed up as a danger along the Pacific Coast (although a couple of Japanese submarines were sighted, and one shot at—and missed—a big gun in Stanley Park), but the politicians and military men did not know such gentleness would reign, and so stood people on guard. Teachers taught children how to use gas masks, although there weren't enough to go around; air raid sirens were tested both day and night, and although it was known that they were only tests, they made for uneasiness. Men, women, and children, too, were reprimanded severely if light from their windows broke into the night's blackness, which gave protection from Japanese bombers. On a minor but, for those involved, an extremely important aspect of daily life, the mansions and semi-mansions of people with whom the Wilsons often dined became awkwardly unmanageable. The cooks and maids who had filled living rooms, hoping for jobs through the Depression, were now gainfully employed monetarily and spiritually—their war efforts applauded across billboards and newspapers. They walked through the gates of shipyards, and their Victory ships rolled down the slips and slid, with a comforting "whoomf," into the harbour waters. Money flowed into nearly everyone's pockets and purses. Never again would so many worried people sit in strangers' living rooms.

There were abuses. Wallace and Ethel particularly struggled with their patriotism when they read in the newspapers that the fishing boats, farms, and houses of Japanese-Canadian families were being sold for pittance to non-Japanese Canadians, and that Japanese-Canadian families were being herded into public buildings and sent off in trains — the men separated from their families — to concentration camps.

Ethel's own way of life was in flux. Audrey needed listening-to and understanding; the Red Cross needed women to knit and roll bandages and pack boxes, which she did, and she edited a bi-monthly mimeographed sheet for the Red Cross which was called "Vancouver Calling." She paid little attention to her fiction now, because the lives of the people she loved were vital to her own living, far more important than lives in her imagination. Wallace could go off any time now. He had let the powers know that he was willing to serve in any way, and they wanted him to become the Royal Canadian Army's Medical Commander for the Pacific Northwest. That took two years to organize, and then they sent him off to eastern Canada and to England, where bombs were falling. Audrey was over there now, too.

"Poor Aunty Ethel," she said to me, "both her eggs in one basket."

Now Chow Lung, ill-tempered, certainly not indispensable Chow Lung, packed his bags and departed forever from the house on Connaught Drive. So the Wilsons decided to move from their pretty, secure house on the hill overlooking the park and the mountains. They would, they said, find a nice, comfortable apartment for at least the period of the war, and what they found they decided was just about perfect, and they stayed there for as long as they could. It was on the fourth floor (later they moved to the fifth) of a handsome ivy-covered building, from which they could see the boats in the harbour and, also, the stone house where they had started their married life. The apartment was generous: three bedrooms, two bathrooms, a high-ceilinged, pleasantly proportioned dining room, and a living room where all their books covered the walls. Ethel found a colourful and capable cook-housekeeper named Mrs. Tufts, who "did" for them for many years, and who they happily rewarded, when she no longer wanted to work, with a piece of land on Bowen Island. That small island was the reason why the transition from house to apartment was so simple.

Early in the war, in 1941, the Wilsons and the Colin Grahams heard that Dr. R.E. McKechnie was putting his property on Bowen Island up for sale. He owned 145 acres of lovely land, most of it timbered, but with some open fields, a small farm, and a charming bay. Dr. McKechnie was now eighty and could no longer visit the island with ease. Wallace and Colin bought his land for $4500.

To reach Bowen Island you drive to the western extremity of West Vancouver, to the ferry terminal at Horseshoe Bay, and then onto a small ferry. You get out of your car, if you have any curiosity about the sea and the land around it, and walk across to the side of the ship and, if it is an early morning in late summer, you stand and watch the gray mist falling and folding into the mountains above you, and the mist seems to be waiting. And then the small ferry starts to move, and its wake is blue. It takes you past gray rocks which are covered with yellow mosses, and behind and above these rocks are hills and mountains. These are green-black with trees which mass together in the mist, and you can not see where one tree stands apart from the others. In only twenty minutes you are at Bowen Island, slipping into Snug Cove, which is appropriately named. This is very different country from the mainland. The hills are softer and lushly green, and remind you of a Henri Rousseau painting with their wildness and mystery and innocence. The ferry bumps and groans against the timbers flanking the dock until it finds its rightful place, and you drive onto the island, along a logging road, turn right onto a narrower road, and then you come to a small dirt road running down to the sea. This road is darkened by enormous trees — except where the sun strikes brilliantly green and oversized ferns — and at the end of the road, on your left, is a bottle-green shingled house with two stove-pipe chimneys and a sway-backed tar-paper roof. You have arrived at Little Rock.

Wallace and Ethel gave it this name because a small rock juts out of the sea in the cove below the house. Seldom does a bird stand on this rock, although many seabirds and a blue heron often stand on the other rocks which rise from this water. The little rock is a pleasant swimming distance from the beach.

The property has been partly put to commercial use now. It is owned by a Vancouver lawyer and has paddocks for his horses and a commercial chicken farm. In the Wilsons' time it had only a small vegetable garden and a lean-to for chopping and storing wood, and the trees (many have been cut down now) marched straight to the small house and threatened to run into it. Inside, the house was snug. The Wilsons white-washed the rough log walls and the stone fireplace, and painted the floors bottle-green, and the window-sills yellow. There were burnt-orange curtains, and candles in bottles, and kerosene lamps because the Wilsons did not need or want electric lights there, even if they had been available. Because this island is usually cold at night, even in the summer, they lit large fires, and so in the fresh morning, the smell of wood-ash lingered in the house. At night Ethel sat in her rocking chair near the fire and knitted or read, and Wallace read or fixed things or chopped wood. One summer night in 1942 he was outside and he called her. She went quickly.

She opened the kitchen door and he was there, holding onto his leg which was spurting blood. The axe had slipped, he said, and he had cut an artery. He was calm. He told Ethel how to apply a tourniquet and then, he said, get a needle, boil it, and thread, yes black thread is fine, whatever you have, and while she held the kerosene lamp, he sutured his leg. It took six stitches. When that was done and he was lying down, she ran through the darkness for three and a half miles in panic until she reached Snug Cove and a telephone. His doctor in Vancouver said he would come right away by boat. But now there was fog and the fog did not lift until late the next morning. It was a story which she told me, still with alarm, ten years later. Wallace was not expendable.

Wallace did recover, although for several years that leg would give him trouble, and, for a while, the drugs they had given him had strange effects.

Sometimes Ethel came up to Little Rock without Wallace, because he was away on the business of war. Sometimes she invited their friend Betty Clegg to join her there. Mrs. Clegg, who was one of Ethel's most trusted friends, and Wallace's too, told me that Ethel used to tell stories to her. The two women would be sitting on a rock by the sea or on the steps to the porch of the small house, and Ethel would simply start talking a story.

"Ethel told me three stories," Betty Clegg said. "I read them later. They were, word for word, what she had told me."

One of these stories, "The Innumerable Laughter," is set on Bowen Island and is a chapter of her novel *The Innocent Traveller*. It was first published in the prestigious English literary periodical *Orion*.

"Word for word, they were the same. I suppose she was practicing on me," Betty Clegg said.

"You're a damfool not to write," said the head of the University of British Columbia's English department, Dr. G.G. Sedgewick, whom she barely knew. He said simply that, at a party early in the war. He subscribed to *The New Statesman* and had read her stories.

"One day I will write down my stories," Ethel said to the former Alex Wilson, "but not until Granny, Aunt Eliza and Aunty Belle are dead."

In 1943 the last of those three women died. Miss Eliza Edge went out at the age of nearly ninety-eight without a bang or a whimper — although she had caused a flurry a few months earlier by having her "drawers" drop around her ankles on busy Granville Street, and screaming out that she was paralyzed. Now she had gone her way, but of course she could not go absolutely into oblivion. There was an incident at her funeral which exists now only as a fragment of Ethel Wilson's unpublished work.

In her last years Miss Edge had a friend whom the family knew as "gentle Dolly Tibbetts," and whom Miss Edge teased without mercy despite, or perhaps because of, the family's protestations. As it happened, the two women died within a day of each other. Ethel Wilson wrote:

When Aunty died, her death—although a relatively trivial event—was mentioned in the obituary column, ending in a request that flowers should not be sent. But, we said, looking at each other and suddenly aware of a depth of feeling, even at that time, for our little great-aunt was the last tenuous filament linking the present suffering volatile generation with the old monumental generations, "We will give Aunty some flowers—a canopy, yes a most beautiful canopy. She would like that."

So someone ordered the canopy and we went to the funeral at the time appointed. . .

Rain fell heavily. I had flu but tottered into the funeral. There we sat with a curious detached feeling that was not sorrow, with which we were so heavily familiar. The feeling became more curious as we saw that there was not a flower on the coffin, not a leaf nor a twig. Where was the ordered canopy? Mutterings and blamings began among the relatives. No one ordered the canopy? Why not? My uncles, fine-looking, dignified, marched up the little aisle. An old woman behind me wheezed to her daughter, "Not a flower! Shameful I call it! And them so rich and stingy." We were neither rich nor stingy and the spectacle of the bleak and naked coffin that hid the tiny body of our centenarian great-aunt smote us.

A cousin sitting next to me bolted out of the chapel and returned. She whispered, "Old Miss Tibbetts was buried this morning and by mistake they put Aunty's flowers on her and they're out at the cemetery now! They said the flowers were lovely!" Two mortuary young men, it seemed, had just leaped into a car to pursue the canopy but that was only a gesture, for it was too late.

What a treat for Miss Dolly Tibbetts, what an incredible ironic postponed delight. Her little smile wafted over us in the chapel air. Not a flower, not a leaf. Pathos is not sorrow but is something like it.[1]

Eleven years after that funeral Ethel was having a holiday in Kelowna at a hotel known as Eldorado Arms. She had recently met Mazo de la Roche, whom she liked, and she wrote to people she liked, as a rule.

I wonder if you ever read my small book [*The Innocent Traveller*] about Topaz [Eliza Edge]. Her loquacious ghost is here but not formidable as she was. It can blow away, as she *couldn't*. She was here in the days of bridge, & circled the tables followed by her distracted Companion. She disturbed everyone by discovering furniture here from the Duke of Southerland's W[est] Staff[ordshire] estate, via one "Duchess Blair" of whom Aunty disapproved, who was the grandmother of the owner—thank God her disturbing presence is removed. But I question whether even the angels can cope—I couldn't. It is really a blessing we don't live forever—even Nebuchadnezzar or Aunt Topaz.

The Literary Editor
Macmillan's[2]
Dear Sir—
I shall venture to send you a few stories, three of which appeared in The New Statesman & Nation, & the fourth in The Canadian Forum, & others—not at all. Dr. Earle Birnie, whom I do not know personally, asked me to send the story ["On Nimpish Lake"] to the Forum. He had intended to incorporate it in a volume of Canadian short stories, but the project was dropped.

Mrs. Robert Lynd (Sylvia Lynd) who I know well, has since the N.S. & N. stories were printed—encouraged me to write a novel, which I know is infinitely more acceptable to a Publisher than a bundle of loosely connected short stories. The work & cares of war have made that impossible, & in any case I do not think it is my métier—yet.

I send these, not with expectations of acceptance, but with plain humility, as I am not sure whether they are good, a little good, or not good, or whether they would interest a public at all.

A very faint awkwardness arises, but not I think a serious one. Following the publishing of the stories in the N.S. & N., I received several letters from an excellent American publishing house, suggesting that I might have a book to show them. I suppose of course they meant a novel. Appreciating this, yet realizing that they might not at all like what I had to offer, I told them that if ever I made a book I would remember, but did not commit myself.—But

now, following these years the bonds with home are too strong, &
if I have any small talent at all I would prefer it to emerge as a
product of home, or at least to remain British. I will write & tell
them what I am doing, as otherwise I'd feel very mean.

I see this bundle of stories under the name A Vancouver
Notebook, or Vancouver Child — or most probably, not at all.

Sincerely yours
Ethel Wilson

Mrs. Wallace Wilson
42 Kensington Place
Vancouver, B.C.
Nov. 18, 1944

Ten days later Ethel sent off another letter. Would Macmillan's please
return the stories. They were not good enough. She "would be glad to
welcome them into obscurity again."

On December 20 the stories were returned as requested, but with an
editor's remark: "If you can not make something out of that Topaz saga
you're not the writer I think you are."

Ethel Wilson stuffed them in a drawer. But she did not stop writing to
Macmillan's. Here were listeners and informers about literature. Besides,
she had to thank them for returning the stories. On December 30 she did
that and added a postscript:

> The post this morning brings an article by V.S. Pritchett whom I
> admire as a privileged & unpedantic critic. He says "I think many
> _____ writers would be better if they were encouraged not to
> write what is called good prose, but to record talk & conversation
> which often has the complexity of a personal style in it." Which was
> quite cheering.

Cheering because this was precisely what she was doing. She felt more
certain now of her work. She had "a small talent" she said, frequently.
Possibly she discouraged a bigger talent. She had known anger,
frustration, fear, and loneliness, which most people experience, but she at
an earlier age than most, and more acutely because of her nature and her
sharp mind. Now she was fifty-six and safe, and possibly did not want to
open herself up and show her selves, imaginative and real, to the world,
which was not always a friendly place.

The head of Macmillan's was Miss Ellen Elliott. Two months after she
received Ethel's thank-you letter, she turned up in Vancouver. The

stories Ethel had sent Macmillan's were discussed face to face over cups of tea. The stories about Topaz were separated from the others and placed under a title, "The Painted Curtain." One story which did not fit the title was "We Have To Sit Opposite" (about Ethel and Kathleen Graham on the train in Germany), and Miss Elliott suggested that Ethel send it to *Chatelaine* magazine. She did. Shortly after it was published, Macmillan's received a letter from a New York agent named David Lloyd, who said he was Pearl Buck's agent. He had read "We Have To Sit Opposite." Would Ethel Wilson have other stories, perhaps a book? He would be interested in being her American agent.

In the summer of 1945, Ethel wrote Miss Elliott that she thought she would have the Topaz stories printed privately, just for the family. Miss Elliott firmly discouraged her. Not only was private publishing an expensive business but, far more important, it might put Ethel Wilson off·doing the Topaz novel. For the second time, Miss Elliott referred her to David Lloyd, and again gave Ethel his address.

On November 8, letters from Ethel and from the American publishers Simon & Schuster reached Miss Elliott, saying that Ethel Wilson had started a novel. Fourteen days later it arrived on Miss Elliott's desk. Its title was *Hetty Dorval.*

Chapter Sixteen

Quiet Machinery

"**I**t is not the least remarkable in a remarkable story," said her publisher John Gray, "that having never served a normal apprentice — no rooms papered with rejection slips, no exercise books filled with juvenile efforts — Mrs. Wilson could without conscious preparation write stories to the standard of these distinguished journals [*The New Statesman and Nation* and *Canadian Forum*]; it is almost unheard of. . . I once questioned Mrs. Wilson rather closely on this point, surely she had always known she wanted to write and had practiced. Her answer was 'I never had, never wanted to'."[1]

Never had what? Practiced or wanted to or known she had wanted to? John Gray took his question to mean practiced. She possibly thought of the lions in the streets of Rome. We have Alex Wilson's remark that she would not try to publish stories while her grandmother and aunts lived, and Betty Clegg's remark that the stories she told her up at Bowen Island were "word for word" what came out later in print. (Incidentally, too, she managed to leave John Gray with the idea that she was two years younger than she was.)

But does such nit-picking matter? Around 1938 and up through 1945, when *Hetty* was delivered by the postman to 77 Bond Street in Toronto, she occasionally found it "imperative" to write, and not in "secrecy but in privacy." She said, "I am sure that the business of writing is one of four or five most private things in the world, excluding the planning of international treaties or crime."

To follow the private events which resulted in what appears to have been the secrecy of the writing of *Hetty Dorval*, let's go back five months before the manuscript arrived at Macmillan's, to June 14, 1945. She then wrote Miss Elliott, whom she'd seen in February.

> Since I saw you, my husband became very much worse, out & out arthritis of a very peculiar kind blew up, all fed by the poison, I suppose, of the accident [the 1942 axing of his leg]. I have been housekeeper, nurse, secretary, shopper, everything for 2 months. In the last 2 weeks a real improvement but still on crutches, & on his way out of the Army & into DVA [Department of Veteran's Affairs] & is now, crutches & all in Montreal or Ottawa. You can't keep a good man down, but his wife can get *quite* down. Making a novel [Miss Elliott was still trying to make her write the Topaz stories into a book] is at the moment a thing that I would have great antipathy to. Given two or three weeks holiday & rejuvenation I may see things in a more amber light, although not, I think, rosy.
>
> How are you...I hope to get away to the cottage next week & spend a little while there while my husband...is still in Ottawa...What beasts writing people are—they either insist on plaguing you with manuscripts, or they do the other thing. I do feel for you.
>
> Very sincerely
Ethel Wilson

On August 17 she wrote Miss Elliott from Bowen Island.

> Even after the complete rest up here my husband's leg shows little improvement. And today we go into town & he has many people waiting to interview him, starts touring western Canada, & is also Pres.-Elect of the Canadian Medical Association, taking office of Pres. next year, but it entails much work this year.

"Suddenly," she explained in a speech which she titled "Somewhere Near the Truth," "in connection with my husband's medical work, I was faced with a long period that involved organization and responsibility in my own particular sphere. I did not like organization and I did not like responsibility, and was not good at either. I was terrified. Moreover, while decisions were waiting to be made, and plans had to be mapped out, my husband was away from home for a month. Nothing could be finally determined until his return. Rain fell by day, rain fell by night. Nightly I sweated with apprehension and funk...I had never contemplated writing a book. Quickly I decided, if I was going to be alive, sane, functioning, and of any earthly use in this work, I must do something that would usurp all my thoughts, and plug or sublimate my unprofitable fright..."

So, early one morning in August, at the age of fifty-seven, she rose from her bed, packed a suitcase, took a taxi down to the Canadian National Railway station, and boarded a train. She got off at Lytton and a man from Brody House, where she and Wallace always stayed on their way Up-Country, was on the platform waiting for her. He took her suitcase and together they walked up the steps to the white clapboard hotel. He showed her to her room and left her, closing the door behind him. She went to the window and looked down at the confluence of the Fraser and the Thompson rivers and across at the pines which "marched" up the sage-covered hills. She prepared the table and chair in her room for work.

In her introduction to the Alcuin Society's limited edition of *Hetty* she said this:

> ...there came an uprush from within. A dream in an early morning took me to the Fraser and Thompson Rivers and the Bridge. During three weeks of rain I sat alone and wrote, and re-wrote, and before my husband had returned I had completed a small amateur piece of work named *Hetty Dorval*.
>
> I knew no one to consult. The manuscript was probably not worth submitting to a publisher. But, in any case, I knew of no publisher in Canada and would not have ventured to send it to a known English publisher. But I remembered a friend of ours, a writer [Robert Lynd] in England...Our friend had read my *Statesman* stories.
>
> "Are you going to write a novel?" he said.
>
> "No. Never," I told him, "that would be impossible."
>
> "Well, if you do," said our friend, regardless, "remember to send it to Macmillans."
>
> And now, I had written a "novel" and Macmillans was far away, in England, long established publishers of Yeats, Lord Acton, of

Mary Kingsley—of many of the nobility of letters. I could not send *Hetty* to them.

I went to one of the then meagre book counters of our town, and looked at the small shelf of Canadian books. There I saw the word "Macmillan." I dared not send my little manuscript to Macmillan of England but I would dare to send it to Toronto, in my country.

I was accepted and was therefore open to the parent firm. I received a kind and lordly letter from Macmillan of London, also taking the book, and requiring that I would alter two inaccurate words in it. I did (a good lesson).

This was the beginning of my long and affectionate association with Macmillan of England and Macmillan of Canada. *Hetty* had grown from the sage brush of British Columbia, from the hills and trees, from two rivers and a bridge, from a skein of honking Canada geese, from love, into anger, all without ambition, with almost passionate concentration, and with amazement, into a small book.

I read *Hetty* again recently. There is something innocent about the book, too innocent to inspire a polysyllabic introduction.

The first news Macmillan's had of *Hetty* was nearly buried in a letter from Ethel that October.

Dear Miss Elliott—

Thank U so much for your truly lovely letter wh. raises me up with its niceness & *sinks* me down with its hope & anticipation [about her writing].

Because U & Mrs. Blochin will be disappointed, I swear it, because there is no Topaz quality in this opus. The story made itself in pedestrian & very homely fashion. Seeking for some association with experience, I can only find a very pure profile of a thoroughly bad creature who still had a true love of nice simple things, but she is entirely different from this "Hetty Dorval" (the name of the tale)—& a derelict bungalow overlooking a lovely & exquisite B.C. river.

By the way I've finished Hetty, & I'll send the works & also to my kind friend Mrs. Leiper of S. & S. [Simon & Schuster], telling her re. reservation to you for Canada, if you both like it...

> This is all very interesting!
> Yours most sincerely
> Ethel Wilson

It's not even funny. And yet as I look at it again perhaps it has something. But mothers are often poor judges about their children.

Miss Elliott took two months to comment on *Hetty*. (The manuscript went out to readers.) On January 16, 1946, she wrote:

I myself don't think it is in the class with the TOPAZ stories, but to my mind...it is a very strong piece of quiet machinery. There has been one dissenting voice from among our readers, but that is not to be wondered at because it seldom happens that there is a novel that is everyone's meat.

On February 11 Miss Elliott comments on Ethel's letters of January 17, 19, and 20, then:

We are prepared to offer you a contract for the book as it originally came to us, incorporating the slight changes we have spoken of, and those to which you agree.

Ethel signed the contract on February 18, but did she make the changes that Miss Elliott wanted? It appears not so. She argued her way out of many of them. Even Miss Winnifred Eayrs, a punctilious small person who read proof and had her grammars constantly at her finger-tips for the decades she inhabited her own untidy office, could quite often lose out to Mrs. Wilson. Yes indeed, Miss Eayrs wrote, Mrs. Wilson seemed to be correct in the spelling of "waggon"; "dashes and dots, we agree, are not desirable if they can be avoided"; but "As to *cannot*, the Oxford and Annadale Dictionaries both give *cannot*, and our understanding is that the only time the two words are used are in such cases as 'I can not only read French; I can talk it as well'...We really think cannot is the correct form almost always."

"On *Oh* all the authorities seem contradictory. To our thinking, 'Oh no, Mother' seems all right, but 'Yes sir' seems wrong—we feel there should be a comma before 'sir.' Could we compromise with you?"

There was lively correspondence over Ethel's use of quotations from John Donne. Macmillan's thought not, Ethel thought so, both lost points and she retained most. And what Ethel did lose of her Donne quotations in the text, she put firmly after the title page. Nobody could quarrel with her right to do that.

Now came the surprise. Ethel did not want her name on the book. Miss Elliott was dismayed: "As you point out yourself there are no real-life characters in HETTY, so I cannot see why you shouldn't use Ethel Wilson." After all, Miss Elliott said, she had not been shy about "Ethel Wilson" on her short stories. Ethel said she wanted to use "Mary Millett Davis" (an obscure, long-dead relation). Letters travelled back and forth. On March 8, Ethel Wilson pleaded: "I pray you, let me wait to decide re. name of author till I see galley proofs! Then I shall know better whether small chunks written in haste & sincerity look like hokum.

> I don't mind Millett Davis getting remarks like "This is a terrible novel—chunks of sentiment & moralizing interspersed with quite good writing. Miss Davis must learn to etc..." because I feel detached about it, but my husband & friends would feel more awful than they need if E.W. got it in the neck, poor woman, for Hetty. About Topaz I'd never mind, because it's all light, yet sincere—and even if anyone didn't like it, there isn't anything that could be *suspected* of being hokum. No criticism there would bother E.W. But I'm not *quite* at home with Hetty.
>
> So *may* we defer decision re. that? I quite understand your natural desire to continue with E.W. who has begun as such. But I do like a *light* touch in my own work.

(My mother and several of her friends thought Hetty was modelled after one of Ethel's cousins, an attractive, vivacious woman with a vicious tongue. I mentioned this once to Ethel Wilson, who nearly defiantly denied it.)

Up at Bowen Island, after dinner with Wallace on July 2, she took her flashlight and walked across the island, three and a half miles, and sent this wire to Miss Eayrs:

THANKS FOR LETTER OF TWENTY SIXTH RE PSEUDONYM PLEASE DISREGARD HAVE DECIDED MY OWN NAME ETHEL WILSON.

Miss Eayrs hurried down narrow corridors (she always hurried) to tell all those involved. She ended in John Gray's office, telegram firmly in hand.

A week passed, then Ethel wrote: "I hope my own name on the book will be *small* print. It would not look well, large."

In Ethel Wilson's time it was "not done" to publicize oneself, unless one was a man and could profit, in a business-like way, from such exposure. That might have been why. But I think not.

The event which had set Hetty into her conception and birth now faced Ethel. She would now have to behave like the wife of the president of the Canadian Medical Association and go through all the frightening socializing which that entailed. But she had been released by the distractions of her book, and been given more confidence in herself by the energy that was still emanating from Macmillan's.

Vancouver did not have the "hospitality industry" (she would have been fascinated by that jargon) to handle the influx of people which this convention would attract. It would best be held in Banff.

In September, she went with Wallace to Banff, to discuss the convention with the proper powers, and then proceeded across Canada, where Wallace gave speeches and talked convention to doctors and to other people, in many cities, for the next six weeks or so. Ethel wrote to Miss Eayrs on September 12, saying that she was sending her and Miss Elliott "a sample of 'Topaz' — Chapt. 4 'In Elder House,' Chapt. 7 'The Majority,' and Chapt. 13 'The Innumerable Laughter'." There would be 25 or 26 chapters, she says, adding that she will be in Toronto in October. Closer to her arrival she writes that she hopes to meet Miss Eayrs and see Miss Elliott, "if her health permits her to be at the office — but she must not make an effort." After five medical conventions in five provinces in four weeks, she says, she would like to "rest up" for a day or two in Toronto. Such a pace must have drained her. She was no longer a young woman, and she still suffered from anaemia. Wallace gave her liver injections, which they believed kept her alive. He would carry along "a harpoon and a quart of liver extract...in other words a good injection," when they were away from home. One of their friends, not knowing of the anaemia, said, "Oh, she was forever going to bed," with distrust of Ethel and distaste for hypochondriacs.

Miss Elliott, who had been ill for some time, gave Ethel a luncheon on October 25. Ethel wrote thanking her, and said she would also write to thank "Mr. Gray — & have to guess at his initial." John Gray had now replaced Miss Elliott as managing director of Macmillan's. He and Ethel would become fast friends. In her letter to him, and also to Miss Elliott, both of which were written in Ottawa, she mentions that she had sat in on the espionage trial of the Russian clerk Igor Gouzenko, who sat through the trial with a hood over his head. She says little about this extraordinarily dramatic and important event, except: "I sat all day yesterday at the espionage trial and marvelled at Gouzenko, being almost *grilled* again. Such a sturdy boy — or man — he compelled my admiration."

That was to Miss Elliott. To John Gray she mentioned that she had visited the National Gallery, and in the same sentence said that Gouzenko "held one spellbound." (No mention of such conditions at the gallery.)

In early 1947 came the CMA convention. Ethel steeled herself. She was responsible for the hundreds of doctors' wives, and for their entertainment. She apparently did her job well, and added a touch of her peculiar consideration and imagination. She asked the wives of the senior CMA members and officers if they would come with her into the shops because there were presents she must bring home and she would like their advice. They went, and on the last day of the convention, what they had admired was wrapped and delivered to their rooms with a note from Ethel.

She slipped from her perch, too. A Mrs. Fuchs was at the convention. Ethel had been told her name several times, but every time she saw this woman her mind seized up and she could not remember, so again had to ask her name, and Mrs. Fuchs became more and more flushed, and Ethel too. But what was dreadful, she told Audrey Butler, was that "Fuchs" was a German name, the war was just over, and so how much better if her name had been Polish or Dutch or English or Norwegian or anything other than German. It was a small faux pas to others, but a dreadful rudeness to Ethel, and to Mrs. Fuchs.

Hetty Dorval was published in April. In its most simple sense, it is a story of an innocent and decent schoolgirl, Frankie, who meets worldliness and selfishness in the form of a beautiful woman. The story takes place largely in the Upper Country of British Columbia, close to the confluence of the Fraser and Thompson Rivers — one a wild river, the other slower and more peaceful — and moves on to England.

The reviews came in:

> A first novel, short, but so remarkable as to convince me that its author should go a long way. Around a comparatively slight plot...Miss Wilson has brought into being an intense atmosphere.
> Elizabeth Bowen, *The Tatler*.

> Written with a sureness of language and a sense of the significant in people denied to many authors of experience Hetty Dorval (Macmillan, 6/-) is a first novel of unusual promise...Miss Wilson has the gift of saying a great deal in little. There is poetry and vision in her book...A longer work from her is something to look forward to, and with confidence.
> E.O.D.K., *Punch*.

An astonishingly good short novel...Rarely in recent reading have I encountered an author who has transferred her love and understanding of a remote and beautiful countryside (B.C.) to paper with such skill. Add to that Miss Wilson's unique knowledge of the human mind and heart and you have what I believe this to be—one of the best novels I have read in a long time.

Victor P. Hass, *Chicago Sunday Tribune*.

Mrs. Wilson's writing has the...singing quality of the early Willa Cather.

San Francisco Chronicle.

Several reviewers compared her to Willa Cather.
And some had contempt for her.

Frankie...is treated shallowly as is the lovely Hetty who at least could have been a little interesting. These people are just pencil sketches, not very clear and there seems no apparent reason for their story having been published.

Halifax Chronicle.

That, with the others quoted above, was pasted into a scrap book. Alongside the *Halifax Chronicle* review, Ethel wrote in pencil, "Tips the scales prettily against the opp. [opposite] page!" There was a three-column review, ecstatic, which ends:

Actually...Miss Wilson for a moment or two has made us think of the subtlety of Henry James, although she has the advantage in interweaving action with introspection, and writing in smooth, uncomplicated language. Bypassing the amateur stage she leaps into the professional class at one bound. Here's to her future!

W.J. Hurlow, Literary Editor, *Ottawa Evening Citizen*.

"It is well not to be too sensitive," Ethel Wilson said, "if we can. The first review of a new book is a bit of a facer. A 'good' review brings guarded pleasure, a sober joy. One rejoices carefully but does not become intoxicated. It is possible that the critic may, on that day, be in love."

The Wilsons' friends bought or borrowed it, read it, and passed through it, according to their natures. A few were impressed and delighted; most discarded it with a laugh or a remark like "how surprising!" For a short time it was the talk of Vancouver society, and then it was forgotten.

On August 22, 1947, Wallace and Ethel, having done with the Canadian Medical Association, sailed from New York on the Cunard luxury liner *Queen Mary* to Europe. Their destination was Paris where Wallace was to represent Canada at the first meeting of the World Health Organization. But first they would go to England and see again her relatives, their friends, and the country they loved.

Chapter Seventeen
Passages

 "Life aboard the Queen Mary...was, I discovered, a luxurious vacuum of living, a flight from reality, and a flight that can only be taken by highly favoured persons. One does not really approve, under certain circumstances, of being a highly favoured person, although it is fun at the time. It induces a faint but real humiliation. Yet one felt that here, in these huge ships of luxury, is a great demonstration of salesmanship—an exhibition of what Great Britain can achieve when she gets half a chance," she wrote in a piece, unfinished but titled "Private Happiness."

Although the war had been over for two years, its wounds were evident and, she wrote me many years later, "had not and would not heal." She and Wallace were driven around Cripplegate and the Roman Wall.

> It is a very silencing scene, as empty and arid as the moon. Here great city buildings became instant rubble in a few hellish hours. All is neatly cleared away long since, but desolation remains all over...There, in a dreadful exposed nakedness lie an infinity of cellars, outlined and laid cleanly bare, sunk beneath the levels of existing bits of streets. All the values and activities that once filled the now empty air have vanished.

They went to see her half-aunt Hannah Atkinson. (Her other half-aunt, Margaret Bryant of *The Observer*, had died during the war.) Hannah now lived "in a spartan little apartment high up in a dark block of flats which reminds one of a prison. . . ."

> She cannot get out because her strength does not permit her to climb up and down the many steep stairs, and she is nervous about the unpredictable behavior of the old and irreplaceable lift. (I was apprehensive too) but there is an inside open-air balcony of sorts where she may walk and get the air — and the roof top, as well.

(Many years later, when she herself was in pain, Ethel was to remember Hannah Atkinson: "And then I say 'Fathead, shut up, how dare you [feel sorry for yourself] with so many blessings & friends! You've only got to think of yourself as living alone in a top room, with joints, & crawling down & back daily for your bottle of milk, to fall on your knobbly knees in gratitude'."[1])

Ethel's England, the ancient seat of law and literature and, yes, courtesy and morality, and possessor of power, was disappearing. She knew that, but she would look for compensation; she found it, to her delight, in the children who, unlike pre-war children, were robust no matter what their class. She remarked, in "Private Happiness":

> Oh what a pretty scene! Outside a pub of old-fashioned appearance stands a baby carriage. I have to revise very hastily my youthful training. I was brought up to regard a pram outside a pub as a shame and a hissing, and a tragedy in embryo and in fact. But this pram is spotless. The King of the pram is the most beautiful red-cheeked clean white-woollied baby imaginable. (British babies have special rations and no country in either hemisphere can show lovelier, healthier children.)

She and Wallace went on to something nearly unreal. One night they dressed with extra care, the doorman whistled them up a taxicab and told the driver to take them to Kettner's in Soho. This was their favourite restaurant in the world and it was still standing. Their dinner, the mood of the restaurant, was everything they remembered and anticipated. After they had finished and paid the bill, they decided to walk for a while.

> Some subdued light came from Kettner's windows but there was not much illumination outside. Light from a high lamp fell on the

figure of a man standing in the street at the far left-hand corner of the intersection. He was tall and large and dressed in a way that gave him a clean but gypsy appearance. Because he kept his head raised, looking up at the lamp or at least toward the sky which was very dark around the light of the lamp, the light fell full on his face and showed it as pale, large, intelligent, with pale gold straight hair that straggled across the large brow. If he had any expression in his face one would say he looked sad, or quenched, and detached from that street corner and from people. He played an accordion and played it very well and, all the time he played, his large pale face was tilted up toward the dark sky as if he did not care for us or our sixpences. He did not court us for sixpences. He looks, I thought, like a young Oscar Wilde, after all the disillusion. Where does he live. I thought, what does he do, and why does he have to play the accordion in Soho with a tin for coins hanging from his shoulder? The tin seemed an affectation of something foreign to him. I said to W., "He looks like a young Oscar Wilde, doesn't he?" but W. was intent on the player.

By this time other people had gathered, and stopped, and stood like shadows on the two other street corners facing the large but not fat pale man playing the accordion. There were shadows where we stood too, but because our eyes had become accustomed we saw in front of us a tall and graceful girl with long hair waving to her shoulders. She stood leaning on a taller young man beside her and suddenly she began to sing. She simply "lifted her voice" and sang. She sang with the accordion player who did not even look at her but all the standing shadows turned to look. Her voice was full of music and she sang with beautiful deliberation. She sang song after song and then, suddenly, she stopped. The accordion player paid no attention and went on playing. A taxi driver with a small dark face, wearing a white cotton coat and a peaked cap, stood beside us, leaning on his taxi.

"That ain't music, miss," said the taxi driver as one who really knows. "Come on now, miss, you can't call *Song of Love* music, now can you. Opra now, that's music, but not *Song of Love*. That's common, *Song of Love* is."

As if the girl knew that someone stood behind her she turned and said to me, "Don't you think *Song of Love* is music?" and I said, "When you sing it is," and so it was. There was that kind of freedom between people standing there.

The girl did not sing anymore...

From the shadows at the opposite corner stepped a small strange man in black...He danced slowly like a marionette, as if invisible strings from the high dark pulled and dropped his legs, his hands, his elbows, ordering his movements. He wheeled and danced and all the while the light fell on him too, we saw his eyes as in caverns, raking the standing shadows for something he wanted that must have been sympathy or at least understanding. He was not drunk.

Then he spoke at intervals.

"I'm a seaman, I am...I bin in ships in them foreign ports...I seen terrible things..."

Everything—light, shadows, time, distance seemed to focus on him. There was silence, somewhere, and we turned to look at the accordion player who seemed to have stopped playing, but he was not there. We turned to look at the dancer, but he had gone. The girl...[was] not there. The shadows were no longer shadows but people walking up and down X and Y streets. Had these things happened? Yes, and they had left no trace as dreams leave no trace. Something had snapped and ended and now everything was ordinary and we all became strangers again, walking up and down Soho. W. and I went pub-crawling after that until we finished up at the Café Royal where there were plenty of ghosts if one could see them.

This year I heard that Oscar Wilde used to frequent Kettner's. I do not understand these things but for ten minutes there had been something simple and complicated and timeless on the corner of X and Y streets.[2]

Hannah Atkinson, once a pupil of Clara Schumann, a pianist set for the concert stage, elegant in her youth and full of promise, was, at the end, like Oscar Wilde, alone and in pain.

Ethel was now summoned to the office of Mr. Daniel Macmillan of The Macmillan Company in London. Their relationship had had an eccentric if brief history.

Early in 1947 John Gray had sent Mr. Daniel the *Hetty Dorval* manuscript. Mr. Daniel had said no thanks, "However, of course you will have to publish it as you are committed to it. It is quite harmless, but it seems to have very little merit."

For some unknown reason, Mr. Daniel changed his mind. He wrote to John Gray, on August 12, that he would not only print his own edition of *Hetty* but he wanted an option on Mrs. Wilson's next book, as well. Thirteen days later, while Ethel and Wallace were aboard the *Queen*

Mary, he wrote to John Gray saying that he would be "very glad to make her acquaintance... Would you be good enough to ask her to telephone me when she gets to London."

On September 7, Mr. Daniel wrote to Mr. Gray:

> I saw Mrs. Wilson the other day and she has signed an agreement for the English edition of *Hetty Dorval*. She seems to be an intelligent person and will, I hope, write more and even better books.

Wallace and Ethel went on to Paris and the birth of the World Health Organization. Such an important event, but it seems that she did not write about it, or if she did, it has not survived. She always had an English person's distrust of the French in worldly matters.

They sailed home, arriving in New York on October 1. They spent two nights in Manhattan, then Wallace flew up to Ottawa to complete his business and Ethel took the train toward home.

She stopped off for a few days to see, again, her Canadian publishers. It was six months since Hetty had been released (at the Toronto press party she had sipped tomato juice instead of good whisky because she did not entirely trust the press). Now she wanted to find out how her book was doing and to be welcomed, so warmly, again.

Hetty Dorval, so quickly conceived and produced (considering publishers' time), was causing a stir.

America's *The Woman Magazine* wanted to buy *Hetty* for $250 and knock seven to ten thousand words out of her, which it did. The book only had sixty thousand words.

"How the dickens can they abbreviate Hetty? I should think it would be like a cousin of mine who was so thin that after he'd shaved you could hardly see him at all," Ethel commented to John Gray.

Americans could cause difficulty, which did not greatly surprise her. Take Simon and Schuster, for example, whose editor, Mrs. Leiper, had been corresponding with Ethel for years now. Mrs. Leiper had found Ethel through the *New Statesman* stories. She now had a copy of Hetty, but despite her persistent sending out to get another reader's report, the readers and the rest of the staff found *Hetty* unworthy of publication. (Later, after an even greater battle from Mrs. Leiper, Simon and Schuster refused *The Innocent Traveller*.) But it didn't really matter about those Americans, because the New York branch of Macmillan's took one thousand copies. (At that time, the American, Indian, Australian, and Canadian houses of Macmillan were tied tightly to the parent company in London.)

Even before *Hetty* had come out, there had been trouble. CBC's women's commentator for B.C., Ellen Harris, asked to interview Ethel Wilson. Mrs. Wilson replied, politely, No, not until publication, anyway. Mrs. Harris was irritated. She was equally polite. She wrote Macmillan's:

> As [your] Mr. Stoddart gave me this book for the purpose [of publicizing it], it seemed to me the author was being overly cautious.

"Publicity is a pill I find hard to swallow," Ethel wrote Macmillan's. "It covers me with gloom & misery...Let it be my idiosyncracy to be still *a private person*—there's a darling!"

In June, the international publishers Gyldendal Bonnier-Glydendal, with offices in Oslo, New York, Copenhagen, and Stockholm, wanted "options and galley proofs," and rejected *Hetty Dorval* in July. In July the persistent New York agent David Lloyd wanted it for Hollywood, and rejected it in September. In late July, Amy Buckerfield, who had "connections," sent it to J. Arthur Rank, and he rejected it. Ethel wrote John Gray that she would have been pleased if Rank, an Englishman, had filmed Hetty, but "wouldn't want Hollywood to do it—it would end up all trollop."

Nevertheless, in November, another agent wanted Hetty for Hollywood. Now she was agitated. She wrote John Gray. As usual, she started off the point, saying, "[Audrey Butler], our evacuee ex-WREN who arrived from London this week to pay us an extended visit...instantly went down with temp. 104 here and so hands get fuller & fuller..."

She says that she is worried about letting Macmillan's down, and tries to explain.

> From your point of view it must be all that is stupid and enraging if I say "No." I understand that absolutely—the standpoint is rightly the business one of Sales—you publish to sell.
>
> My whole feeling is so strong against it, I cannot argue it away, & the bad experiences of eminent writers like Thurber and Waugh, recently, made it stronger than ever. My responsibilities are many but I do wish to continue writing, with as clear & fresh a mind as possible. Cluttered up with Hollywood in this connection—& my feeling about it—in addition to everything else, I would be defeated...

Three pages later she concludes:

> With a sinking feeling, because I am letting you down & you are
> always so considerate to me—in fact with woe I remain very
> sincerely Ethel Wilson.

A CBC radio adaptation by Joseph Schull allowed Ethel to be
reasonable.

> I do not conceive of H., cool, smooth, pleasant & nasty, being
> nearly as sweet etc.—Nevertheless an awful lot of people seem to
> find that allright...but I feel that Mr. Schull took it to pieces & put
> it together so well, for so simple & precarious a tale would present
> difficulties.

After that broadcast she did not refuse to answer the telephone, as she
would later, and she was amazed that callers, strangers to her, "wanted
to know the end of the story...& both sexes." She wrote to
Macmillan's:

> One boy of 7 who will no doubt be sending you manuscripts twenty
> years hence—by name of Bren.
>   *Bren.* She never finished the story.
>   *Grandpa.* No they don't always. You'll have to finish it
> yourself.
>   *Bren.* Allright.
>   And he did—the bothersome one was killed in a train accident on
> her way to Vienna, her shoe caught in the train & she was not
> saved, but was tossed over the white cliffs of Dover.
>   The other two joined the RAF. They decided to get married &
> were just having their finger prints taken in preparation when a
> German bomb killed them both.
>   Good enough, I think, don't you.

Then a poet and English professor whom she had heard of, A.J.M.
Smith, approached her about taking one of her stories for a Canadian
anthology, and she wrote John Gray that she "would get some foolish
pleasure to think that possibly a future generation of bright eyed
innocents (or not) might perhaps study 'me' in University, which
possibly they might do..." That was the farthest she ever went in
public, and I think in private, to place herself in the future.

Smith had appeared earlier in her writing life. In 1942 he had told the poet Earle Birney, who was then teaching English at the University of Toronto, that the American literary journal *Story* was planning a Canadian edition, and asked if he would be interested in editing it. Birney went into action. He started by lining up Morley Callaghan, Emily Carr, Stephen Leacock, Hugh MacLennan, Mary Lowry Ross, Ethel Wilson, and others, offering $25 or $35 a story, except for Leacock and Callaghan who were accustomed to $100. Ethel sent him several stories, including "Nimpish Lake," which arrived in the midst of a flurry of anger and protests of misunderstandings. Whit Burnett, *Story*'s editor, had written Earle Birney: "The times are not ripe for a Canadian issue...I am very regretful of course that the good work you did has at the moment no use in the dimension we had hoped...the idea got underway a little too fast..."

"This taught me about contracts, that it's a writer's business to have a contract. I never got a dime," Birney said to me, still irate after nearly forty years.

"Nimpish Lake" was the first story she wrote about that small, pretty, fishing lake, Lac Le Jeune. Birney suggested that she send it to *Canadian Forum*, where it was quickly accepted. And, ironically, many years later, Whit Burnett's wife, Martha Foley, chose another Ethel Wilson story, "The Window," for *Martha Foley's Best American Short Stories*.

Chapter Eighteen

"Most Things are Dangerous. Nothing is Safe!"

Ethel's mother had died before she could remember her; her father had died when she was nine. She had been passed from relative to relative until her grandmother, whom she had never seen before, had come to claim her, and then she had been taken across an ocean and a continent of wilderness to live in a raw town on the edge of another ocean. She knew the threat of the unexpected, and so she embraced happiness when she found it. Her husband was what she had one of her characters say: "He is everything that I could ever love, not perfect, altogether charming for me, unpredictable, yet to be trusted, perfect."[1]

In late October or November of 1947, a few weeks after they were home from Europe, Wallace developed an angry skin rash. He went to see Dr. Donald H. Williams, a Vancouver specialist trained at University College Hospital in London and at the Mayo Clinic in Rochester, Minnesota. Dr. Williams could not make a diagnosis, but gave Wallace a prescription to ease the irritation and, he hoped, take down the infection. Wallace went about his business, sometimes in misery.

In 1980, when I talked to him, Dr. Williams "clearly" remembered that late autumn day in 1947 when he got what he called "an S.O.S." from Ethel. She was telephoning from Bowen Island, she said, and Wallace was in anguish. Dr. Williams told her that he would catch the next ferry over. He saw Wallace, brought him back with him on the boat, and drove him to Vancouver General Hospital.

"Every square inch of his skin was covered with a red, dreadfully itchy condition which plagued him day and night," Dr. Williams said. "The most exhaustive medical examinations revealed nothing that we could pin-point.

"Atopic Dermatitis is the best of many terms given to this condition. No more is known about it now than was then. It is seen from the cradle to the grave—it can occur in little babies three months old. It is sometimes called Neuro Dermatitis—I have purposely avoided that term with you. One school thinks it is brought on by inner stress. I didn't and don't think so in Wallace's case, although that was an idea I continually entertained."

I told Dr. Williams that two women, who had known the Wilsons well, told me that Ethel was "too intense," and that while Wallace was in hospital "she was driving him crazy" with her long daily visits.

("I took up his major meal, cooked or planned, every single day. He had three nurses and one prepared it and I think the tasty meals helped," she told Alan Crawley.)

"No," Dr. Williams said. "I never at any time saw any stress between the two of them. And I'd be a pretty sharp observer because I rarely missed a day of seeing him."

He said that he never saw any patient "handle a difficult, distressing skin problem better than Wallace." Ethel was the more difficult of the two, he said. "She was constantly hovering over us, dissecting and analyzing us.

"Perhaps she was oversolicitous. But you can't have anything else in a loving relationship."

For eighteen months Wallace might have died. His whole body was inflamed. His hair fell out. Anything that touched his body was torture, so a sheet had to be draped over the sides of the hospital cot, without touching his naked body. Ethel was to write of "the nights of anguish waiting for the telephone to ring." He telephoned her each night at ten-thirty on the dot from his hospital bed. She told me that she might have started to drink too much whisky if he hadn't always done that. She had to be alert and calm for him.

After nine months and no improvement, Wallace was very weak. The doctors asked Ethel to take a holiday away from him.

"I don't remember that," Dr. Williams said, "but it would be in order because I was surrounded by Wallace's solicitous doctor-friends and it may have been that one of them said, 'Give it a try'."

For a month in the summer of 1948, Ethel stayed with Alex Wilson and her second husband, Massy Goolden, in their large, comfortable house by the sea on Vancouver Island. They were familiar, affectionate friends, and because of this, Ethel broke.

"Massy, Ethel, and I would be sitting in the living room, just as you are now. It happened two or three times," Alex said. "Suddenly she would flee to her room, weeping.

"I would follow her up and I had to be very firm with her, and say that she *had* to control herself so that she could help Wallace when he got better and came home." She paused and added, "But I didn't know that he would come home."

Outside that living room, which had enormous panes of glass, a family of owls was living, above, in the eaves. Ethel, Alex said, was fascinated by these birds and sometimes would be so preoccupied that she would not hear the tinkle of ice as Massy stirred the martinis, and he would have to call, "For goodness sake Ethel I have a lovely martini here for you. Will you forget about those owls?"

"She was fascinated by them, and by all the birds," Alex said. In a story, "The Birds," Ethel wrote about the birds which she could see so easily, without being seen, from that large living room.

> The house...faced west and south and there were great sheets of glass of the kind called view windows...
>
> I looked out of the window at the living birds who were tossing themselves in the air and flying from tree to tree, and a moment of revelation came to me and I was a bird and the birds were I. The birds flew and flew with speed and attack in the clear air, and in the clear window was reflected to them the familiar sky and the flowers and the trees, and so each day some little bird flew into this familiar reflection and dashed itself against the real glass and fell, with its mouth split and its bones broken by the passion of its flight. Here was the dim mark of its death. And yesterday I had bashed my head against the reality that was waiting for me, invisible, and had nearly broken my neck. The thought of the merry birds and the birds in the years to be, falling outside the window, sickened me. A bird is so free.[2]

Ethel did try to control herself because she was a guest, and her husband's wife. Her husband was astonishing.

"To keep his courage up at night, and night was the most dreadful part of his day, the most tortuous part of his day," Dr. Williams said, "I heard that he would sing hymns, if you could believe it!"

And the nights, alone with her premonitions and imaginings, were dreadful for Ethel. She had a dream when he was so ill, and she told it to the Crawleys nearly twenty years later:[3]

> ...I was alone in the flat, he in hosp. with 3 nurses a day. Life was terrible. One night, unaware, standing in the middle of the bedroom, I said loudly "We Are Cut Off!"...[Some time later Wallace was travelling across Canada and] I was again alone in the flat. One night I had an extraordinary dream—not a nightmare. We were in the train, on the prairie, as so often [we were actually] & something happened. There was mental confusion...We were at a station called Cut Off...there were irrelevant happenings. The other passenger was [Boris] Pasternak. When I woke up I wasn't exactly frightened, but I felt I had all but died. Some time later I wrote the story ["A Visit to the Frontier"] & added & subtracted, because you can't write that wispy, shadowy kind of thing *echt* all by itself.

She said that she thought it was "a queer tale." Robert Weaver, editor of *The Tamarack Review* where it was published, "found it more than mysterious," and "it almost terrified Isabel Tupper," she said. It is both terrifying and not terrifying. It ends with the train crashing and then confusion:

> Please, she said to the poet—for she felt somehow that he was a poet or kin to a poet—have you seen my husband? I have lost him.
>
> I saw him, said the passenger, but he is not here now. He came back to the train and looked for you. He told me, She always likes water and she must have followed the river. So he took the far footbridge and followed down the stream. I am very sorry, said the passenger deliberately and with compassion.
>
> Lucy turned and went back with great difficulty to the steps. It seemed as though she fell, and lay there, on the tawny prairie.
>
> In the course of time, or of time and a time, all memory and strange pictures and confusion of human experience left her, and she died.
>
> When those who were killed in the train wreck had at last recovered from the fatigues of death, it may be that some of them met again with a transfigured delight in that beautiful and happy country, with death past and over. We do not know.[4]

A year of Wallace's illness passed. In October 1948, without doctors' request, she went away, not far, but up the valley to Harrison Hot Springs. She felt that she needed distance, to think at rest, to prepare for the time to come. With her she took some novels of Anthony Trollope. "I have been Trolloping along—as I told Wallace, taking a Trollope to bed every night with me [it was not too far or expensive for nightly telephone calls for those few days]—and what a help they are," she wrote her librarian friend Dorothy Jeffers. And then she gave the real news:

> ...The doctors decided that nothing more can be done in hospital, in fact further stay there is a detriment, & although there is not the longed for "normal recovery"—indeed the skin is often more violent than ever & Wallace suffers greatly but imperturbably (his steadiness/stability is a marvel to them) he is *in himself* very much better...The result is that I have got the flat geared to the very complicated business of his return, & though even that short journey [from hospital to apartment] will work a hardship on him, & although we know—he & I—that there is no *miracle* in *"place,"* there may be real benefit. It is as near happiness as one can imagine that he shall be back in his own home again, seeing the familiar things.

She says that she will now be "more than ever out of touch with friends—as he said, we'll just write this year off," and ends the letter: "We hope however to make life in this apartment as normal as possible, and not a *sick* life. He's on his way, we both know—bless him for a great good dear man."

In October 1949, she wrote Earle Birney on literary business, and said that Wallace was still very ill, but getting better, "slowly, but too slowly."

What is extraordinary to me now is how little I have known about this woman. I knew her for more than a quarter of a century, and she was confident that I was her friend. She left me and my children—as did Wallace—the things, not in essence material, which they most valued. But she spoke so little about herself and about her work, although she knew I was interested, that it has come with shocks, more than surprises, to see certain details. Among them, that when her greatest concern—Wallace—was dangerously ill, she had the discipline to carry on what she had started—the story of Topaz, her great aunt, the Innocent Traveller. Her pain over Wallace was so great that this ability to work is incomprehensible except as being extraordinarily sensible. If it was constructive and distracting for her, it would be for Wallace, she understood. He would find ease in knowing that his most vulnerable wife was not only coping, she was alive.

I have a letter from her, written after *Love and Salt Water* was published, in which she says a reviewer doubted that people in a gale at sea behave calmly.

> Has he never been to sea? Very likely not, & certainly not in a dire storm, because the worse the storm, the more violent the facts, the more you try to control yourself, however awful you feel. Does he really think, the good man, that people rush up & down shrieking? Not so.

With her emotions it was the same.

Wallace's illness ran dangerously from the autumn of 1947 to the late spring of 1949, when it seemed to subside. She started then to relax, but it is interesting to see what she did during that eighteen month crisis.

She worked on and completed *The Innocent Traveller*, her second book, which had started off as some of the stories she had sent Macmillan's in 1944. The final draft, except for an additional chapter which came a month later, arrived on John Gray's desk in February 1948.

But for many months before that final draft arrived, Ethel Wilson worried over its title. She simply could not make a decision. Earlier and later in her life she made quick and definite decisions. But now it seemed she could not decide on a title. On March 17, 1947, she said the book was to be called *The Dancer*. On May 21, *Portrait of Topaz*. In August, *Topaz, The Dancer*. In October, Macmillan's of London said they had "decided" on *Portrait of Topaz*, but that was not to be. Frank Upjohn, who was in charge of trade books at Macmillan's, received this letter on CNR stationery which, as usual, was not dated (it was probably October):

Out of Winnipeg, Sunday

> Quite a new line of thought came to me this a.m. — & flashes in the pan are
> Unimportant Journey
>   or
> The Long Journey of Topaz
>   or
> The Youngest Daughter

or
Journey to Vancouver of a Small Bird
or
Topaz in Vancouver
or some such.

On November 6, John Gray heard from her again:

What a plaguing thing that title is. I now have
A Portrait of Vancouver
Told in Vancouver
Vancouver Tale
A Vancouver Story
Vancouver Aunt
& the old *Portrait of Topaz*

In November, John Gray wrote her to say, "[*Down at English Bay*] seems to have everything that goes to make a good title."

Apparently she didn't agree because on December 12, 1947, he received a letter which, after four pages of talk, got down again to the subject:

I have the name for Topaz, without further examination, & will write soon to Mr. Daniel [Macmillan]. When the time comes, one knows! It is *The Innocent Traveller* or better *Topaz the Innocent Traveller*. The latter sounded too long, till I recalled again that little-read but remarkable book of Defoe's *Roxana the Fortunate Mistress*, which has a lovely flow as a title.

On December 22, 1947, John Gray wrote to her with considerable tact and just a suggestion of firmness:

I do like the title "The Innocent Traveller" and, although in some ways I should be reluctant to see "Topaz" go, I suspect that "Topaz the Innocent Traveller" may be considered too long for a modern title. After all, "The Fortunate Mistress" is surely a definitive sub-title for "Roxana," which is I think usually known by the one word only.

The Innocent Traveller was never again questioned.

Three months later, in March 1948, parts of a new manuscript arrived on John Gray's desk. "It is pouring itself out with great ease & pleasure," she wrote him, and its title was definite: *Tuesday and Wednesday*.

Ethel used her rare imagination and extraordinary eye for character and ear for language when she wrote this novella. That may be why she said she liked *Tuesday and Wednesday* best of her novels. The story is about a short time in the lives of three uneducated people in the east end of Vancouver: Mort, a sometimes logger and gardener; his egocentric wife, Myrtle; and a shy spinster who touches their lives but is not changed by them. It is full of sharp humour and gentle delights.

In April, the readers' reports came in: "marked degeneration in the writing here," "the mannerisms tend to run to seed," "looking at these chapters by themselves I must say that I find them very irritating. They are sentimentalized, cut down to pattern, so ruthlessly that only the author's unquestionable charm of style saves them from being bad," "here is a danger that what might be a leisurely, easy style will become a wandering, tiring thing..."

John Gray must have mentioned the reports because on May 16 she asked him to please return the manuscript because she had sent it just for him "to have a look at." She would send it out to him again two years later.

> This obscure, savage & capricious illness continues & the anxiety is the most terrible thing—complete hell. It changes with savage rapidity—it is simply unbearable & yet one has to bear it & keep "serene," & match his courage.

She was failing at her craft right now.

In April 1948, she sent the new chapter for insertion in *The Innocent Traveller*.

In July 1948, she wrote Mr. Daniel Macmillan and—perhaps because *The Innocent Traveller* was now at the Canadian printers—asked the big boss to tell John Gray, whom she did not like to tell, to insert the dedication, "To Wallace, my dear husband." Although the book was then being printed, it was held for release until spring 1949. England took 2500 copies; New York, 1000.

In April 1949, Wallace's night nurse could be let go.

Nearly a year passed, and then she had to answer a letter from John Gray. She said the American Printing House for the Blind could have *The Innocent Traveller* for its Talking Books, "gratis of course," and she goes on:

Am poking along at intervals of "leisure" (which it ain't) at something called, perhaps, *The Journey of A White Lady Friend* — did I tell you? It should be & could be a novel proper as far as material goes, but I don't think Lilly rates a good novel. I have got quite fond of her — the slut.

Ethel Wilson

More than a year later, July 19, 1950:

Hounded by Wallace ("Have you *nothing* to show Mr. Gray?") I send you (a) Tuesday & Wednesday which I haven't looked at for an age,
   (b) an unpleasant little story called *Mr. Sleepwalker* in which I hope to have clearly conveyed Mr. Sleepwalker,
   & (c) two parts of *The White Lady Friend...*
   It is curious, but both *Tues. & Wed.* & the *W.L.F.* are, really, studies in self-deception & lies. I became much interested in this, having observed how influential deceptions (self & otherwise) are in personal, group & national relations. Personal relations, however, come within the scope of our own study. Truth is sometimes absolute, but very often a relative matter, as we know — gets frightfully important. Both stories are perhaps unethical (because the lies win)...Oh, and I'll enclose A Visit To The Frontier for your perusal...We're revelling in health, freedom, happiness, friends, & Little Rock again. One closes one's shutters (at my age) to the horrors. Really, we are like the sands of the sea — what can we do? It seems to me I've spent most of my life getting worked up over things. Now no longer, if possible...

November 15, 1950, to John Gray:

I have seldom felt excited at the conclusion of writing anything. I do, over finished The White Lady Friend. [She says that it is now at the typist's and it will be some time before that is finished.] However, you'll survive the wait, & then you will say what I learned as a small child & have never forgotten, "Much cry but little wool, said the Devil when he sheared pig."

January 12, 1951, to John Gray:

Yes, I will be glad to have another go at the *W.L.F.* I don't quite know what will result. I *care* about Lilly, & know her, & she is prosaic, stupid except for self-interest, no heroine of romance, but courageous, & many people are like that. I quite see about her un-natural lack of interest in men. Either it is un-natural, or I have not made clear the consuming intention (one can hardly call it ambition) that nothing shall come into life that might interfere with—not child & mother necessarily (for she had no ego & no urge to power) but—with child & position in life. (*Must* have folks, like other people, *must* be "like folks")...Re. her mode of speech. I also thought of that. And proved it to myself by our dear Mrs. T. [Tufts] who has served us on and off for 20 years & before that served highly superior persons. She has the fatal gift of intimacy but has never made a woman friend—deliberately—outside her employers who love her & her shrewdness & converse for ages with her—far more than Lilly's would. And yet, although she has seldom conversed with an illiterate woman, Mrs. T. still speaks incorrectly, & when W. was away so long & I was immured with her—I caught it & had to check "I been" & "I seen" & "I gotta" in my own speech.

Room 220—Private Ward Pavilion—Vancouver General Hospital
                            Monday, Feb. 26 [1951]
Dear Mr. Gray—no, I'm not ill, & not bored, only thought I wanted a little fun.

I've been here a week & have 3 to go, as lazy as on board ship & well & kindly looked after. But not attempting "writing" because this costly & whimsical drug cortisone has to be given full opportunity. "They" are at last trying it although it doesn't usually apply to this kind of arthritis. "You are warned" not to be exhilerated too much if pain goes, so I'm not, it may be so temporary. But I have only a shadow of the pain I had, & on my nightly short walk have very little limp...Well, my fun I thought up is to send the little short chapter of Mr. Sprockett on the train [in *Lilly's Story*], which stands alone, & tells nothing, to the *Northern Review* for amusement & you know me, I don't repine if they send it back...

They didn't.

Chapter Nineteen

Truth and Creation

"T hey" thought that Ethel's arthritis probably started when Wallace was so ill, in the late 1940s. She was up at Little Rock. It was raining hard that day and she put on her gum-boots to go outside. She slipped on a wet rock and fell hard on the hip, which now at times could cause her exhausting pain. There is a quality about the appearance of people in nearly constant pain. If they do not frown and pull down their mouths, they take on a look which seems to put them at a slight distance, and they set their lips in a near-smile. Ethel Wilson did that. It gave her an appearance, with those piercing eyes of hers, of being extraordinarily astute, and also wise.

The night I met her, in 1951, she was in a wheelchair and, except for a few occasions when relief miraculously and inexplicably occurred, she was seldom out of it for the purpose of moving about. Once I ran into her at a Vancouver Art Gallery opening and, probably in order to give Wallace a chance to talk to some people and herself to talk to others, she asked me to wheel her around. If she saw someone she wanted to talk to, she would say so, and then, with a gentle, graceful, nearly regal gesture of her arm and hand, she would indicate the direction we should take. She could enjoy herself.

She did not discuss her pain with me, except occasionally when it impeded her and so had to be mentioned as a fact, but she did write about pain in her first draft of *Love and Salt Water*. Here, she wrote, is "a good working philosophy...[which] you take in addition to your pills...I am speaking only of severe and continuous pain."

> This is an old-fashioned recipe known as Counting Your Blessings. In the rich fabric of human life, my dear girl, the blessings and the sorrows and the bereavements...are there together and hope and faith and love spring from them...When I say Count Your Blessings I mean of course those blessings which you can look around and see in the past, the future and certainly the present. Books—and I place them near the top—and music and the arts and history past and present, and always friends of all ages and both sexes...ring the bell will you my dear? [Ethel Wilson had a small silver bell whose handle was in the shape of a lady in a long skirt]—we'll have a little drink—no—it won't hurt me.

She discarded that passage from her book, perhaps because it was not as well said as she would like, or because it broke a rhythm, or for other, possibly professional, reasons. But one day at Little Rock, when Geoffrey and Margaret Andrew were there, she brought out her copy of Colette's *Le Fanal Bleu* and gave it to Margaret. She had marked a passage—both women read and spoke French—which is translated here by Robin Phelps:

> My juniors in the prime of life sometimes look sternly at me; they feel anxious. They gather the recalcitrant fold of a shawl across my shoulder [Ethel often wore a blue boucle shawl] with a "You're not feeling a draft?" No, I am not feeling chilly, I am not feeling *that particular* draft you have in mind. My thoughts are too out of joint for me to feel it. I have so many reasons for avoiding what you tactfully call "the dangerous draft." Chief among them is pain, pain ever young and active, instigator of astonishment, of anger, imposing its rhythm on me, provoking me to defy it; the pain that enjoys an occasional respite but does not want my life to end: happily I have pain. Oh, I know perfectly well that by using the adverb "happily" I sound affected, like someone putting on the brave smile of an invalid! Very few invalids so remain entirely natural, but I would not like it thought that I am making my infirmity an occasion for sinful pride, that I require respect and special consideration, or that it fosters an inferiority complex, that

root cause of acerbity. I am not referring to those who pretend to be sufferers, who are of no interest and are in any case a small minority, nor am I alluding to a category of sufferers who are far from reluctant when surprised or discovered in the very act of suffering. My doctor brother summed up in a few words the pleasure enjoyed by such as these. "It is," he said, "a kind of ecstasy. It's akin to scratching the hollow of your ear with a matchstick. Aphrodisiacal, almost."

So, as luck will have it, I am fated to suffer pain, which I reconcile with a gambler's spirit, my ultra-feminine gambler's spirit, my instinct for the game of life, if you prefer it; the Last Cat, toward the end of her life, gave every indication by the movement of a paw, by the smile on her face, that a trailing piece of string was still for her a plaything, food for feline thought and illusion.

Whichever way it came about — before or after reading — her behavior was nearly a model of that passage.

"There is truth and there is creation, the outward eye and the inward eye," she wrote in an essay, "A Cat Among the Falcons." She went on to talk about herself as a person, who appeared now to have some authority. At least she was now being asked to appear this way in public.

I find that in talking about novelists, their lasting or passing fame, and their critics (who are an undetermined factor in fame), I am thinking first and always as one of "the Great Variety of Readers"; in a small but definite degree as a writer; but not at all as a qualified critic. I am not a cat among the pigeons. I am a country cat among my friends the falcons who are handsome, formidable and trained birds, equipped to detect and pounce upon error. It will be better, now, to take my convictions safely indoors and sit looking out of the window at what I can see, and at the sky which is beautiful.[1]

That's what she tried to do, and sometimes adamantly insisted on doing, but she was courteous and had been brought up as a child to give what she could. Here she was not unusual; she had not put away all childish ways. She was also innately, insatiably curious, and so it was natural that when Earle Birney and his group of mainly-young writers asked her to join them, she did.

After that correspondence over *Story* magazine several years earlier, she met the poet and writer Earle Birney when he came west, in 1946, to the

University of British Columbia, to teach English and give a course in Creative Writing. He was, and is, a man who tries to help writers, particularly if they are or have been his students, and he is passionate about his art and craft. I was one of his students and was occasionally asked to the meetings, and then asked by Ethel Wilson whenever they were held at her apartment. Although I knew and felt easy with some of the people—Earle Birney, Bob Harlow, Dorothy Livesay, Eric Nicol, Bob Patchell, Ernie Perrault, Mario Prizek—the ones I knew appeared to be different when they walked into that apartment. They seemed to be both more aggressive and more subdued, quite loud at times, in bursts.

"She could strike terror, I suppose, into the hearts of people who were not 'properly brought up'," Bob Patchell said. "When we walked in the door we were trying to be Edwardian gentlemen and trying at least to keep the language of our own criticism to polite English rather than the usual Anglo-Saxonisms that most of the time we hurled at each other about our literary efforts.

"The apartment was impeccable. I have never seen so much silver. She was the most gracious person I have ever met. It's funny, she was very modest about her writing, yet she wanted you to know what she had done. I remember she gave me her short story 'Hurry, Hurry,' which she'd written about fifteen years before, and later she asked me what I thought of it."

The purpose of the group, which called itself Writers Anonymous, but which she quietly called The Lit'ry Group, was to criticize each others work.

"These children of mine," Earle Birney told me in 1982, "my ex-students, wanted their own generation's advice, not necessarily mine. We met in each others' homes. I don't remember how it happened—perhaps we invited her one night. After that, we met often in her apartment. That's when I got to know her."

I asked him what struck him about her, when he first met her.

"Oh, a very intelligent, sensitive, almost a Katherine Mansfield type of woman."

"In what way?"

"Her antenna was out. She was sensitive. She was very modest. I didn't feel that she valued herself as a writer as she should."

Before anyone started reading, just after the last person—or what was probably the last person—had arrived, Wallace would stride in, warmly welcome their guests, and then, sometimes with his wife's prodding (but it had been agreed that he should come in and go out quickly), he would leave them to their business. He had much to do himself. After he retired from active practice he started the Second Mile Club, for men who lived in bleak rooms and had nowhere to go after the city had boarded up the old Carnegie Library in the East End. He chaired the committee of Ethics of the Canadian Medical Association and lectured in medical ethics at UBC. He was a founder of the Narcotics Association and president of UBC's Friends of the Library Association, and he was honorary consultant at Shaughnessy and at Vancouver General hospitals. At around eleven, Wallace would come back into the room of writers, and that was the signal that it was time to go; possibly, we thought, she needed her rest.

I remember only impressions about those meetings, among them, that she was comparatively easy about reading her work, and that she couched her criticisms in care and courtesy. Her pen was sharper than her tongue.

An aspiring writer could go to creative writing classes until he was black in the face, but if he has not a sound and critical knowledge of the construction and working power of the English sentence and the English language, he had better stay at home. He will become muddled and waste his time, because he has not been given the basic tools.[2]

She was respected now, she was being praised, and she was becoming more bold, shedding her uncertainties. She distinctly disliked what she called "contemporary double-talk," which became absolutely fashionable in the 1950s.

Our language is now being assailed on all sides. . . . "Gracious living," which has to do with the mind and the spirit and with good and kindly manners, has become one with bathtubs, window curtains, soft drinks and household equipment. Turkeys are no longer "cleaned," as they have been for hundreds of years; they are now "eviscerated" or perhaps even "eviscerized," and they don't taste any better for it. As I stood looking at some turkeys labelled "oviscerated," the woman next to me said, "Goodness, what's *that*? Some sort of special grain-fed, I suppose." You see how these fancy words can muddle people. People (we) are hospitalized, concertized, catagorized, sanforized, accessorized, janitorized (yes, I once saw that), deregionalized, dis-oriented, and goodness knows what else. Deals are "finalized" instead of being concluded, closed, ended, finished, completed.[3]

She said that publicly. Privately she played with it too. In an unpublished essay she tossed up a quotation and watched George Orwell bring it down.

"I returned and saw under the sun, that the race is not to the swift, nor the battle to the strong, neither yet bread to the wise, nor yet riches to men of understanding, nor yet favour to men of skill; but time and chance happeneth to all." This passage is a model of good language, from the first perfect phrase to the terse powerful conclusion. Here is Orwell's translation into contemporary jargon:

Objective consideration of contemporary phenomena compels the conclusion that success or failure in competitive activities exhibits no tendency to be commensurate with innate capacity, but that a considerable element of the unpredictable must invariably be taken into account.

Oh God, oh Ph.D.! You are both mighty and can surely prevail over this kind of thing!

One of George Orwell's biographers, George Woodcock, was teaching English at UBC and was editing the magazine he started, *Canadian Literature*, to which she contributed. She greatly respected him and knew, to her delight, that he did not have a doctorate. In a letter to me she mentioned him.

George Woodcock spoke at the Humanities on some aspect — I forget which — of Tolstoy. "They" asked me to introduce him & of course we couldn't go — but I was heartily glad & heartily sorry not to — glad because I'm not competent to know & assess his achievements properly, & sorry because it would be a pleasure to say how lucky UBC is etc. etc. etc. to have him. In a place where Ph.D.s are a dime a dozen imagine having a man of his mental gifts & calibre who has no degree at all. Magnificent & quite emancipated. But the [University of Toronto] Alumni dinner was no consolation prize...Someone at the dinner spoke seriously of University graduates as the "intellectual elite." As I looked at them they looked more like prosperous young executives out for the evening. I wrote & destroyed a bad story about executives & expense accounts & "prestige" cars etc. etc. They are a sign of the times & make me sick, they do. There's a "prestige" house going up on Beach Avenue & Mrs. Abbott's nice old wooden house is coming down & another "prestige" job two blocks east of it. Too bad.

She preferred to give up the Humanities meetings, which she did enjoy, to attend Wallace's university alumni dinner. There is no doubt about that word, preferred. It was in the nature of their marriage.

Chapter Twenty

An Indecent Commotion

That slut Lilly, the white lady friend, was between hard covers in 1952, a year after Ethel had told John Gray that she would take another look at her.

She had become a novella, *Lilly's Story*, and was published with the other, formerly rejected novella, *Tuesday and Wednesday* (which was also about people from what society women called "the wrong side of the tracks"), under the title *The Equations of Love* in Canada and England. The American publisher wanted only *Lilly's Story*, so she came out alone in the United States.

Lilly was the instigator of a little extra cash and a burst of scandal, which was appropriate if only because she was born, Ethel said, out of a phrase: "and formed other connections." This phrase, she said, was "dropped almost at random in a previous book." And then, she said, she started to think about the words. "What connections? I had never seen and did not know the girl in question. She did not exist in my knowledge any more than a fly in the next room, but I considered certain aspects and likelihoods...characters multiplied, their outlines at first dim, later clear."[1]

An immediate critical success, Lilly was quickly adapted into a radio play by the CBC. And this is what started her infamy.

At the end of 1952, a special committee of the Canadian Senate had been struck to investigate "the sale and distribution of salacious and indecent literature" in Canada. One member of the committee was R.W. Keyserlingk, who regularly put B.A. after his name, and who was publisher and editor of *The Ensign*, a small weekly newspaper.

Mr. Keyserlingk rose to his feet at 10.30 a.m., February 12, 1953, and told his fellow members that Lilly's was "a sordid story, told graphically and with extreme poor taste."

"Basically," Mr. Keyserlingk said, "this was the story: Lilly, described by the CBC narrator as 'a pale slut,' is in her middle teens when a Chinese cook (speaking dreadful 'pigin' English) tries to seduce her by offering her gifts. He gives her silk stockings, for instance, in a public restaurant, makes her take off her old stockings and put on the new ones while he watches her legs. She agrees to go to his room to spend the night in exchange for a bicycle. Police, looking for a stolen bike, intervene.

"Time of broadcast was 9 to 10 p.m. Sunday evening when many children were still listening to radios.

"Are we not aware," he continued, "that a war in Asia is being fought, not only against communist soldiers, but also for the respect and esteem our world hopes to gain from the peoples of Asia? If so, does the representation of a lecherous Chinese, seducing a pale young slut not imply a false impression of our Chinese friends?

"Whichever way you look at it, the thing looks bad. Or maybe I am just old-fashioned, and there is not bad or good anymore, just what the CBC thinks should amuse us."[2]

Ethel Wilson did not comment publicly, although she was asked to, and I don't know what she said privately, but I imagine that she enjoyed the absurdity and disliked Mr. Keyserlingk—even though she had not met him—with equal intensity.

Lilly had attracted other attentions. Ethel, her pen moving rapidly, spasmodically across the page, wrote Margaret Andrew.

> I shouldn't gossip about reviews but will. *Observer* was intoxicating, *Times Litt. Supp.* (Eng.) was a model, I thought, of a critical review of a novel & was a delight. *The Listener*, well I won't believe it till I see it (a friend [Hannah Atkinson] copied it out & sent) for it was incredibly good, too good, right overboard. *The Spectator* tore into the first story [*Tuesday and Wednesday*] something fierce, & then subsided, growling, about Lilly & granted me "a most assured irony" etc. I quiver a little in case the *N. Statesman* does a neat job of

ripping-up (if it notices)...The fascination of the thing—by the giants—is unique, & happily I'm detached enough to hold it the right of good reviewers to think & say what they jolly well like, & oneself (that precious creature) can take it with everyone else.

Marghanita Laski, in *The Observer*, had written: "...But no reservations need diminish *The Equations of Love* by a Canadian writer. There are two stories in this book, both set in and around Vancouver; the second is good and the first, 'Tuesday and Wednesday,' is excellent. This story of the sluttish vixen Myrtle and her indolent husband, Mort, is told with a smooth, critical and yet unjudging delight in humanity. Miss Wilson can communicate the enjoyment of observing, of understanding as much the drunken logger Eddie as the delicious happy old lady Mrs. Emblem."

When she opened her copy of *The Listener*, the British Broadcasting Corporation's periodical, she saw that her half-aunt had transcribed accurately. Sean O'Faolain, the distinguished Irish writer of fiction, had said this:

> It is enough to make any critic lose his sense of proportion when he comes on a writer and novel that he can put forward as an example of how English ought to be written, and of an original and unspoiled mind. I have just had this immense joy and I hope that I shall not lose my sense of proportion in the delight of the discovery. The writer is Miss—or is it Mrs? I know nothing of her except that she is Canadian...The publishers tell us she has written two other works (Hetty Dorval and The Innocent Traveller). If they are as good as this book, if this is not a chance success, which I cannot believe possible, and if she continues to produce books as good as this one we may take it that, within her gamut, Ethel Wilson is one of the most charming and accomplished writers of English fiction now living. Indeed this opinion is inadequate to her merits...[*The Equations of Love*] is, in short, a rare book...from a new and lovely star.

Her reservations about American publications stopped short of *The New York Times*. She clipped its review, which was written by another British Columbian, Stuart Keate.

> In a few magic moments she is able to illuminate a mood or a life; a movement in a darkened hall; a child's eye-view of a fight among

eagle, robin and snake; a first revelation of love to an unnoticed mother, as she watches her daughter greet her husband. The result is a moving and eloquent saga.

As most people who knew Ethel only from a distance—and that was most people—thought her cold, and those who knew her quite well indeed thought she did not much like children, it is worth really looking at *Lilly's Story*. It could not have been written by a woman who was incapable of feeling love for a child. *Lilly's Story* has humour and compassion, irony and a sharp eye, and it is a triumphant assertion of life. Its several settings are dramatic—the Chinatown area of a seaport flanked by mountains, a pretty small town on the west coast of Vancouver Island, dry cattle country of sage-brush and jackpines, the convergence of two great rivers, and a wind which is never still. So it is not surprising that Hollywood again approached Ethel Wilson. Again she rejected the idea of a film. And then John Patrick, who had won the Pulitzer Prize for his stage adaptation of *The Tea House of the August Moon*, approached. That was different. She gave him screen rights to Lilly.

For seven years, it looked as if Lilly would find stardom. John Patrick sent Ethel a tidy sum, and later Metro Goldwyn Mayer studios sent her $2500 to secure Lilly for its studio. Ethel Wilson enjoyed thinking about it, and told me that she was sure that, with John Patrick writing and directing, it would be a good film and in the spirit of Lilly. She liked the money, too, and as soon as it came in, she dispersed it. To Nan Cheney, whose husband was now dead and who was having a thin time financially, she sent off this letter which, if not convincing, shows her impulsiveness and fun in giving. She disguised her handwriting.

Dear Madam
    There is a nice gentleman in N.Y has ast me if he can try to get me a job on the Movies. He hassent got the job yet but he sent me some money today in Case he gets it Bless his kind Hart.
    I am getting my dear Husband a nise hat and maybe a case of wisky tho I don't use licker myself.
    I have ast my sekerterry name of Wilson to make me a check to send you with love to sellerbate same and maybe you will buy a hat or some wisky or put by for your holiday wichever you prefer.
    Humbly remaining with love and oblidge and pleese to share the Fun—Lilly.

Lilly never reached the screen, but she did cause one last uproar. It came from the quick and contrary novelist and short story writer Morley Callaghan, who had boxed with Ernest Hemingway and played with Scott and Zelda Fitzgerald in Paris, whose books were noticed by the best American and English critics, and who was considered a prize by his distinguished editor Maxwell Perkins. Callaghan, now living in Toronto, was on the alert. In anger he roared out against the people on the selection committee for the Governor General's awards. How could they pass by *The Equations of Love*? Was it, he bellowed, that they had been intimidated by the inanities of Mr. Keyserlingk and the rest of the Senate's morality-rousers? Did they too consider the book obscene? Morley Callaghan went full-tilt and the windmill didn't topple.

Ethel Wilson went on with her writing. In February 1953, in the midst of the Senate and Callaghan uproars, she sent off a new novel to Macmillan's. Revisions were suggested and completed within six months. The novel was *Swamp Angel* and was another story of a woman escaping her identity.

Usually considered the best and most intricate of Ethel Wilson's novels, *Swamp Angel* is the story of Maggie Vardoe, who leaves Vancouver and her unlikable husband, and disappears into British Columbia's Upper Country. She works in a fishing camp, spending her easy hours casting her fly on the lake in something close to pure contentment. She naturally becomes involved in the lives of the people around her, and because she is alive, strong, and noticeable, she makes changes, sometimes unconsciously, in those people's lives.

"You know, John," she wrote her publisher that year, "although I write chiefly of women I don't want to write 'women's books' — fie upon them. And I am interested that, so far, more men, and young men, than women seem to like them, which is pleasing — I've had more letters from them — because it disproves the women's book thing."

1953 and 1954 were years of taking and storing up pleasures. Of course there was a flaw and, not unnaturally, it came from the USA. For the sake of dryness and heat — the miraculous relief given by the cortisone and hospital-rest quickly passed back into pain — and at the insistent urging of their friends, the Wilsons decided, after unusual hesitation, to go to California in March. This is when the rains in Vancouver seem most black and torrential, although that is only an illusion which comes from having them pour down for so long. They went where their friends advised, to the desert around Palm Springs. They did not stay at fashionable hotels because they liked quieter ones, and they admitted that they dined well, but they disliked the brashness of the places. After two weeks they gave up seeking pleasure on the desert, and never again went to the United States of America.

Eight months later they took a different way out.

On November 23, I went down to a Vancouver dock and boarded a deep-sea freighter. I asked a sailor where I would find the Wilsons. He said they were in the saloon and I simply followed the noise. Some of the Wilsons' many friends had formed a farewell party. In those days, Vancouver people talked extraordinarily loudly, as if to still the silence of the mountains. Wallace and Ethel were surrounded by flowers and colourfully-wrapped presents, and Wallace kept the drinks flowing. It was a very good party.

Now they would find the sun in the more quietly rich civilization of Portugal. They would sail past the coast of California, through the locks of the Panama Canal (presumably all in sunshine), and then enter the unpredictable, swollen, gray Atlantic. She wrote Margaret Andrew:

The first day the ship did this

& this

& everything fell down flat & was propped up & fell down again. I would have, too, but did not dare to stand or would have been hurled about, so rolled merrily in my bunk & watched things fall as the ship shuddered.

Next day a quiet sea, & it was such fun to see whales ("blackfish" kind) & porpoises who are the prettiest sight playing in the ocean. Their life is one long game.

...Our food is much too good & plentiful—in a way. Irrational, it seems to us. Too much delicious unsalted butter, fattening doughy rolls, pots & pots of creamy, hot milk with good coffee, magnificent Dutch cheese—but 6 courses at dinner of varying interest, & our nice young steward who has long, curling eyelashes, nearly breaks down when we can only take 4. Two kills him.

The passenger list—assorted. W. & I went in a fool's paradise at first saying, Imagine, no radio, how heavenly! But oh dear me, we realize as never before that most people like a roaring radio, broadcast till it invades your cabin, the calm of deck, no matter what it is yelling about. We have sourpussed around a bit & the radio has become a little abashed. Otherwise I would say everything perfect...

Not much reading done, not all letters yet written, far too much yackety yack in smoke room or on deck (can't nobody *never* say nothing?) too much "What will you have?" & of course my lack of mobility makes me a sitting duck. However it is nice not to be completely ignored—but there is always this nice cabin when the facial muscles need a rest. Do not let me mislead you—I wouldn't have missed this for anything but am thankful we don't play bridge anymore. So is W.

"Young people," she was to write in *Love and Salt Water*, "cannot usually afford either time or money to travel by freighter; but toward the end of life, when one has less time, one has, strangely, more time."

Ethel's friend from her youth, Marion Ward, was in England, and she was not having an easy time. How nice, Ethel and Wallace agreed, if she would come to them in Portugal. So they invited her to fly to them, at their expense of course, and stay with them at the Estoril Hotel in Lisbon, which she did. They took trips out with their hired limousine and chauffeur, and of course they went to the beach and swam, and they spent the nights in restaurants and bars listening to fado, and they explored the market in the cool of mornings. There they bought some good Portuguese marmalade and every day, before the boy came to their rooms to clear away the breakfast trays, they decided, between them, where to hide the marmalade to keep it safely for tomorrow.[3]

Their chauffeur drove Ethel and Wallace to Coimbre and she wrote of it in an essay:

As I sit on this balcony and the old-fashioned trams go roaring past, and the oxen go silently past, I see that the townspeople—who no longer walk with burdens on the head but carry dispatch cases—walk more slowly than the country people. City life is less urgent. I see also a pig. An aged woman in black has a string attached to the pig who is grey and pink. She drives and teases it continually with a switch. The thin pig stops at intervals to root, it seems, in the tessellated pavements of Coimbre. No luck in this life, pig.[4]

In April, five months after leaving home, they flew back to Canada. Governor General Vincent Massey, an admirer of Mrs. Wilson's work, invited them to stop off in Ottawa and spend a few days at Rideau Hall before starting the last lap of their journey home. They did this, with delight.

And in September they went again, for the first time in thirteen years,

to their favourite small lake, Lac Le Jeune, to cast their flies among the
tule weeds. It was agonizing with her arthritic hip, but she was
determined to fish those pretty waters once more with Wallace. She was
too crippled to walk the short distance between their cabin and the lip of
the lake, so Wallace drove her down to the water, and he and a man
from the lodge lifted her into a rowboat. They stayed out for hours,
casting their flies. She must have been stiff and in pain; she didn't say that
she was. Some years earlier she had written about Lac Le Jeune, calling it
Nimpish Lake.

> An osprey circled overhead...Vigour had gone out of the day. Sky
> and silent lake breathed a charm...The osprey circled above. Not
> far from the boat floated a loon and her two big babies. Out of the
> silence the loon uttered her startled and melancholy laughing cry.
> Her laugh clattered over the lake and was thrown back by the
> shores. The vacuous but musical cry of the loon spoke to all the
> creatures on the lake. All the creatures listened. The laugh ceased
> abruptly and the two big babies swam closer to their mother. Then
> the loons dived. One. Two. Three. The sky and the lake blazed
> with the outrageous colours of the setting sun...The trout,
> beautiful and exasperating, began to jump and jump from the
> shining surface of the lake...Splash here. Splash there. Little
> fountains of water arose far and near in the placid lake, and there
> came the delayed "plop" of the jumping fish. The osprey dropped
> from high and hit the water in an explosion of flying spray. The
> osprey shook itself like a dog, and flew up carrying in its talons a
> silver fish. It was getting cold, so...[they] rowed through the
> coloured water out into the lake towards home.
> Overhead came the sound of high music. They looked up. High
> in the flaming sky drove a spearhead of great birds flying south. The
> clamour came nearer..."Oh...it's geese isn't it?"
> "Yes. Geese. Just look at them," said the lame man, gazing
> upwards. He gazed until the clamourous flying shaft had passed like
> a filament from sight and sound. He felt a queer exaltation, a sudden
> flash that was deepest envy of the wild geese, strongly flying and
> crying together on their known way, a most secret pain.[5]

Chapter Twenty-one

Nothing Is Safe

In 1954 Wallace Wilson was attending a medical convention which was being held at Harrison Lake, less than a hundred miles from Vancouver. In a meeting, he felt heavy pressure in his chest and a sharp pain down his left arm. He left the convention hall, went to his room, packed his suitcase, and assembled his papers. He checked out at the desk, got into his car, and drove home, a three-hour drive. Mrs. Marshall, their housekeeper, said that Mrs. Wilson was out at a luncheon. He went into the study, where the telephone was, and closed the door. He had telephoned to his doctor, he told Mrs. Marshall when he came out of the study. It was an attack of angina. He drove himself to hospital.

Chapter Twenty-two

Public and Private Crises

Times come when a person does not dare to look or feel because she is too vulnerable. Now, again, Ethel was in that time. And, again, she did not do either, and did both intently and intensely.

For two months, Wallace, who was now sixty-six, was in hospital and daily, again, she visited him for four or five hours. Nearly every evening, when she came home, and again when she woke the next morning, she went into that "desert of loneliness...it is the emptiness," she would write, "of time and occupation, the desert that lies between now and sleep."[1]

Wallace was allowed to come home for Christmas. They could not go this year to Victoria. For the last few years they had spent the holiday there, staying in comfort at the Empress Hotel, a chateau-style Canadian Pacific Railway hotel, whose like is seen in pleasantly eccentric variations in the major CPR train-stops and CPR boat-stops across Canada. In the afternoons, the Wilsons would settle down for tea in the hotel's lounge, where people to be watched included not just the rich, but the displaced titled (Lady Swetenham caused excitement once by toppling a potted plant off the sill and out of her window, just missing a pedestrian), and where William Tickle and His Orchestra muffled the rattle of silver sugar-tongs and tea-spoons against china teacups. At night, William Tickle and His Orchestra miraculously were transformed to Billy Tickle and His Band, and the Wilsons enjoyed that, too, although not as much. But this Christmas of 1954 they would stay at home and, as far as their housekeeper, Mrs. Phyllis Marshall, remembers, Sir Ouvry and Lady Roberts were there for the turkey and flaming Christmas pudding.

The flat was good for Christmas. It was handsome, high-ceilinged, and rich in colour, and Mrs. Marshall kept the dark oak and mahogany tables, the silver and glass, polished to brilliance. This remarkable woman lived with the Wilsons for twenty-two years, and in 1956 Ethel Wilson mentioned her to me—as she did often, and with immense appreciation—in a letter.

"During our manifold afflictions Mrs. M. has been wonderful past belief, a support indeed. I am so grateful to her, & will never be inwardly cross again at her allergy to 'entertaining.' She has contributed very much to our weathering our gales." Wallace and Ethel loved to have friends in for tea, drinks, dinner, and lunch.

With Wallace better again, Ethel returned to her writing. She wrote in bed from approximately eight to noon. She corrected galleys at the dining room table. It was not until she was in the small study that overlooked the sea and the stone bungalow where she and Wallace and old Mrs. Wilson had all lived together, that she could look "down on the water of False Creek flowing out with the tide to mingle with the water of English Bay" and watch the "hundreds of small nameless ducks" that flowed with it. "I shall never tire of these water matters, seen from this nearness and height."

She could also see where old Mrs. Abbott's house had been demolished and replaced by a "prestige" house. She was going through some prestige herself. At the spring convocation of 1955 at the University of B.C. she was awarded an honourary doctorate of literature, and more honours would follow shortly after: a special Canada Council Medal, the Lorne Pearce Medal, the Order of Canada. She felt truly honoured, but she did not particularly enjoy what she called the "severe onslaughts of fame." Public events plucked at her nerves. She was on television ("I hate it"), on radio ("My voice is thin and too high"), and she stared into photographers' popping bulbs. "I suddenly realized that when you're old, stand up (or lie on your face!) because sitting photographs are of your chin, bust and tummy. So I spent the p.m. [being photographed] leaning casual like against walls and chairs..."

She was interviewed by the Vancouver *Sun*'s best feature writer, but she found it "an asinine silly piece...To call a woman 'stately' is as near an insult as you can get, the ass! A nice and very he-man big person to talk to, I thought, quiet, pleasant, but it was difficult to know what he wanted." She was so reserved she must have been nearly impossible to get through to.

Ethel wrote Alan Crawley, too, about her onslaught of fame. She was, she complained, at a partly-publicity party for Robert Weaver, who at the time was doing more for writers in Canada than anyone had ever done. Jack Wasserman wrote a gossip/personalities column for the *Sun*, and he was there. He was, she told Alan Crawley, "an objectionable but more 'reputable' Walter Winchell of local snoopings." She said she was trapped in her wheelchair when "a young friend [probably the bookseller Bill Duthie] came up and said, 'May I introduce Mr. Wasserman?' "

> Well. . .I was horrified because the man can be pizen. . .So I said "How do you do Mr. Wasserman" counting 10 I assure you—
> My young friend said, "Of course you read Mr. Wasserman's column?"
> I was silent. Mr. W. watching, I counted 10, & laughed & said "I don't have to answer your question. I don't need to tell you what I read or what I don't read." (I didn't want to open the door to discussion. "Yes" would elicit "Do you like it?" "No" would elicit "Why?")
> My young friend said "No, really, *do* you or *don't* you read the column?" I didn't take him seriously.
> And I said again "But I have reached an age when I don't have to answer questions unless I want to!"
> So Wasserman said, "And what age is that?"
> And I said "Oh about 90."

"It was not a tasty morsel to see my name in that column," she concluded, although Mr. Wasserman, no doubt bewildered, was innocuous in what he reported.

Her pleasure in a touch of drama came with her, on another occasion, into a university lecture hall. In 1956 she was speaking at a writer's conference which was being held at the University of B.C. She looked dramatic under the light, perched on a high stool, tall and still beautiful. She had just started reading from her paper when a door at the back of the hall opened, and light came through along with the darting figure of a woman. Ethel stopped reading and looked toward the door. The audience turned to look too. And then Ethel smiled, suddenly and broadly, and said "Hello Nan" to Nan Cheney, who was dropping as quickly as possible into her seat and obscurity. Ethel let out her high trilling laugh, the audience followed, and then she continued with her paper.

Ethel's short story "The Window" was chosen for *Martha Foley's Best American Short Stories of 1959*, and this made her even more prestigious. What literary lions arrived now in Vancouver, she was brought out to meet, when she would come. She didn't for W.H. Auden. She explained that she and Wallace were not particularly well, and added, "If I knew more about his poetry *and* the man I might induce W. to bust a gut & have a too-crowded party here. But I haven't the warmth for him...But I do hope a true patron of the arts will." Some would have bust their guts to have him.

And then Angus Wilson appeared. She had a telephone call from her friend Ella Fell, a kindly woman who happened to be rich. Ethel wrote the Crawleys in July 1962.

> E. (Ella)..."Ethoo (she is really saying Ethel but Ethoo is what it is) — Ethoo, *do* you know a writer called Angus Wilson?"
> Me, "Yes."
> E. (very cautious), "Tell me is he a good writer?"
> Me. "Yes, he has a wide good reputation. You might or might not like his novels."
> Ella. "Tell me some of the names" — and so on. Then "Well this morning a man's nice voice rang me up & said he was Angus Wilson & friends of mine are neighbours of his in the country, in England, (& who *is* he?) & they want him to come & see me, & he's lecturing at UBC this weekend & he's coming to lunch tomorrow, & I haven't a cook, only a housemaid, & I can't ask anyone else to lunch but I do want you & Wallace to — etc.
> "Well, would we take coffee in the garden & we did, and drove him back to UBC...
> Angus W. "I never knew you lived in Vancouver, I thought you lived in Toronto," he kept on saying that.
> Me. "I never knew that you never knew that I lived anywhere."
> A.W. "Oh yes, you & I had our photographs on the same page of the *N.Y. Times*. Don't you remember?"
> Me. "I never saw it & what's more I don't believe it" & more to that effect but apparently we did, circa Lilly's Story time, I think...
> Me. "I'm so glad to see you. You know you rebuked me once in the *Sunday Times*, was it?"
> A.W. in a tone that didn't think much of the *Sunday Times*, too

Establishment/smug, I expect, "No, no, not the *Sunday Times*. In the *Observer*. What did I rebuke you about?"

Me. "You rebuked me for giving Chinese people un-Chinese names, but they do that here. Second Generation Chinese *do* choose un-Chinese names. Our member of Parliament was Douglas Jung & the nearby druggist is Wesley Koo & my favourite Chinese vegetable man is Angus, just like you."

A.W. "Well!!!"...

...he talks fast & audibly & things & opinions come pouring out. He's a funny looking little man aged 49 but looks older. I have always understood that he has a characteristic common to many bachelor artists & writers, but of course I do not know. Even if so, that does not prevent him from being a very interesting person to talk to. Very genial...

P.S. Comedy. Ella instantly, after telephoning, got 3 paper backs from Duthies [a book store] & quoted them so knowledgeably & tenderly to him ("As you said in..."). I, so unworldly & innocent, was amazed, yet shouldn't have been. What games we play!

Despite illnesses (between 1954 and 1966 Wallace suffered eight heart attacks, and she too was ill), they fought to continue their way of total life—"our absurd & pleasant life 4 times out to dinner last week." One of those was dinner with the assistant editor of *The Times*, Maurice Green.

"My one desire," she wrote me, "was to ask Mr. Green why for Heaven's sake the *Times* (in these days) was so innocently & idiotically snob as to advertise themselves as the paper that 'all the Top People read,' a statement perfectly on a par with the use on our continent of the word 'prestige,' as 'a prestige car,' a 'prestige suit,' a 'prestige office'—v. vulgar.

"However, I didn't have the courage or rudeness. He was a pleasant soft spoken man, with opinions, which he expressed disarmingly—or did not express...But oh golly, the difference in spending a p.m. with Kingsley Martin! Full of delights—However, being K.M. was not his function."

When, in 1946, Ethel Wilson knew that *Hetty Dorval* was coming out, she became strangely upset. She asked Macmillan's to let her use a pseudonym; she talked of "knowing" Hetty, although, she said, the fictional Hetty differed from the living woman. She threw a shawl of mystery around Hetty. Now, nine years later, she was doing the same thing, only differently. The girl Gypsy in her last novel, *Love and Salt*

Water, was based on me, or so she told John Gray and two other mutual friends.

It started before the book was published. I had come after work this day, as I did two or three times a week, to the Wilsons' flat. She was not lying on the day-bed, which looked like a couch, in the study, which is where I usually found her. She was sitting in a chair, not her wheelchair, in the living room. As usual, she greeted me with her arm stretched out, palm upward, a broad smile, and "Hello Ducks."[2] I asked if someone else was coming to tea, and she said No. A manuscript lay on the table beside her. (Usually, there was no sign of a manuscript by tea-time.) She said she wanted to read me something. There were two possible endings, she said, to this new novel which she called Miss Cuppy. She would like to read them both to me—they were only a few paragraphs—and would I please tell her which I thought best. I was alarmed. I was afraid that her mind was in trouble. She was too independent, too professional, to ask my opinion on such an issue.

She read. One ending left Gypsy alive, the other dead. I said, embarrassed for her as well as for myself, that I couldn't say which was best because I hadn't read the book. She smiled and we went on to other matters. A few weeks later she sent both endings to John Gray, who chose to have Gypsy live. It's conjecture of course, but my only explanation for that curious event is her superstition. She had become fond of me.

Then she set a false trail. By the time the book was out in 1956, I was working in London. For ten days I worked for Macmillan's, but could not afford to stay. Through her and those ten days, I got to know several editors, including Sylvia Farrow. One day I had an unusually brief letter from Ethel Wilson. She said that Sylvia Farrow was Gypsy. I told Sylvia this and she was as surprised as I had been, and I remember that she said, "It couldn't be. How astonishing. She's nothing like me." In fact, she was nearly angry that Ethel Wilson had so misinterpreted her.

Perhaps Ethel Wilson was afraid that I would see similarities and become self-conscious with her, or suffer some other effect from identity. So she decided to propagate a mystery. I didn't find out the truth for many years, and then the things which seemed familiar to me made sense. It is just not natural to think a character is based on you.

The story, which is not based on me except for one incident, opens with a girl, Ellen Cuppy, her mother and father all making up a happy family. The mother dies and Ellen takes a trip with her father, and they live through a storm at sea (which is taken directly from Ethel Wilson's experience). Later her father falls in love and marries again, and Ellen

Ellen grows up. In her turn she falls in love and is loved, but an accident, in another ocean, scars her face and could, she is nearly convinced, destroy her happiness. That is the essence of the plot.

She mentioned briefly, in a letter, the critics' reaction to *Love and Salt Water*.

> The better Can. reviews of *L. & S.W.* are quite rightly unanimous in the too-thin-ness of the story (how I agree!) but give unqualified & surprising praise to the thing called "style," "language," "magic" (which of course is not enough) to an extent that informs me that I have that place in writing in this country—which I was not aware of. *Eve.[ning] Standard* was brief & much too good, *Sunday Times*, as perhaps you know, less than tepid, a very poor review. —The thing I'm working on, when poss., has an awful lot of content (begun last Jan.) & will be pleasantly difficult to do. Can only do snatches, 2 chaps yesterday, wh. is bad because no further immediate prospect.

That book was *The Vat and The Brew*, the only book which John Gray suggested was not good enough, considering the high standard she had already set. She asked him to return the manuscript, and did not try again to publish it. It is the story of violence and children.

Meaningless, useless violence to people who were no threat to anyone—like the Chinese man who ran the small store which sold chocolate bars to children and perhaps a bottle of milk late at night to solitary adults—had now started its way into a prosperous western world. It was too foreign, and too dangerous to be ignored.

Now another part of the world looked as if it, too, were about to change character, in fact, had changed character, and that was Great Britain. In the autumn of 1956, Britain and France joined forces and sent them into the Middle East, and this threatened to ignite a third world war. It was called the Suez Crisis. I had been sending reports from London to the Vancouver *Sun*. She wrote me, her pen moving jerkily, in haste:

> I have never been so unhappy about world and national affairs in my life—because always, before, whatever the anxieties & blows, I always felt that Britain was *right*, & this time I was, & am, shocked beyond measure. I feel I never knew what "shock" was before, that the U.K. (with France! indeed) would land troops without notice & call it "Police Action." When W. returned from Toronto he said

"Wait, you don't know everything" & I said "I know that the U.K. has shocked the world and the world's very shifty conscience, earned the hatred of the Moslem world, set a precedent of return to bad old ways, etc., etc." W., deeply distressed, still said "Wait"...I've become oh in the months past very apathetic to [Prime Minister] Eden, and again W. says "Wait"...Is it the inheritance of past stupidities and vacillations? Russia growls on nearer and nearer & revealing herself as more & more odious.

Then she tacked on a P.S..."Oh how sensible W. is! He says that Lord Acton said that the Greek democracies fell to pieces because they fought each other, not the enemy, & it behooves us not to do a silly thing like that. That seems the higher wisdom—& as W. says...Eden was in the position that you're damned if you do & damned if you don't.

"Golly, a lifetime's not long enough to grow up in!"

Never before had she doubted Britain; neither had she been aware of the violence in children. She was sixty-eight and her world was shaking, and she felt inadequate.

That year the doctors thought they had found a malignancy in her breast. She went into hospital and into the operating room. She wrote me a note from the hospital on February 4, 1956.

I've been a very lucky woman—reports all good. Post-operative pains in chest & throat quite hellish but nearly subsided, the amputation itself being the least of it—so how fortunate. [In a February 19 letter to John Gray she said that, after the breast was removed, the tumour was found to be benign, not malignant.]

And then she talks about the possibility of a new literary magazine in Canada, and doubts that there is enough material to justify it having a good and long life.[3]

"We have to face the fact," she wrote Mazo de la Roche, whom she had met through their mutual publisher John Gray, "that with Wallace's coronary and my lameness our own place [on Bowen Island] is not safe any more for us. I have on several occasions had to walk out 3½ miles for communication & after illness or accident to others; we're completely cut off. That used to be a joy, normally, the cut-offness I mean, but not now. Also 'help' is impossible to get, & W. must no longer haul, dig,

174

axe, & all the things he loves doing."

So they thought it out for a long time and then gave the University of B.C. a gift of Little Rock, saying that it was to be used by the professors and other teachers and their families. (A few years later, to their disappointment, UBC decided to sell Little Rock because it was not a money-maker, or so Ethel Wilson told me.) The first guest, who came alone, was the now-famous architect, Arthur Erickson. After that it was booked on all weekends and throughout the university holidays, year after year.

They left behind her book of recipes because the things in it were, in her mind, easy and quick for island living, and probably because she wanted to leave something of herself there. The contents are catholic: Goose or Duck Stuffing, Mrs. Leslie's Ham Dish, Jean's Peasant Soup, Chili Sauce, Crab Souffle, Raspberry Ice Cream, Rose's Christmas Cake, Mrs. Bourne's Chocolate Cake, Milk Jelly, Clam Juice Cocktail from H.R. Macmillan (the lumber baron, not spiked), Canned Beans. The one I picked out for you, the Reader, is "Mrs. TUFTS Crab Cocktail" which calls for:

    ¼ c. whip cream   )
    worchester sauce   )
    Ketchup   )   All combine to make about
    lemon   )   a cupfull
    2 or 3 drops onion juice)
    salt pepper
    chili sauce
    thick salad dressing

That's the end of the recipe. You could add some crab.

So now, with Little Rock gone, they looked for another haven on another island, and found it in an old-fashioned hotel with a spectacular view, Island Hall, near Parksville on Vancouver Island. Now they would get into their car, Wallace would light his cigar, and they would drive onto the ferry in Vancouver and off again in Victoria. Slowly they drove up the ribbon road, which was framed by tall dark trees, and cut through the eastern, sheltered side of the still-wild island.

The hotel, which stands today but now has plastic decorations, is a rambling wooden structure of no discipline at all, which makes it odd and attractive. The Wilsons always took the same adjoining rooms with a balcony which looked across at the sea and enormous expanse of beaches. They took two rooms because then they could entertain their friends in greater comfort. Roderick and Ann Haig-Brown came from Campbell River, Nan Cheney came from Vancouver, and Alan and Jean Crawley, and their son Michael, who drove them, came from Victoria. Ethel, confined to her wheelchair, sat on the balcony and watched the children, people, and dogs, and the seabirds strutting and pecking on the sands which stretched for miles both north and south. And she watched Wallace and Alan take off their shoes and roll up their trousers and walk across the sun-warmed sands and through the lip of the sea. It frustrated her that she could not walk and talk with them.

"Ethel had her imagination and her consort," Geoffrey Andrew said, "and that was enough for her."

Her consort now disappeared for weeks at a time on trips across Canada because, although he had retired and was not entirely well, he had taken up an immense amount of non-paying work. He wrote her every day when he was away. On October 23, 1956, a few weeks before the Suez Crisis, he was on the train to Edmonton, where he was to attend a meeting of the Narcotics Foundation, of which he was a founder. He wrote to her, his hand jiggling with the train's rocking motion. First he described his pleasures from the scenery, and then his impatience erupted. He said that he had been reading a social worker's report which would be given at the meeting.

> Here are a few atrocities. He [the social worker] goes out to do some work at Oakalla [a penitentiary in B.C.] & refers to that work as his "extra-mural orientation programme." He regrets his inability to follow-up on an addict who had left town because of her "Geographical location"...Surely it is bad enough to be a drug addict & in Oakalla without having an additional cross to bear in the form of such a pest.
>
> And in addition that man is speaking to public groups about Addiction & the Foundation & is certain to be using the same esoteric jargon.
>
> I will certainly speak out at the next Board meeting & if our fine social worker can't revert to the simple words he learned at his mother's knee he should be prevented from either appearing in public or writing any more reports for us.

On this and previous and subsequent trips, Wallace went into bookstores, occasionally to buy a book, but usually to check on his wife's latest book. If it was not on the shelves, he would go to the bookseller and ask if he or she had it. Should the answer be No,

Wallace would say that it had had excellent reviews and would imply—he was too courteous to say—that the bookseller had been remiss.

Students of Ethel Wilson believe that he did not read her books. I think I know how this misconception came about. She broadcast something near the truth over the CBC. This is what she said:

I am glad that my husband does not read novels—if he can help it . . .

I cherish the time when a man said to him, "I hear that your wife has published a novel!"

My husband, pleased at such réclame, said "Yes, she has."

His friend said, "What is it about?" My husband, rather uncomfortably, "I—er—don't know."

"Don't *know*!" exclaimed the friend. "Do you mean to say you haven't *read* it?" and he hadn't.

However, I know that later he tried to, for I saw him sleeping like a child one day with the book open on his chest. He has done better since then.

Now that is a wholesome, pleasant, entertaining and not too shattering relationship. Much mutual pleasure is derived therefrom and too much gratifying self-deception is not liable to occur.

Chapter Twenty-three

Visiting the Past

With her cancer operation, his heart attack, both set firmly in the past but not lying still in their minds, they would live now. They would go again to Portugal, they would see their war-time daughter Audrey, they would explore the streets and shops and museums of London. In the early spring of 1956 they flew over the North Pole, and she wrote to me that "the flight is an experience in itself—pleasant, indeed luxurious (lunch 4 courses, 4 wines, dinner 6 courses, 4 wines!!!)—one stodges away on filet mignon, you (or we) don't sleep much in spite of black eye shades and 'composing oneself to slumber,' so that to our surprise we woke in mid-afternoon next day in the hotel, having slept 15 hours..."

At the hotel, luxurious but not expensive because of the rate of exchange, she says that her wheelchair "as usual exhorts general rushes of assistance and overpowering of attentions, and I *do* feel a phony. I respond graciously, feeling a perfect fool—bowings in all directions." They dine and sightsee, she sends me ideas for radio documentaries, Wallace steers her in her wheelchair through the art galleries, and she comments, "As we look at Rembrandt and Vermeer and Jan Steen and the rest, beside the perfection of art it is a revelation of contemporary humanity with an implied continuity to life." They fly Audrey to Amsterdam. They haven't seen her in nine years and Ethel writes, "What a darling she is — so sincere, unaffected, of deep affection, very intelligent, a woman of the world but artless too. Since we have the same kind of sense of humour, natural hilarity, the simplest, silliest things occur all the time..."

They fly to Portugal and, at the Lisbon airport, their old driver, Antonio, greets them, picks up their baggage, and settles them into the car.

" 'Are you married now, Antonio?' asks W.

" 'No-no-no-no, doctor,' says Antonio in his rapid staccato. 'I still sing, I still sing.' Of course, he means that he is still a single man, although another interpretation could be taken," Ethel writes in her essay "On A Portuguese Balcony."

They fill their days and their nights, she ignoring her pain as much as possible, he agreeing that life is a precious commodity.

Last night we went to Lisbon again to listen to the *fado*. *Fado* is the traditional type of song beloved by the town workers. I have enquired of many people and cannot find its origin...The lights are lowered in the winecellar — for it is really a winecellar in a black narrow street, with an unedifying dark entrance, a light in a window (good wine needs no bush). The guitar players tune and pluck their strings. The room goes silent. The *fado* singer stands beside the guitars. She is one of the great singers and she is not young. She is dressed in black, of course, and her shawl is clasped around her. Her face has an arrogant aquiline look of an Iroquois Indian. The men sitting at tables gaze at her; then lean their faces on their hands. The singer stands proud and erect, raises her head, closes her eyes, and lets go with a tragic piercing note that fills the room. She draws upon some inner unhappy intensity and sings loudly. There is a kind of rage. You can detect the metre; it is simple and you could write it down. The room seems to be full of suffering which is not entirely phony. If a whisper were heard between verses, that *fado* singer would stop singing and turn her back, but no whisper is heard. Enjoyment of this melancholy is intense and complete. The song ends; we drink our wine...

Tonight we go down to the little restaurant in Cascais for our dinner. There is no advertisement anywhere as you approach a town, a restaurant, and that is one thing that the visitor from the North American continent finds refreshing. There are fewer pictures here than with us, except in the shiny *azulejos* tiles where there are saints and angels, animals and people and things of the sea — which you will find everywhere in coastal Portuguese decoration, since and perhaps before the days of Prince Henry the Navigator who was the grandson of John of Gaunt and greatly directed the seafaring explorers on their way to the coasts of Africa and the Atlantic islands. In the bar of this small restaurant is only one picture and it is of an innocent vulgarity. The name of the restaurant is Fim do Mundo, the End of the World, because this village of Cascais, this point of land which we see from our balcony was the end of a world, the end of an ancient world.

All this is peculiarly beautiful, but I would like, now, to return home to my own country.[1]

Not yet, not yet. There was business to be done in London that had to do with William Shakespeare. Somewhere in the old city there was a church, the Church of St. Mary the Virgin Aldermanbury, which she and Wallace must find. The morning after they flew into London from Portugal, a fine May morning, they got into a taxi and asked to be taken there. The driver took them to St. Mary Aldermary. No, Aldermanbury. It too is by Christopher Wren. The church was not known to the driver, nor to the people he stopped to ask, but a long time later they found it. Here it was, but only its shell, and that not complete. An incendiary bomb had dropped close to it in the Blitz of 1940. It now stood without roof or windows, simply with broken walls. They walked into its enclosure, also of broken stone walls. They found a plaque lying flat to the ground (once a small, pretty garden), which stated that this garden was "full of memories of Shakespeare, and his friends, Heminge and Condell, wardens of this church." On a simple pedestal, two plaques recorded the parish and domestic events in the lives of John Heminge and Henry Condell, who had been buried here.

These two men were friends of William Shakespeare and partners with him in the Globe Theatre in Southwark. After he died, they collected his work and had it printed and so preserved for all time. Wallace and Ethel walked through the small enclosure where the garden had been, and stepped into the roofless, doorless church which opened dramatically to the sky, and then sat together for a long time on the bench in that garden. When they were ready, they went back to the taxi-man, who had been waiting, and they drove back to the hotel. Soon after that they flew home, and she wrote of this church on some flimsy, blue, air-mail paper, gave it to her typist, and her agent, Ruth Bendukov, in New York, sold it to the American periodical *The Reporter*.[2] (It was intended for the CBC, but they did not want it.)

She sent me to find St. Mary the Virgin Aldermanbury and sit in the garden. It had a strange peace.

One afternoon, about a year later, she opened one of the English periodicals which had come with the day's mail, and read that St. Mary the Virgin Aldermanbury was to be taken apart, stone by stone, and sent across the Atlantic Ocean to the United States of America, which was not Shakespeare's or Heminge's or Condell's country. It was to be built up again in a place called Fulton, in Missouri, which was Harry Truman's country. This, apparently, was because Winston Churchill (whose portrait, clipped from a magazine, was framed and hung on her living room wall) had made a speech there in 1946, and that was not a good reason. She dispatched letters of protest to the Lord Mayor of London, to the small, broken church's diocese, to Parliament, the Ecclesiastical Board, London County Council, and *The Times*. Even *The Times*, she commented, "seemed ignorant and indifferent." The church, stone by stone, was moved, and the world seemed to her a foreign place.

Chapter Twenty-four

Some Pussy

"**I**t interests me," she wrote me in the early 1960s, "to look back at—say—1938, when the person 'writing' here was a two-headed calf—and where do stories go? There was literally nowhere...That is the only thing I'm proud of, that with absolutely *no* outlet [here] I was just the same—published. And here we are! I think people have to make their own way a bit—one can*not* make too many outlets for too many not good enough 'stories.' The 'stories' must come first.

> I even remember feeling almost ashamed with conventional sassiety friends at having written a story. "She writes!" they said askance, and I remember one friend writing and saying "How brave you are! None of our lot ever do that!"—Really it was a piece of daring-do that young women writers, whipped and urged on now by Creative Writing classes and awards and "outlets" cannot know. One cannot picture it now—so soon!

She was passionate in her dislike, really distrust, of Creative Writing courses, which were springing up all over North American campuses. In a brilliant essay, "A Cat Among the Falcons," she defended her unfashionable stance. Writer Eric Nicol read it and commented, "Some pussy!" Her admirer and considered friend, the poet Earle Birney, who taught Creative Writing, felt betrayed and bewildered.

"I got a body blow from Ethel Wilson," he said more than twenty years later. "I had never known she had those opinions. I was then taking the offensive—battling UBC to have Creative Writing continue.

"It was quite clear that she liked me. Why did she do it? Well, I thought, she just doesn't understand the politics of the university. I felt and still feel that it was worthwhile to teach writing. If people have no talent you can't teach them to write. I quite agree with her. But that applies to all fields—chemistry—engineering. At least I selected my students.

"The very people who were fighting me were so gleeful—they would quote Ethel Wilson. Why did she attack me? I put it down to a certain naivity on her part."

She wrote George Woodcock, editor of *Canadian Literature* where the pussy appeared.

I am aware of speaking perhaps too confidently & impudently, chiefly about early & later education & the matter of instruction in the art of writing, about which I feel strongly. But I think you would wish your contributors to say what they mean, not Nothing...

Chiefly I feel diffident because my own basis of justification & achievement is very small, & then I bolstered courage by saying to myself, "Your first story appeared in the *Best British Short Stories* of that year, your last story is appearing in the *Best American Short Stories* of this year, & some of your small books have been published in various countries & languages[1]... That is nothing much, but it is a working basis of experience & opinion. Come now, take courage."

So I've said what I think about a tendency in letters on this continent that disturbs me—at least as regards my own country—because, entre nous, it seems earnest yet superficial, perhaps leading to a guided mediocrity, & likely to inhibit spontaneous expression & great achievement. You will realize that I do not think well of "creative writing."

...I hope you do not object to this expression of opinion...I remain gratefully but still with diffidence, Sincerely, Ethel Wilson.

She admired George Woodcock for his odds and ends, like erudition and humanity. She liked his magazine because it presented "opinions, divergencies, ideas of the kind we need," and she trusted him—"You do know—and of this I'm sure—that being published is not intrinsically important to me, but being published out of kindness would be unbearable." She once asked him to return a manuscript which she had sent him because she had since re-read it and found she disliked it. "It's jotty and spotty, ill-made and put together, and purely for personal interest. So please use the stamps enclosed and return it. Many thanks—Sincerely, Ethel Wilson."

It was returned and destroyed.

This new business of being a writer disturbed her. She wrote an essay, it seems for herself, because she never sent it out for publication. She called it "Admissions, Seabirds and People."[2]

> I have read and re-read with sympathetic pleasure a piece named *The Office*, by Alice Munro, appearing in *The Montrealer*. Why my heart warmed and expanded towards Mrs. Munro is because I have never before seen in print an admission of a frailty, a peculiarity, a folly, or an honesty which I share with her. I had thought that perhaps I alone—
>
> Alice Munro tells us of her difficulty in uttering the simple words "I am a writer." Oh how my heart warms to her. She says (better than I can) ". . . here comes the disclosure which I never find easy to make: I am a writer. That does not sound right. It sounds presumptuous, if not downright false. If only I could say with some workmanlike pride: I am a dentist. Try again. I write. Is that better? I *try* to write. Oh, worse: that makes it into some sort of cosy female hobby, and slathers on the hypocritical humility as well. There is no way—"
>
> This is true. There is the initial statement or question to be met—"I believe you write," or "Are you a writer?" That requires response of some kind. "Yes" or "No" avail nothing, for then you are prophetically aware of the follow-up. I am not ashamed that I write. I am glad, engrossed, and happy or frustrated, but something invades me and I cannot reply spontaneously that I write. My malaise is surely not due to the asker's obvious unfamiliarity with my books or is it? Surely surely not. I had not thought of that, but—one is human and confused, for it is not natural to introduce oneself and present qualifications. I have invented discouraging replies, such as "Sometimes," or "Oh yes," or even "I don't quite know," but any answer sounds gauche and presumptuous. I try to prevent further sociable enquiry when it is for the sake of

conversation, unless the asker really seems to want to know. As Rebecca West's little boy said "Change a subject, change a subject." I have my rights haven't I?

Some of my friends care a little for reading and not at all for writing. It is not necessary that they should care. They are always interesting and beloved without that. They ask no questions because they take such an activity as writing for granted (books are full of it), like coffee for breakfast. There are other friends who can easily permit or offer question and answer. Between us that is natural and very pleasant. They probably write. They certainly read. There is a rapport which does not fall down or turn away and there is never enough time. Doors are open, and if these simple questions are asked, they are answered without hesitations and equivocations on either side. Perhaps in the world of poets, all questions are simpler still. I do not know. Among poets it seems to me that there is a frank honesty to the point of furious difference, but no evasion except for the sake of amusement. Workers in prose seem to be milder than poets by nature, although no poet could be as furious as Dr. Leavis [F.R. Leavis, English critic and Cambridge University fellow].

It is in another world, the great ceaselessly vocal world known as "the social world," where conversation never stops, that the inhibiting difficulty arises, and the simple words "I believe you are a writer" and "What are you writing about?" — it is these simple words that can disconcert. The easiest question to answer in the world of drinks and conversation and the social and personal column is "Do tell me what you are writing now" in its various forms. It is engagingly spoken and you can detect the indulgence. The askers are often — not always — of those who do not in any case read what I write (why should they), but propinquity requires something suitable to be said, so they say it. It is undoubtedly kind. The askers are polite and sometimes beautiful. I like them but I do not want to tell them what I am writing. They cannot guess that their simple question is difficult to answer. The shame of reticence lies entirely on me. The questions may even be relatively sincere and it is I who am the phony.

I find writing to be a private and avidly solitary affair which I do not disclose even to my nearest and dearest one who does not accuse me by asking. He is busy too and does not really mind what I am writing about. That is perfect. Therefore the purely social question has a strangely un-private and stripping aspect. I have learned to deal with it fairly easily, thus:

"*Do* tell me, what are you writing about?"

"I am writing about an elephant."

"An elephant?"

"Yes."

This is a lie. The asker sheers off and murmurs, "Imagine, she says she is writing about an elephant! Why an *elephant*?" The good news spreads. I have been rude, and although my job is to know what goes on in people's inner selves, I do not know what goes on—not even in my own self with which I have lived so long. There is a risk in frequenting society however much you like people, but it is—on the whole—worth that minimal risk.

But in medical conventions—which I have attended for decades—when meeting with questioning doctor friends, for whom I have an unusual affection, I find it easy to answer, "You'd never ask a woman at a cocktail party if she was pregnant and if you did, she wouldn't tell you. It's really the same thing and I shall not tell you either." Defences are down and conversation goes merrily along. Is it perhaps that a writing woman is like a preaching dog—abnormal?

I have wondered, after these brief and frequent dodging encounters—why and whence comes this aversion to speaking the truth and answering a reasonable and polite question politely. Is it because one deeply reveres, and at so great a distance from achievement, the act and substance of writing? Whether the work is to be bought and sold, does not matter. It is the writing itself that matters. Therefore although one's efforts are by no means sacred, they are a trifle inviolate—however—in that they come from a place undefined and are being transmitted into a semi-permanence by some strange communication (unpatented) and during that process of curious transmission you are unable to explain. Leave it alone. I would be proud to be, but am not, a journalist, or an historian, or that magical person a good biographer. The answers might then be more frank. I am simply a writer but cannot easily say so. Why?

When faced with a document that demands one's occupation, I say "housewife" although I am not a very good housewife. If the document is of a literary nature, I hesitate, and then write "housewife," adding the words "and writer," although I know this is carrying veracity too far. But that is what the document wants to know—writer. Perhaps I am a better writer than housewife. This hesitancy may come from a divided life. One accuses oneself of amateurism as against professionalism by this absurd hesitancy. But I am a writer and had better admit it.

I have always found it difficult to join a society or club which is a writer's club. It denotes something organized and semi-public. A fear descends. The Society of Authors of Great Britain makes joining easy. Either you are an author or you are not an author, good or bad. You pay your fee if invited to do so, that is all. There is no hesitation, no self-consciousness. Much business is achieved. The air is cold, prosaic, competent and fresh. You sit down again and write, if you can.

The most teazing comment to encounter is "I do so envy you your writing—it's such a *lovely* hobby!" Curses rise within you—"It's not a hobby, damn you, it's next but one to my life. If I were a man you'd never say that." But you do not or should not utter those words. It is better to smile, or smirk if you cannot smile, and say No, it is not a lovely hobby.

How is it that true words can be suspect? The years provide only ambiguous answers.

A heron flies past the window and all hesitancies and ambiguities vanish. Look, his wings flap widely as no other bird flaps, he proceeds deliberately yet with strength and smooth speed on great gray flannel wings. How different are the characteristic flights of birds—slow, fast, agitated, calm. They fly alone or in companies. The Canada geese are flying south. I see them, now, this minute as they go together in a pointed arrowed skein, crying as they go. The heart lifts to where these bad tempered geese are flying. The heron flies alone, saying nothing, and even when—outside my bedroom window—two herons fly past each other, going to and coming from the fishing grounds, they do not stop to speak. On arrival at his heronry, the heron sometimes screams harshly in response to a chittering that is heard from the trees. The gulls, fine and carnal, and the small white terns, wheel and cut the air with beauty as with a superb line of Max Beerbohm's pen. Small seabirds appear agitated and speed away together above the water as if escaping from danger. The cormorants, who are really ugly birds, fly alone, a single handsome black arrow low above the water, never touching a wave, or they fly together when alarmed, with the utmost elegance in a low straight line. When they separate and go each to his own deadhead or rock, they sometimes stretch their black wings and hold them out like washing or the American eagle, for 40 or 60 odd seconds. Why? The answers do not reconcile. If the cormorants alight on a rock where there are gulls, the gulls—with a strange docility—occupy the upper part of the rock because the cormorants prefer the lower part. The gulls stand near but do not venture into the cormorants' area. They are much wiser than the children of men; they do not invade. The small black and white ducks swim slowly forwards in a straight and accurate line of 10, 20, 30 ducks, one behind the other like beads on a string. They turn as one and proceed back again but there is no visible sergeant-major. We do not know their means of communication from the head to the other end of the line. It is a mystery. They are cleverer in their own way than we are. Mallards are too domestic to be interesting. Sometimes an eagle sails very high, for some reason scrutinizing the ocean which is of a silken gray today, innocent and menacing.

All these birds we do indeed see from our high waterside windows in the city. Are we not lucky?

"And what are you writing about now?" People and seabirds. Of the visible and sub-visible world there is no end.

Chapter Twenty-five

Reading and Writing

As her arthritic pain became more debilitating, she escaped more and more into other people's writing. Virginia Woolf, she wrote Desmond Pacey, irritated her—although she was quick to say that this irritation could come, in part at least, from their different upbringings.

> An extremely feminine & narrow prejudice reminds me as I read her that her view of life is patrician to the point, sometimes, of not understanding. Perhaps my memory plays me false—but it seemed to me that she mis-read entirely Arnold Bennett (not in his more florid novels) and his view of poor persons, poor houses, poor places, mean streets, and their relative beauty and importance to those concerned—both dwellers and observers. She was surprisingly blind to all that. She was very noble in character, enormously gifted, fascinating, I think. I cannot maintain interest in the longer books although she has a heavenly pen. *To The Lighthouse* is written with a heavenly pen.

Ethel Wilson was not blind to the values of the poor, the undignified (in the eyes of the rich only), and of people with intensely colourful personalities. She wrote about a Miss Casey "bringing into the muted shop a blazing of bright eyes and [red] hair and leopard coat and humanity."[1]

She knew, and repeated, when addressing the Vancouver Institute on November 5, 1958, what Forster knew:

> To trust people is a luxury in which only the wealthy can indulge...

> ...The poor cannot always reach those they want to love, and they can hardly ever escape from those whom they love no longer...[But she had Maggie escape from Edward Vardoe in *Swamp Angel*.]

> ...I know that personal relations are the real life, for ever and ever...

> ...[The voice in the gondola] was the voice of one who had never been dirty or hungry, and had not guessed successfully what dirt and hunger are...

"Have you heard that voice?" Ethel Wilson asked her audience. "I have."

How that voice angered her despite, and amused her because of, its proximity. In "A Drink With Adolphus":

> An embarrassing moment occurred at once. Owing to the strike among waiters, all available experienced waiters are employed in the various hotels and restaurants and very few can be found for private parties. This accounts, I think, for the young hobbledehoy who served us at Mr. Adolphus Bond's party. When this Mrs. Gormer asked him (very rudely, I thought) what certain of the hors d'oeuvres contained, he said he did not know but thought they were hot ovaries. Mrs. Gormer seemed very much amused at this, but that shows the kind of woman she is.

And in another story, "Truth and Mrs. Forrester":

> "What did you do to Mrs. [Lee] Lorimer Smith?" asked Laura.
> "I sat beside her at lunch...and I said a terribly stupid thing. I said, 'Do you like Dylan Thomas?' And Lee stopped short and said 'Do I like what, who?' and I said, 'Dylan Thomas' and Lee said 'Does he live in town?' and she was terribly upset and thought that

there was someone I knew and she didn't, and she said 'For goodness sake Fanny, if this Thomas man is nice, do bring him to dinner. Your cousin Max is a dear of course, but living in the club he's always out when I want him, and sometimes I *do* need an extra man so badly.' And then she said to Margaret Fensom, 'What do you suppose, Fanny has a stray man up her sleeve, some Mr. Thomas,' and I said 'Oh he wasn't really in town but...' 'Well,' she said, 'if he doesn't live here he's no good to me,' and then she forgot all about him and was off on something else. It was very silly of me, because you can't make worlds mix, not at luncheons anyway; you've got to move into one or the other. I think 'social life,' Laura, is a most peculiar erection built of imponderables and invisibles..."

(Shortly before that story was written, Dylan Thomas was in fact in Vancouver and, rumour ran, took a society matron, possibly two, and someone mentioned a third, into his bed; otherwise he behaved with drunken abandon.)

Social pretence was nearly acceptable and sometimes fun. Literary pretence was something else, and she condemned it. She shuddered over the Canadian Authors Association, particularly in the early 1950s. Although she destroyed nearly all her papers before she died, she kept a special supplement of a trade journal, *The Canadian Author and Bookman*, which was devoted to the Canadian Author's Association Annual Meeting 1948. It contains a poem, "The Convention," by Lorraine Hooker.

> They pinned a ribbon on me
> And my name was rimmed in gold
> And I might have been an author
> Of some famous story told.
>
> There were brilliant minds about me,
> There was Costain, Pratt and Child.
> Such marvelous, famous people
> Brushed my shoulder — and they smiled.
>
> There were speeches, teas and chatting
> With the gayest social flair,
> And the great and little mingled
> And their "shop-talk" filled the air.

Now you ask me — how did it happen?
How come you were there to see?
Why, my dear, I am an author...
Or, at least...I'm going to be!

Alongside the poem she has scrawled, "This awful poem caused me to resign from such a jejune society." (But below that, she has written "1965 — Improved since — E.W.") The fact that she kept this among the papers which were for possible public scrutiny uncovers her passion. Even the word "author" sent her flying for her pen. She wrote (to Earle Birney) that "the collective idea of 'Writers' is pleasurably free from pretentiousness & possibly? — smugness. A room full of 'authors' is a thing to flee from — a room full of 'writers' presents free and disarming possibilities of flexibility. What is there that is grim & humourless about 'authors' en masse. Something, undoubtedly. But one must make allowances for taste." (The Society of Authors in Great Britain was an old and venerable association and was not to be compared to the Canadian Authors' Association in her own young country. Great Britain's "authors" were writers to her mind.)

She did not like the way the novel, in the 1950s, was developing. She was open to change, it was not that. She admired the coldness and ruthlessness of I. Compton Burnett and her extraordinary presentation of "plot," if it could be called that. And she had been quick to recognize the brilliance of Joyce. What worried her now was that some writers were examining their belly-buttons rather than their imaginings. She wrote an unpublished essay which she named "Enemies of Promise."

This may not be the great day of the novel or — more specifically — the great day of characters in a novel; I don't think it is; but it is an exciting day of the novel and we scuttle hopefully around this enchanting ploy and try to find out what is happening. A young boy fixed me with his eye some time ago and said: "I'm glad to see you, Mrs. Wilson. I am told you are an author. I have never seen an author before. I thought they were all dead." I was modestly pleased by this remark until I thought "Perhaps they are."

Now too there was the nearly orgasmic arrival of Symbolism and, in answer to a university student who had written for her opinions, she said, "[I] began to think that the preoccupation with symbolism, which had begun to manifest itself in critical work (of which I have always read a great deal, with pleasure and detachment) was becoming rather silly. A conscious fashion, no less."

She continues the thought in an unpublished essay, "On Not Being Educated":

> "We cannot live by Freud alone, there is still the mystery," says Christopher Fry who is not a rationalist. And Bertrand Russell who is, I suppose, a rationalist, says the same thing with his own devastating elegance. And I, living for decades non-educated on this new charming brash and wooded shore of the gulf of Georgia, I say so too.[2]

And then she had fun, in an essay which she didn't bother even to have typed. She named it "Hunt the Symbol."

> My first active experience with S. [symbolism] in its vogue form was while talking to an adult student of writing. He said to me, "Gosh, why do they bother all the time with symbol, mostly sexual. I'm getting so that I can't even look at a boiled egg without blushing."
>
> Now I skip many S. experiences including my own alleged and unmeaning perpetration thereof and move to a copy of the *Spectator* a year or two ago. In it there is a delightful piece by that terrifying writer William Golding. In this piece, which he named Grades and Parnassum he has abandoned terror. He had been for some months a travelling lecturer at some universities on this continent. He was impressed by the pervading impact of S. as found in the Eng. Lit. courses of these universities. He had never met that kind of S. before, only the natural kind. He recounts...his experiences as a listener at a writing class—"Jake, I didn't quite get the symbolism of the hair on the bathmat."
>
> "I was a bit worried about the plumbing, Jake."
>
> "It's a sex image."
>
> "I don't quite get the symbolism of the stars throwing down their spears."
>
> "Well Harry I think it's an obvious sex image."

But of course she was not blind to symbolism. It could lie, unconsciously on the part of the writer, and do its powerful work. But it must be "for those masters who feel its power," she said in a talk which she called "Somewhere Near The Truth." "If it is there, you can't stop it; but it cannot, I think, be satisfactorily imported."

In *Swamp Angel* she thought that she might have found it, although perhaps not. In a "Ms. note" she wrote:

Was it because we ourselves had a little revolver inscribed with the words Swamp Angel which had belonged to my husband's grandfather and to someone before him; & because in my enraging and unforgiveable folly we have lost it irretrieveably? Or was it because, once, I had to make a decision, alone, and tossed a small and lethal looking steel revolver from a high rock into the sea so that it should do no more harm? I assure you, it was a delightful and unique sensation, tossing a strange revolver up into the sky and seeing it fall down into and through the blue ocean — or did the book arise because?

I have tried, very hard, to find out about both those incidents, asking everyone who knew her and Wallace, both slightly and very well, but nobody knew when or why they came about. In a letter to John Gray from Bowen Island (August 22, 1953) Ethel Wilson alludes to throwing a gun into the sea, saying it was done by her on a bright day and was a wonderful experience, "but this was not our Swamp Angel." Eleven years later, in a letter to Desmond Pacey, she tells a tale about the gun.

I hope you have time to listen to this little story. My husband's grandfather (who was old when Wallace knew him) had a little nickel and mother of pearl revolver, very old, and on this little gun were inscribed in a flowing script the words Swamp Angel. He gave it to my husband. I became very much attached to this object — very very interesting to me because there it lay, inert, incompetent, but with a story (perhaps danger, defense, death) implicit. We know nothing of its origins, I had it always in sight.

When the last war came and my husband joined up again, at the time of his joining there appeared in the papers a very peremptory order from the police that the possessor of any kind of firearm whatever must turn it in on pain of penalty. Well, I never thought the police would keep a useless outdated weapon, and I asked my husband to take it in for registry.

He said "What nonsense! no one could fire that revolver!" And I said, "Oh, please! If you're going away and for some reason I got into trouble over not having turned in our little gun, it'll be just one thing more — I couldn't bear it." So he thought I was very silly but, to oblige me, took the gun in, and they kept it!

Well, there was too much to occupy me, but I did grieve for my little gun, and eventually it became more mine and more alive because I could make a book about it, and I didn't miss it any more. The gun continued to live again, in a sense. (Very soon of course, the book itself took over.)

And although she mentioned the Swamp Angel revolver again, she said no more about it. It and the other were part of her person not to be revealed, perhaps because it was secret, perhaps because it could still harm another person. She was too careful.

Now she was speaking out about herself within her craft, and about her craft itself. These are some of the observations she shared with audiences and friends:

I understand so well [she said and repeated, using different words, more than several times] what the Canadian novelist Mordecai Richler said when he was asked "Are you a Jewish writer or a Canadian writer?"
He answered, "Neither. I am a writer."

Now I regard region as a very rich and potent affair in writing—for those writers who are affected by Place; some are not...[it is] quite different from what we regard as provincialism. I can only illustrate my clumsy remarks by great examples of regional writers. One may, of course, say that Proust really wrote about Time. But Proust took his text from Place—a room, a limited area of his particular Paris, the 2 little towns of Cambray and Balbec. [She points to the regionalism of Mark Twain, Thomas Hardy, and of Emily Bronte who was "bounded narrowly by space & unbounded in herself"]...there it is, writers of books that are both regional & universal, all writing with great and various power, but none of them writing with an eye on home or a national public. And so I think it should be in Canada. A "writer" simply writes.[3]

We all—at different stages in our lives—undergo inner conflict, or, at least we should. This is inescapable unless we are complete simpletons...I believe that fictional books are also sometimes written for sheer delight in writing—just as a person swims for the love of it—from a joy in and the selective use of our language, and because of an abiding interest in, partial understanding of, projection into, curiosity about (—what would one do without prepositions?), identification with and compassion for our fellow human beings, and not through our own conflicts alone—which may, none the less, have given power, and understanding of the strange human predicament. The human predicament is universal and also intensely personal and curious, and is the subject of all serious fiction.

And when her novels were done and published and criticized, she said that they had come about in these ways:

The Innocent Traveller
...I wrote the book on account of my great interest in [my] family, also for the benefit of unborn generations if they should chance to be born and cared to read the record which might otherwise be lost; and because this story was typical of many families coming to British Columbia from the United Kingdom, for of such is *this* kingdom, here, in this place, to a large degree.

Tuesday and Wednesday
I cannot truly say how I came to write it. Perhaps it was because I observed increasingly the irrelevance of cause and effect amongst us, outside the world of science and inside the world of human relations—and the instability and suggestibility of emotion and behavior...Or perhaps it was through my observation of a certain man and a certain woman at different times and places in the town. I do not know who they were...They never saw me and I do not exist for them. I'm sure they never met each other. Yet I seemed to know wherein the fabric of their lives consisted.

Lilly's Story
I know exactly how this book came to be written. In *The Innocent Traveller* there occurs a character called Yow who gives some colour to the book. I recollected, some time after *The Innocent Traveller* was published, a terminal sentence in a chapter. It ran something like this: "Yow stole the bride's trousseau, bit by bit, and gave it to a white lady friend. Yow, unfortunately, had to go to prison, and so the white lady friend formed other connections."
What connections? (I thought).

Swamp Angel
I don't know how it originated except that I love fly-fishing which is a marvelous thing in life, unique in the deep communion of the senses and rich in contemplation and memory; it is all that.

196

Love and Salt Water

...my reason for writing the book was peremptory. I have a life-long love for this province of ours which I share with many people, this British Columbia, as if it were a person, as it is—and a person with infinite variety and inference. I had already written with some verisimilitude about the Upper Country which I most love, but there is that about the salt sea and our own coasts...[and] I found it desireable—for my own peace, I think, or at least for my own satisfaction—to commit this to paper. Thinking of that, I saw, one day, in Stanley Park...a father, mother, and little daughter, walking together in health, companionship and unusual physical beauty...I had never written about just such people as this before...but I decided to make them my story, by the sea, whatever might happen to them. Nothing much, I thought, might happen to them, any more than happens to most such pleasant people whom we meet daily in our lives...I wanted nothing identifiable with any one amongst the many hundred such whom I might know, and, in some sort, do know, in Vancouver; these were anonymous people...they would, no doubt, fall into some of the traps that life sets for us all...In the course of the story I made three or four fair-sized deletions of sections which gave the story more depth, it is true, and this I did for reasons important to myself, technical or other.

She ended by saying to her audience: "There may be some questions which I will try to answer, or evade."[4]

Chapter Twenty-six

Happinesses

Eldorado Arms in the 1960s was an old hotel overlooking Okanagan Lake. It had the same rambling generosity as their hotel on Vancouver Island, which overlooked the sea. Between their last trip to Portugal, in 1956, and 1962, Wallace had been hospitalized by four more heart attacks, and so they retreated to this quiet hotel Up Country. It was not far from their fishing places, but they did not fish now because she could not get into a boat and he should not be far from help.

The hotel had a tradition of good plain food and generally well-behaved and well-heeled guests, whose children, if only by osmosis, were usually quietly behaved and played ball and croquet on the green lawn which moved softly down to the sky-blue lake. (In the lake they shrieked to all the heavens.) Beyond the lake, the hills were scorched brown, and beyond them was a valley of green orchards. The history of the valley is English. At the turn of this century, Remittance Men, as they were called, came out from England and cleared the valley and planted apple, pear, and plum trees. They made wooden troughs to bring rain and river water down from the hills, they prospered a little, and then they went off to fight for King and Country in the first world war. During their absence nearly all of the orchards died. The troughs coming down from the hills rotted. It wasn't until the end of the second world war that young people began to look again at the land, plant vigorous young trees, pipe up water from the lake, spray their trees with pesticides, and prosper. It was again a pleasant valley of green promise, and the Wilsons enjoyed driving through it.

Eldorado Arms had a few cabins which stretched across the lawn. The Wilsons always took the one farthest from the hotel. Here they were far enough away from the other guests, some of whom they knew slightly in town and did not want to strain to know better here. They sat in two deck-chairs on the grass, and read, and watched the children and birds and swimmers without being disturbed.

Early in the 1960s, not long after I was married and caring for two boys and suddenly two babies, the Wilsons invited me up to Eldorado and enclosed an aeroplane ticket. They met me at the small airport outside of Kelowna and, it being a searing mid-afternoon, we went straight into town and a cool beer parlour. It was unusually garish, but the biggest and most cheerful in town. They thought this would please me. They themselves loved a beer on a hot day, and they liked watching people. Someone misbehaved nearly every time they went in. Then we drove to Eldorado Arms, parked, and walked to their small cabin. They apologized. They had tried to get me a room of my own in the main hotel, but all the rooms were booked. They showed me to a tiny half-room at the back of the cabin, which is where I slept.

In such tight quarters you notice even small irritations which erupt, or don't erupt but are nevertheless there, between the other people. I stayed with the Wilsons for four days and nights and know that they were easily content with each other. Some years earlier I must have had an inkling of this, because I asked her if she and Dr. Wilson had ever had a fight. "No. I could not stand that," she answered, nearly passionately. Up at Eldorado, another person asked Wallace the same question, and he replied as if he were shocked, "No. Why should we?"

That person, Peggy MacIntosh (who had noticed Ethel writing in the car when Dr. Wilson was seeing her sick husband in the 1930s), mentioned an incident which she found revealing about Wallace and Ethel. She was helping to manage the hotel when a long-distance call came through for Wallace. She hurried across to the cabin, but only Ethel was there. Ethel said that she thought he had gone into town.

"They said it was an urgent call. Do you know where he'd be in town?" Mrs. MacIntosh asked. Mrs. Wilson said that she didn't really know but, "You might look in the park — on the bench which looks over the lake." He was there.

Those days, for me, went as quickly as only easy days go. Wallace and

I swam—he with an inflated belt around him in case of another heart attack—while she sat in her deck-chair and watched. We read silently, and he and she in flashes aloud, and talked aimlessly but sometimes with purpose about babies and fishing and Hamlet and Neville Cardus, the extraordinary music and cricket critic for the Manchester *Guardian*, whose autobiography they had bought at Hatchard's in Piccadilly when they were in London in 1947, and which was one of the first books they loaned me. And many of the things that I have told you, she told me during that holiday. Both were thoughtful in all ways, seemingly wise, never prying, sensitive to me and themselves.

A few months later, in September 1961, she received a telegram, which she first took over the telephone.

TAKE GREAT PLEASURE IN INFORMING YOU OF YOUR SPECIAL SELECTION OF ONE OF TEN CANADIANS TO RECEIVE SPECIAL CANADA COUNCIL MEDAL FOR DISTINGUISHED WORK IN ARTS HUMANITIES OR SOCIAL SCIENCES stop FURTHER DETAILS IN LETTER stop ANNOUNCEMENT WILL BE MADE IN PRESS IMMEDIATELY
CLAUDE BISSELL CHAIRMAN THE CANADA COUNCIL

A few days later she received a cheque for $2000. Half of it she kept for herself and Wallace, the other half she gave to the library at UBC ($200), two small literary magazines, *Tamarack Review* and *Prism*, and individual people whose names she and Wallace did not mention. She wrote to the Council's director.

September 30

Dear Dr. Trueman—

I wonder if you can realize the surprised pleasure that the Canada Council has conferred on an individual who now, perforce, lives quietly & does not expect to make much appearance in the great world. (I'm talking of arthritis, really.)

The large cheque arrived today. May I tell you that it will give me further pleasure to be able to return a certain amount into the cultural stream in ways I had wished to do—but I assure you that most of this generous cheque will be kept & applied to my—our—opportunities, or needs, or pleasures. You will think it is superfluous to tell you this—but I am overcome with the

possibilities & *charm* of this large cheque from the Canada Council.
  I only wish that my attainments were greater & more pertinent, but it is an old truth that one can only do well what one can do.
  Again my acknowledgement & my thanks—sincerely
                                                    Ethel Wilson

She was now seventy-four, and too crippled to go out to buy a dress specially for the presentation. So she went into her closet and chose a long, gray-blue dress with long sleeves and a full, pleated skirt, which she had bought in London in 1955. And then, in February 1962, she and Wallace flew across Canada, coming down first in Toronto. They saw their friends and came to dinner at our house, and for some reason I remember that she asked me to have only a simple dinner because she and Wallace could no longer eat rich or spicy foods. So I had roast beef and Yorkshire puddings. I think I remember because they acted as if they hadn't eaten for days and never so well.

They flew on to Ottawa, then drove through streets banked high with snow to the CPR's Chateau Laurier, which Ethel Bryant the orphan had seen sixty-four years earlier, as she sailed up the St. Lawrence River with her grandmother. On the night of February 19, Ethel put on her London dress and Wallace his dinner jacket, and they took a taxi out to the Country Club on Aylmer Road. With most of the other special medal winners—former Governor General Vincent Massey, the ethnologist Marius Barbeau (who had caused her dismay at Nan Cheney's house over tea nearly a quarter of a century earlier), historian and French Canadian nationalist Lionel Groulx, painter A.Y. Jackson, Bess Harris (who accepted the medal on behalf of her husband Lawren, who was too ill to attend), musician Wilfred Pelletier, composer Healey Willan, poet E.J. Pratt, and, posthumously, Brooke Claxton, the Council's first chairman—they sat down among eighty people to dine on green turtle soup, sole meunière, braised beef tenderloin, green peas, buttered onions, parsley potatoes, heart of lettuce salad, and frozen rum mousse, and their glasses were kept brimming with fine French wines. Returning home, for the last time by train, they were most content.

About the time that they were on the train I was told, in confidence, by someone of dubious reliability, that the young novelist Mordecai Richler had proposed her for that special medal. (I wrote him recently, but he did not answer that particular question.) I wrote and told her, in confidence of course. A few weeks later I received a confusing letter from her. It took several readings to realize that she was referring to the enormous pleasure she received through learning that this young and clever writer, Mr. Richler, whom she thought, incidentally, might like B.C. better than Ontario, had such respect for her work.

She never did become smug with honours, not even when she received the Lorne Pierce Medal from the Learned Societies. And when Queen Elizabeth herself gave her (and others) a silver pin for being the wife of a former president of the Canadian Medical Association, she simply wrote me that it was "a lovely surprise," and "gosh we do deserve it for 1½ years' hard work," but that the Queen, "poor lamb," must have been much too busy for such a slight occasion.

Chapter Twenty-seven

A Last Bird

In 1964 she wrote me that, once more, Dr. Wilson had been sent to hospital, but now he was home again. He had "been ill most of the year," she said, "but now hope plain sailing."

"He is too unconquerable, & if a friend in trouble wanted him he would try to get the car out & go. I've forbidden him to answer the telephone, as already he's got enmeshed — But he does seem promisingly better . . ."

In 1965 she wrote her friend Margaret Laurence, whom she had praised and encouraged privately and in print, that, although the Learned Societies were then meeting in Vancouver, she could not get to the meetings.

"I am appallingly & painfully lame, hardly walkable, have been in hosp. & all kinds of things — better in some respects, worse in others — so I wasn't able to attend — Wallace is better enough — a coronary is not a thing easily & safely recovered from." In that same letter, toward the end, she scrawls, "another attack this a.m."

Several months later she again wrote to Margaret Laurence. "If only my dear W. would go straight ahead. It is really hard to hear sensibly & brightly. Much love — E.W." (For several years now she had been reluctantly and impatiently wearing a hearing aid, whose high-pitched buzz could sometimes be heard nearly across the room. She despised it.)

That year they sold the car (a big 1957 Buick with power steering) and left Kensington Place because both had fallen on the stairs there. They moved into a light-filled apartment on Point Grey Road, which gave them a spectacular view of the sea and mountains, but not as intimate a sight of the boats and seabirds. Because both were in nearly constant physical distress, they were restless in their beds and so had to separate at night. Wallace, with nurses attending around the clock, slept in the bedroom. Ethel slept in the den.

In January 1966, one of Wallace's nurses had just finished helping Ethel bathe, and had got her into her wheelchair, when she suddenly said to Mrs. Marshall, "There's something wrong here." Ethel was having a stroke. Mrs. Marshall and the nurse got her back to the den and into her bed, and called the doctor.

"He did not come for a long time," Mrs. Marshall told me. "Dr. Wilson did not go in to see her. He waited until the doctor had come, and he had talked to him, and he still didn't go in. He was frightened that her features were altered. They weren't."

A few weeks later, Ethel, determined to fight, wrote Margaret Laurence in a shaky but legible hand:

> Margaret — you darling —
> What a happy-making letter. Bless you for it. And I needed it, not having experienced a *stroke* before. Believe me it's hellish — No moving, no can do, no walking, no sitting! even, everything on left is immobile (fingers etc. and/or cruelly painful, therapy a torture. Rt. hand more or less O.K. No squinting, etc., but sight deteriorating, cutting down blessed reading. I see W. seldom — the brave darling is very frail — he has no stroke thank God. A glimpse of him my joy...Can write a little but how nice it wd. be to write a book. But not today thank you. Lots of love and luck.

There was no signature.
On March 8 Wallace wrote John Gray.

> Hark the Herald Angels Sing!
> We secured a wonderful physiotherapist and she is really doing wonders with Ethel's left arm and leg. Ethel can now hold things in her left hand, close and open her fist, and even, with an effort, scratch her nose.
> She is also getting some movement out of her leg and her eyesight

is steadily improving; so the goose hangs high in the Wilson family, and the next stage which will take time, of course, will be for the physiotherapist to get Ethel standing and then in the wheelchair and out into the living room...

By the way I am reading with great interest Barbara Tuchman's "The Proud Tower"...

Wallace once told their friend Reggie Tupper, whose wife Isabel was ill, that there was nothing as easy to bear as someone else's pain, which was a way to help a man gather courage and strength. So he gathered his fortitude now. But he was intensely worried about what would happen to Ethel if he died. Soon after Ethel's stroke, Mrs. Marshall came into his bedroom and found him weeping.

"I had never seen him weep. I have never seen anyone weep like that," she said to me. " 'Marsh [my children's name for Mrs. Marshall],' he said. 'Look after her for me. Please look after her'."

He had dinner in the study with Ethel on the night of March 11 and, as he came out of the room, Mrs. Marshall was in the living room and heard him say, "Goodbye Ethel."

"He did not say goodnight, as he always said. He never saw her again."

The next morning Mrs. Marshall did "a big wash." When she came back into the apartment, she saw Dr. Wilson in his bedroom, sitting in a chair. He asked Mrs. Marshall to put him to bed. She said she would get one of the nurses and he said, firmly, "No, will you put me back to bed?"

"He slept," Mrs. Marshall said, "and then he had lunch. I was filling tobacco in his pipe. He complained of pain and the nurse gave him a needle. And he died then."

Sunday, March 13

John [Gray] Dear — my Darling died yesterday. How glad I would be to join him —

Yours with love —
Ethel

Dr. Wallace Wilson's funeral was held in Christ Church Cathedral, which is directly across the street from the Methodist Church (which now did not exist) where he and Ethel had been quietly married forty-five years before. The church was packed with people who paid tribute to a man who, to some, was a kind doctor, to some a great man, to others a loved man, and other things too. Ethel was too ill to go, and Mrs. Marshall stayed home with her. It would have been Dr. Wilson's wish that she do this, Mrs. Marshall thought. She said that Mrs. Wilson did not know, or did not want to know, that a funeral was being performed for her husband.

Because she knew Wallace would want this, and so did she, and that he would be firm about it, Ethel Wilson tried to live with patience for the present, and gratitude for the past. But she could not always do this. She wrote her friends:

In my heart there is a kind of fighting.

I read & re-read your wonderful present of Mike Pearson's Memoirs; after reading it three times, I embarked on it the fourth time.

I look back & adore my 45 years of intense happiness, more than most women have. How wonderful he was. The doctors have published a marvelous memorium of him, which helps me daily.

A horrid Socred called Waldo Skillings has called Dr. Macdonald [UBC's president] a "lame duck" in public because he said the Provincial Government should give more to UBC. Now, although one may or may not have been wildly enthusiastic about Dr. M., what a nasty thing to say, & highly smellingly political.

I have been so silent, I've *felt* so silent & not just to you my dear love but all those I love...

To tell the truth, my dear, my one great desire is to join him, & every day when I look at him [his photographs were around her] my heart aches to join him.

Mrs. Marshall has looked after us in a way to make one humble & grateful.

That first summer, when I came out from Toronto, I went to see her right away. We had, as usual, tea, and then I had a whisky and she a sherry. She turned to me and said, "If I am not here when you come back again, don't be sad. It is what I want." She looked me directly in the eye and without sadness.

On December 6, 1967, I received a letter from her: "I never, never thought that the absence of my dear, accompanied by physical helplessness would be so unbearable—*and* so inexcusable. He planned everything for my happiness. I am just very stupid & ashamed, because it would be hard for him. But the days pass—'a day's march nearer home,' that is incontrovertible...

"I'm sorry, Mary, that stories don't pour forth as by nature. It enrages me that now that I have more spare time than ever in my life, I have no desire or ability to 'write'...A bare desert, & nothing growing in it, not a weed, nor a flower, nor a ponderosa pine."

On Christmas day 1967, she wrote Margaret Laurence that the editor of the magazine *Habitat* had asked her for an article on Vancouver as a young city. "I pleaded the stroke but he bade me try—so I tried. It appeared last week. My small finale."

In February 1969 she wrote me:

> I had today one of Wallace's letters, just *perfect* & charming sent to a friend...& the copy was taken off with one of those [photostat] machines, hand-written & all, it has filled me (the sight & words of it) with joy & sorrow. Yes, Life can be unbearable—& also how divine...
>
> It is marvelous to have that letter with his ordinary...signature but shattering too.
>
> Dammit, having too much imagination & vision.

She tried, sometimes valiantly, to get on with life, or at least to make a pretence at it, but she had written that she would like to have the freedom of a bird and she was confined by pain.

Seven years after Wallace's death, Ethel was moved to a nursing home. She astonished her nurses and friends because she went without a murmur, perhaps still exercising the orphan's self-discipline.

A few days after she was moved in, I went to see her. She had taken her photographs of Wallace and her favourite books, some from her childhood, and several small pieces of oak furniture which fitted into the small room. When I arrived, she was sitting in her wheelchair, meticulously groomed, watching the door. She beckoned to me, and smiled. The whisky and sherry decanters and two of her cut-glass whisky glasses were out, and there was fresh ice in her Chinese green bowl which they had always used for ice. We started to talk, and then I saw her eyes on the door, which was still open to the corridor. Our conversation stopped. I turned to see what she was looking at and saw a very old and thin woman who was peering, with oddly unseeing eyes, into the room. Then the woman turned and started to walk away, her profile to us. She slowly opened, closed, opened her mouth, and disappeared. I turned back to Ethel Wilson, who was watching me.

"Look," she said. She opened, closed, opened her mouth, her face turned in profile to me. "You see," she said, letting out that high laugh, "a trout going upstream."

She had not been there long when her mind seemed to fail. Many people complained that she did not know them, and yet she did know those she was very fond of. Then she had recurring strokes and she and the world shut each other out.

Ethel Wilson died in the nursing home at 7:30 on a Monday morning, December 22, 1980, a few weeks before her ninety-third birthday. Two days after Christmas, the retired Anglican Archbishop Somerville took her funeral at Christ Church Cathedral. He had taken Wallace's funeral fourteen years earlier, and the church had been packed. Now there were no more than forty people in the chapel on the west side of the church, and most of these were the children and grandchildren of her cousins. She had asked, in a letter attached to her will, that one of Elgar's "Variations" and "Sheep May Safely Graze" be played, and that was done by the organist, but not well. She was cremated, as she had instructed, with a used cigar box containing some of Wallace's letters.

One of the greatest of all field naturalists formed the theory that the birds of these migrations—leaving their habitat at a season when food was ample and the climate salubrious, leaving as it were against their will—were drawn in migration by a sense of polarity, that is, by the strong influence of the magnetic poles exerted upon their species at certain times. The birds are uncertain, restless; they are forced to go. One last bird remains alone, restless, nervous, undecided, wishing to go, awaiting something. After pitiful agitation the bird at last rises and follows the flight with confidence. There are certain things about which one can only form a theory.[1]

Epilogue

George Santayana said, "Even what we still think we remember will be remembered differently; so that a man's memory may almost become the art of continually varying and misrepresenting his past, according to his interests in the present. This, when it is not intentional or dishonest, involves no deception. A point of view and a special lighting are not distortions."

Appendix

Ethel Wilson: A Profile

by Dorothy Livesay

Ethel Wilson's comments
1 *that*

When a doctor's wife begs her husband to leave the room, "so[1] he won't be bored," while she reads a chapter of her book to some younger writers, an echo comes to mind of other scenes, other drawing rooms. Is the voice that of Jane Austen? Or Mrs. Gaskell? You pinch yourself and realize that this is Vancouver, 1952: and the quiet, well-modulated voice, the chiselled face with its serenity and poise, the well-groomed grey hair, belong to Ethel Wilson: and this story about "Lily" which holds the young people intensely interested, is a novella to be published this spring by Macmillan, under the title: "The Equations of Love." Before that the titles were "Hetty Dorval" and "The Innocent Traveller."

Ethel Wilson's style is in her voice. She never wrote at all, nor thought of doing so, until she was in her forties. But as a girl she

2 *I'm so sorry. I never crocodiled with Crofton House being a day girl— any old City girl would exclaim! It was at boarding school in England.*
3 *delete—pioneer.*
4 *delete and say Southport.*

5 *May I say "one who loves & cultivates fine writing," loving as in "aimer" rather than the "pastime." I did it more for a private passion than a pastime.*

6 *delete "had to take" and say "took"*
7 *add "the"*
8 *delete and add "lousy doctor's—actually W. was not a gen. pract. although he so greatly [sic]*

9 *delete-and add "a sense of proportion"*

remembers walking "in crocodile"[2] with Vancouver's Crofton House Students and as soon as the walk was well under way a friend would cry: "Now Ethel, begin!" And she would start on the next instalment of a story made up as she went along, through the decorous pioneer[3] streets of the West End[4]. This habit of "talking a story" out loud undoubtedly helped to establish that simple and conversational style, classic rather than modern, so evident in "The Innocent Traveller." But because she was not brought up in an age or social environment that expected young girls to become artists, the girl Ethel Bryant never perhaps took herself seriously. She has remained, even now, with a growing body of work behind her, a happy amateur. An amateur, not in the debased sense of the word today, but in the true French sense: "one who cultivates fine writing as a pastime."[5]

When her first book appeared, in 1947, a former schoolmate wrote: "I am so pleased that at least one of us has had the courage to do something queer." But to Mrs. Wilson herself there is nothing queer about her interest in writing. True, she was brought up in a protected and conventional way by elderly aunts—the pioneer Malkin family. Later, by marrying Dr. Wallace Wilson, she had to take[6] on[7] social and professional responsibilities as a general practitioner's[8] wife. But her writing, she feels, has never been an escape from all this, but "simply an extension of it."

"I am proud of my strict upbringing," she explains, "because as long as one feels loved, a conventional home life is salutary, gives assurance[9]. And then," her eyes twinkle, "One can always move outwards from it!" She did move outwards, finding life "terribly interesting," both actually and vicariously. "I never thought of writing in all those early years because I enjoyed so many things in life; tennis, badminton, swimming—before this arthritis came! And even now I[10] can manage to go fly-fishing with my husband...But of course the one[11] interest (that has kept us so close together, and)[12] that has kept me aware of writing, has been reading[13]. Reading aloud, reading in bed..." and here an Irishism burst out as she spoke for a moment of Proust: "I was reading him before I was awake!"

The habit of reading started early in the little girl, daughter of a Methodist minister, The Rev. R.W. Bryant, a native of Staffordshire[14]. She had been born in South Africa where her mother died. The widower took the child back to England and was for a time in Wales, then in London. At[15] six (or so) she remembers sitting in his study as he wrote a sermon, and pulling out a book (to read)[16]: "Ivanhoe."[17] From then on, without stop or stint, Ethel read.

The great break in her life occurred after the death of her father, when as a child of eight her maternal grandmother brought her out to Canada; to the rigours of raw new life in Vancouver. Her aunts, particularly the "Topaz" of "The Innocent Traveller," were themselves great readers and Matthew Arnold was table talk. But the delights of Shakespeare the young Ethel was to discover for herself. Along with Samuel Butler and Anthony Trollope, Shakespeare is the one she turns to most often; and of him she has written, (in a letter to the writer:)

"Of course when one says 'one does not like novels'—it is (only the goodish or the good current novel)[18]. Because the Great Novels are incredible masterpieces, aren't

10 add "hope"

11 delete "one"
12 bracketted phrase means delete—"I'd like to keep our personal relation out— they're too private & important
13 add "decades of reading"

14 Lincolnshire—really irrelevant but my mother was Staffordshire
15 add "the age of" & delete bracketted words—
16 delete bracketted phrase & add "and reading"
17 sitting there on the floor, skipping the big words, but engrossed from beginning to end—

18 delete she comments— "not quite a fair statement is

212

it?" Although I was frank with you personally I'm afraid the statement in public sounds superior & pretentious — may we change it? — equally true.

they, to be read and re-read. I feel first Hamlet, second, Hamlet...third, Antony and Cleopatra...and then the Great Novels and of course many others such as the Old Wives Tale. And then a big big drop."

A love of English literature in its great variety, a respect for "the integrity of the language" came early to this girl with her English roots. In her 'teens she was sent back to England to a girls' school of high academic standing, and there wrote her Junior Cambridge[19] examinations, (specializing in English and French)[20]. On her return to Canada there was nothing very dramatic for her to do in a Vancouver that scarcely stood on its economic, let alone cultural feet.

19 and London Matriculation.
20 delete this phrase — to be quite accurate in spite of getting what were called "honors" it was just the regular course.
21 add — "in the public school"

"I taught[21] school for some years; there were 50 or 60 little ones in the classes there. I remember, when Point Grey was forest, that a big boy — big among little children, not educated — used to walk in three miles and one time he had just killed a bear who was after the pigs." But that period of outward independence, when she was still living in the circle of aunts, left no very strong impression. She was swept into a different life of domesticity, travel and social activity when she married Dr. Wilson. "One had to be phone[22] conscious, (planning each day according to the doctor's hours)[23]. I had little time to myself." But there is little doubt that the time was well spent, (absorbing a "feel" for other people's troubles as seen through the eyes of a gentle, sympathetic doctor)[24]; and developing sympathy and interest in people, in the eccentricities of character. Eventually it was to come out.

22 I like a prig, cannot use the word "phone" so that as a quotation I have to change it
23 brackets mean delete
24 Again throughout I fear a "posture" — & I know W. would maybe delete — the sentence works out all right without it.

"My first story, written in the thirties, was in the "*asinine genre*." It was called *I Just Love Dogs* and I sent it (for fun)[25] to the New Statesman and Nation. What a delight when

25 delete

they took it and when later O'Brien re-printed it in his *Best British Short Stories*, 1938 — beside writers like Eric Knight, James Hanley, Elizabeth Bowen and H.E. Bates."

Mrs. Wilson's first written book was actually her second to be published: "The Innocent Traveller." It was drawn largely from family history, re-constructed with a loving and ironic touch. At first the book took the form of sketches, but when some of these were published in England, the publisher suggested there was material here for a novel. In the meantime, while under (great)[26] stress (helping her husband organize)[27] a medical convention, (Dr. Wilson was President of the Canadian Medical Association, 1946-47), Mrs. Wilson was seized with what might be called "an escape mechanism." At any rate, the heroine "Hetty Dorval" took possession of her. In three weeks of pouring British Columbia rain, the book was written. After Canadian publication it appeared in England under the Macmillan impress, in 1948. "The Innocent Traveller" was published in 1949.

Also set in British Columbia, but dealing with very different social strata, is the new book, "The Equations of Love." The characters in it, denisons of Vancouver's Hastings Street have simply "come" to the writer's mind and taken possession. "Of course," she explains, "I have *seen* them — coming out of a hotel, a beer parlour, a bus, and[28] once I have seen the face, then the character and life (of these people)[29] has unrolled before me."

In the same perfectly natural way, Mrs. Wilson feels her Canadianism is apparent in her work. "There is nothing conscious about this process; it is simply inevitable. You live in a place and become a part of it." (Since 1946, when her husband gave up his general

26 delete
27 delete and say instead —
"of responsibility in"

28 delete   "bus" — interject
"and I knew them at once,"
29 delete this phrase —
replace with "and story" —
again that feeling that "these
people" may have another
inference — tho' your state-
ment is quite correct!

30 *better left out — will explain below*

31 *delete and say "her husband"*

32 *delete*

33 *delete — "would give"*

34 *I'm afraid 1 or 2 of our young friends mightn't like being called "beginners" by one who is so much a beginner herself — shall we delete? — or change?*

practice for a position with the Department of Veterans' Affairs)[30], Mrs. Wilson has had opportunity several times to tour with (him)[31] the length and breadth of Canada. "When you make journeys like that, the name *Dominion* seems so splendidly right, and although our country divides into such strangely different empires...the word *Dominion* unites them all. I think a vision has gone when that word has gone."

But the vision exists, if anywhere at all, with the writers in a country. The work Mrs. Wilson is doing, along with her contemporaries in Canada, is, she feels (merely)[32] spade work. "We are preparing the ground for that real roaring talent — that genius who will be here we hope; but who perhaps may choose to spring from some other commonwealth soil." Thus, in the matter of her own writing of novels Ethel Wilson is neither ambitious or pretentious. "I know I have only a teaspoon of talent," she smiles: "So what little I have must be good if it can."

This then is the advice she (gives)[33] to beginners: (the young people who gather once a month to read their work and hers, in that airy apartment overlooking English Bay)[34]: "Pretentiousness is the worst sin.... write simply of what is close to you...read and read and *read*, not for the purpose of emulating any style, but to develop a critical faculty so keen that you yourself cannot write badly. You will know by instinct, what to leave out. But of course a thing equally fundamental, for a writer, is to have an interest in people, to centre as it were your whole eye and mind on people, and on springs of human action."

The people who move through Mrs. Wilson's novel and novelettes are so full of vitality that they seem to carry the story

35 delete

(through)[35] themselves. This sometimes leads to an unevenness, noticeable in "The Innocent Traveller"; or to a melodramatic climax, as in "Hetty Dorval." But, in the new book, the story of Mort, called "Tuesday and Wednesday"; and "Lilly's Story" — two novellas — possess qualities of intensity and irony that hold even critical young people, as they sit in a circle, (in a modern drawing room)[36],

36 delete
37 delete — say "would not seem"

spellbound. In their elders this (is not)[37] astonishing, for Ethel Wilson's style has the clarity and irony of a Jane Austen, a Samuel Butler; it is part of that tradition. When young people are so moved, one can predict greater things for this quietly forceful Canadian writer.

Notes

Chapter 2

Information about Ethel's ancestors comes through the late Lucile Malkin Parsons, who compiled a Malkin family tree; from the University of B.C. Library; from Barbara Wild's paper given at the University of Ottawa Symposium on Ethel Wilson; and from talking to various members of the Malkin family.

1. Robert Bryant called his journal, of which he made two drafts, "My First African Circuit, or Life & Work in the Orange Free State." It is at the University of B.C.

2. The story of Verlaine comes from her essay, "Reflections in a Pool" (*Canadian Literature* No. 22), and so does the story of Tom and the description of Robert's family.

3. Margaret Bryant's accomplishments were reviewed in *The Observer*. Ethel Wilson cut out the article, framed it, and hung it on her living room wall.

4. Trollope arrived in Cape Town on "a wintry Sunday," July 28, 1877. He sailed from Cape Town on August 4 and arrived in Port Elizabeth on August 6, 1877. (Trollope, Anthony. *South Africa* reprint of 1878 edition. [Cape Town: A.A. Balkema, 1973]).

5. These quotations are from, in order of appearance: "Reflections in a Pool" ("Life was luminous"); Crofton House School speech, March 1, 1957 ("I remember"); "Duchess" ("...and because Father"); her letter to H. Richardson Malkin, October 23, 1960 ("With all [Uncle Sydney's]"); and *Lilly's Story* ("the strong taste of sorrow").

6. Her conversation with her grandmother is taken from an unpublished talk, as far as I know never given, which she titled "Seen Through the Waves."

7. The description of coming into the station is from her essay "Young Vancouver Seen Through the Eyes of Youth," *Habitat*, 1967, Centennial issue.

Chapter 3

1. From her letter to H.R. Malkin, 1960.

2. Information on her arrival in Vancouver was taken from photographs of the time and other research, from *The Innocent Traveller*, and from some relatives' memories of tales their mothers told them.

3. The chain gang fear is from "Young Vancouver Seen Through the Eyes of Youth."

4. The "pretty ladies" and Joe Fortes stories are in *The Innocent Traveller*.

5. Girton is a college of Oxford University.

6. Information on Miss Gordon's school comes from a piece Ethel Wilson did for the Vancouver *Daily Province*, February 5, 1948.

Chapter 4

The chapter title is a quotation from Edwin Muir and was used as the epigraph to *Mrs. Golightly and other stories.*

1. Her remarks about her homesickness and her teacher come from her essay "In Defence of A Little Learning."

2. This poem, "The Trance of Light," is in Ted Hughes' *Remains of Elmet*. Although Ethel Wilson would not have read it, the poem is appropriate to her time and sensibility.

3. The description of Trinity Hall School, which was opened in 1872 and closed in 1970, and the reference to Nina Ward, were taken from Prof. C.M. Armitage's paper, delivered to the University of Ottawa Symposium on Ethel Wilson, 1981.

4. Her comments on the rich are in a letter to John Gray written on April 10, probably 1960. She rarely dated letters.

Chapter 5

1. "When the mountains beyond..." is from "Hurry, Hurry," *Mrs. Golightly and other stories*.

2. The story of Mr. Burns is from "Seen Through the Waves."

3. She told this story about Emily Carr when she opened a B.C. Society of Artists exhibit in Vancouver.

4. The Pauline Johnson story comes from an article in *Canadian Literature*, Summer 1961.

5. The description of the laying of the cornerstone comes from Irene Howard's essay "Shocking and Unshockable Methodists in *The Innocent Traveller*."

6. Amy's letters were loaned to me by her daughter, Mary White.

7. The passage "as she hurried along the dark wet pavements" comes from *Tuesday and Wednesday*.

Chapter 6

Much of the information in this chapter comes from Amy Wilson Buckerfield's scrap books and from Mary White's memory of things her mother and the Wilsons told her.

1. Although there is no record of Algie and Ethel meeting at that time, it would have been difficult for them not to. Their social connections were the same, and both were outgoing people.

2. Sarah Bernhardt and her company that evening—if they kept to the printed programme—played excerpts from *Lucrece Borgia*; *Phedre*; *Elizabeth, Reine d'Angleterre*; and *Un Nuit de Noel*, a one-act play by Maurice Bernhardt and Henri Cain.

3. Dr. Wilson also served in England with the 4th Canadian General Hospital from Toronto and with the Ontario General Hospital.

Chapter 7

1. From April 17 until July 23, 1917, more than 200 employees struck at the B.C. Sugar Refinery. They were protesting against another employee's dismissal, and demanding a 20 percent raise. (They settled for 10 percent.)

Chapter 8

1. These stories ran between March 3 and June 13, 1919, and are in the Ethel Wilson Special Collection at the University of B.C. Library.

2. The information about Dinesen comes from Judith Therman's *Isak Dinesen*.

3. Belloc's *Cautionary Tales* is now among her godchild Lucinda's books.

4. "the nuptial hour approaches" is from her letter to the Crawleys on January 4, 1965.

5. She told Audrey Butler about the long underwear.

6. According to Muriel Whitaker, whose grandfather once owned the resort, the lake was renamed in 1932 in honour of Father Le Jeune, a pioneer Roman Catholic missionary in the Kamloops area.

7. "It is true. Say Lytton Bridge..." is from *Swamp Angel*.

8. "When I got there, I tell you my heart..." is from "Beware the Jabberwock, My Son..." *Mrs. Golightly and other stories*.

9. "Isn't it strange..." is from *Swamp Angel*.

Chapter 9

1. "Cards were unknown..." is from "Young Vancouver Seen Through the Eyes of Youth."

2. "the incorporeal presence in air..." is from *Lilly's Story*.

3. "Polite and fashionable Vancouver..." is from *The Innocent Traveller*.

4. The "Algie has gone to heaven" story was told me by my godmother, Maidie Murray Daniel.

5. Dorothy Livesay was the interviewer; her story ran in *Mayfair*, November 4, 1947.

6. The people I spoke to about her being childless would be hurt if I named them.

7. Adopting a child was difficult—a two year wait for most people—although doctors could often get babies more quickly. But in those days, family doctors often saw adoptions turn out badly. Sometimes they blamed it on heredity; a few thought it was because these babies were unwanted and were affected by this while still in the womb, and sometimes later when they were told they were adopted.

8. "A child is still one with reality..." is from *Swamp Angel*.

9. The story of Tom Tokunaga comes from her essay, "Series of Combination of Events & Where is John Godwin?" *Tamarack Review*, Autumn 1964.

10. Audrey Butler told me about the death bed scene.

Chapter 10

1. "His lateness made the house too quiet..." comes from "Beware the Jabberwock, My Son..."

2. "I think 'social life'..." is from her story, "Truth and Mrs. Forrester," *Mrs. Golightly and other stories*.

3. "The isles of Greece..." is from *The Innocent Traveller*.

4. "Up the broad steps..." is from an unpublished fragment titled "Words and Places." This and her travel notes are in the University of B.C. Library.

5. Forster's comment was quoted in P.N. Furbank's *E.M. Forster: A Life*. As it was published in 1979, Ethel wouldn't have read it. Still, she would have sympathized with him.

Chapter 11

1. These three doctors were interviewed by Mary McAlpine in 1980.

2. Uncle Phil's son, Philip Malkin, told me this story in 1980.

Chapter 12

1. She went to England in 1913, but what she did (aside from visiting Burslem) or how long she stayed is not known.

Chapter 13
1. Audrey Butler told me the Chow Lung and cook general stories in September 1980.
2. Sister Beverley Mitchell, Ph.D., who has studied Ethel Wilson's work for many years, gives an interesting argument that the novella *Tuesday and Wednesday* in *The Equations of Love* was written as a game; that Mrs. Wilson was playing with the structure of Joyce's *Ulysses*. Whatever may be true, Ethel Wilson said that *Tuesday and Wednesday* was the work she liked best.

Chapter 15
1. The Eliza and Dolly Tibbett story is in the Ethel Wilson Special Collection at the University of B.C. Library.
2. Letters to Macmillan's are also in the Ethel Wilson Special Collection.

Chapter 16
1. "It is not the least remarkable..." is from John Gray's talk "An Evening With Ethel Wilson," given on November 10, 1961.

Chapter 17
1. "and then I say Fathead..." is from a letter to Alan and Jean Crawley, January 28, 1963.
2. This is an excerpt from her story "Corner of X and Y Streets," *Mrs. Golightly and other stories*.

Chapter 18
The chapter title is a quote from *Love and Salt Water*.
1. "He is everything..." is from *Swamp Angel*.
2. "The Birds" is from *Mrs. Golightly and other stories*.
3. Dreams were very important to Ethel. She once, with anxiety, asked Audrey Butler if she knew a man named Al Nobel. If she did now, or in the future, she must not marry him; she had had a dream. *Hetty Dorval* came to her, she said, in a dream — "beginning, middle and end."
4. "A Visit to the Frontier" appeared in *The Tamarack Review*, Autumn 1964.

Chapter 19
1. "A Cat Among the Falcons" appeared in *Canadian Literature* No. 2.
2. "An aspiring writer..." is from her talk to the Soroptomists' Club. It was titled "The tool that fits the hand," and is in the Ethel Wilson Special Collection, University of B.C. Library.
3. "Our language is now being assailed..." Ibid.

Chapter 20
1. "What connections..." is from a talk given to the Humanities Association on 1/12/60.
2. Mr. Keyserlingk's speech is from the Senate Proceedings of the Special Committee on Sale and Distribution of Salacious and Indecent Literature 1952-53.
3. The hidden marmalade story was told in a letter to Mary McAlpine from Marion Ward's daughter, Vivien Maitland, August 5, 1980.
4. "As I sit on this balcony..." is from her essay "On a Portuguese Balcony," *Tamarack Review*, Issue 1, Autumn 1956.

5. "An osprey circled overhead" is from "Nimpish Lake," *Mrs. Golightly and other stories*.

Chapter 22
1. "desert of loneliness" is from *Tuesday and Wednesday*.
2. In *Hetty Dorval*: "She held up her hand, palm upwards, and there was all giving, all welcome in the gesture." Art imitates life or life art?
3. *Tamarack Review* was first published in Autumn 1956. In his final editorial (Winter 1982, issue 83 and 84) its editor Robert Weaver pointed out that *The New Statesman* once "suggested that the useful life of 'a little magazine' was forty or fifty issues." And then he says, "The only real sadness I feel as I write this final editorial is that the magazine has outlived too many of its friends and contributors: Anne Wilkinson, Ethel Wilson, Nathan Cohen, Hugh Garner, Alan Crawley, A.J.M. Smith, John Glassco, Peter Dwyer."

Chapter 23
1. The description of fado is from "On a Portuguese Balcony."
2. "To Keep the Memory of So Worthy a Friend" was in *The Reporter* of December 13, 1956. It is also in *Mrs. Golightly and other stories*.

Chapter 24
1. All her books were available in Canada and England; *Swamp Angel*, *Lilly's Story*, and *Mrs. Golightly* in U.S.A.; *Equations of Love* in Italian; *Lilly's Story* in German and Danish; *Swamp Angel* and *Hetty Dorval* in Phonotape, Canada, *Innocent Traveller* in Talking Books, and *Hetty Dorval* in Braille.
2. "Admissions, Seabirds and People" is in the Ethel Wilson Special Collection at the University of B.C. Library.

Chapter 25
1. Miss Casey appears in the story "Fog," *Mrs. Golightly and other stories*. "A Drink With Adolphus" is also in this collection.
2. "On Not Being Educated" is in the Ethel Wilson Special Collection at the University of B.C. Library.
3. "Now I regard region..." is from her letter to Desmond Pacey of July 12, 1953.
4. "We all at different stages in our lives undergo...," and her remarks about how she came to write her novels, are from "Somewhere Near The Truth," Ethel Wilson Special Collection, University of B.C. Library.

Chapter 27
1. "One of the greatest of all field naturalists" is from *The Innocent Traveller*.

Index

222

A Note On Sources

Most of the information for this life of Ethel Wilson has come through the University of B.C. Library's special collection of Ethel Wilson's correspondence, typescripts, diaries, and photographs, and through my letters, photographs, and memories, which have remained vivid because of her nature and her unusual mind and way of talking. (She spoke the way she wrote.) Our friendship extended over nearly thirty years.

People who knew her have been remarkably open and honest in what they have told me, and they have been generous with their letters. (She much preferred writing notes to talking on the telephone and her letters rambled over many pages.) Among these people are the late Geoffrey C. Andrew, former vice-president of University of B.C., and his wife, the late Margaret Andrew; the late Nan Cheney, medical illustrator; writers Earle Birney, the late Margaret Laurence, and George Woodcock; Canadian Broadcasting Corporation producers Robert Weaver and the late Robert Patchell; anthropologist Audrey Hawthorn; and many relatives and friends of Wallace and Ethel Wilson, particularly Mary Buckerfield White, Audrey Butler, the late Amy Buckerfield, Betty Clegg, Michael Crawley, Gwynneth Rogers, Colin Graham, Peggy Macintosh, Vivien Maitland, the late Philip Malkin, Richard Malkin, Ursula Malkin, Alex Goolden, the late Lucille Parsons, David W.H. Tupper, Q.C., and Muriel Whitaker.

Of great importance to the work on this book was Mrs. Phyllis Marshall, who was more than housekeeper to the Wilsons.

The late John Morgan Gray, who was Ethel Wilson's publisher and friend to both the Wilsons, asked me to take over his job as her literary executor and so unwittingly led me into this book.

Beverley Mitchell, SSA, has been helpful to me, and to many others interested in Ethel Wilson.

Other important sources have been the Earle Birney and Mazo de la Roche collections of letters at the University of Toronto Library, and the Ethel Wilson Symposium held at the University of Ottawa in 1981.